DATE DUE

OC 11 '01			

DEMCO 38-296

FILMS AS CRITIQUES OF NOVELS

Transformational Criticism

FILMS AS CRITIQUES OF NOVELS

Transformational Criticism

C. Kenneth Pellow

The Edwin Mellen Press
Lewiston/Queenston/Lampeter

Library of Congress Cataloging-in-Publication Data

Pellow, C. Kenneth.
  Films as critiques of novels : transformational criticism / C.
Kenneth Pellow.
       p.   cm.
  Includes bibliographical references (p.) and index.
  ISBN 0-7734-9067-1
  1. American fiction--History and criticism. 2. American fiction-
-Film and video adaptations. 3. English fiction--Film and video
adaptations. 4. English fiction--History and criticism. 5. Motion
pictures and literature. I. Title.
PS374.M55P45 1994
813.009--dc20   94-31631
                                                              CIP

A CIP catalog record for this book is available from the British Library.

The Edwin Mellen Press   The Edwin Mellen Press
        Box 450   Box 67
  Lewiston, New York   Queenston, Ontario
  USA 14092-0450   CANADA L0S 1L0

                    The Edwin Mellen Press, Ltd.
                      Lampeter, Dyfed, Wales
                    UNITED KINGDOM SA48 7DY

                Printed in the United States of America

DEDICATION

To Marie

TABLE OF CONTENTS

Acknowledgements

Portions of this book have appeared previously, in varyingly different form, in <u>Arete</u>, <u>Aethlon</u>, and <u>Literature/Film</u> Quarterly. I am grateful to the editors for their permission to re-create the material and for their having started this work on its way. I would also like to thank James A. Null, Dean of Letters, Arts, & Sciences at the University of Colorado at Colorado Springs, for assistance with the purchase and rental of films. Lastly, I thank all the students in my "Film & Novel" classes at UCCS for their aid in the formulation of some of the arguments here.

C. Kenneth Pellow
English Department
U. C. C. S.

> "I can't think of any
> film ever adapted from
> any work of literature
> that I or other people
> feel has any quality
> to it that even
> approaches the
> original work of
> literature that was
> its source."
>   --Joseph Heller [1]

INTRODUCTION

Writing a preface to a collection of his film reviews, John Simon asserted that "the ideal critique is itself a work of art as well as an explication of and meditation on the work of art it examines." [2] This book hopes to demonstrate the converse of Simon's thesis: a film that is based upon a novel--though it may be artistic in its own right--also serves as a critique of that novel. What the film-makers do with their source material helps to explicate and cause meditation upon that source. The film can always be seen as an interpretation of the original work which will shed light upon that work.

Each chapter here examines a particular transformation from novel to film. Each attempts to juxtapose the film and the novel and, by seeing what did and did not "translate" to the visual medium, to understand the novel a bit better. There is an admittedly odd logic to the argument, for close scrutiny of the film will emphasize elements of the novel by what the film retains, what it alters, and what it omits. Always, one is taken back, consciously or otherwise, to the importance to the novel of its particular elements--how the novel did what it did, and why. In some cases, this compare-and-contrast method will shed light upon the novel's theme(s); at other times, it will emphasize the novel's structure, its style, its methods of characterization. Necessarily, there will be some concentration upon the films. But always the main intent is to come to a better comprehension of the novel. Ideally, these essays will also have something to say about all such transformations. How well that ideal is achieved, the reader shall have to decide. The film will always serve, in these examinings of the transformation, as a critique, as another way of looking at the author's material and methods, and as an interpretation of the original work which will shed light upon that work.

For a host of reasons, the film is almost invariably a shrunken version of the novel, a precis of sorts. Mainly, this is a difference of time allotted. Most of us as readers will give twenty hours or more to a novel--a bit more to _Moby Dick_, somewhat less to _The Great Gatsby_. Few of us will allow a "feature film," meant for a single theatre showing, to hold us for over three hours. This is mainly what accounts for the truth of John Nichols's statement, quoted here in the essay on Bang the Drum Slowly, that "Movies are not novels; movies are short-story." This point is sufficiently obvious to make one wonder why all film-makers rush to film the great American (or European, or Asian, etc.) novel, while thousands of excellent and perfectly adaptable short-stories remain unadapted. The artistic success of such films as "Babette's Feast" and "The Dead" make this an even more pertinent question, as do the repeated failures to adapt Moby Dick, The Trial, or The Sound and the Fury.

In addition, films and novels must operate by vastly different media. This too is obvious enough; yet the difference seems surmountable, since, as everyone knows, "a picture is worth a thousand words." Worked one way, that old saw makes perfect sense: to summarize all that one "sees," all the "meaning" that one apprehends in a Bosch or a Van Gogh, might well require a thousand words and more. When the process is reversed, however, the cliche becomes ludicrous. How would one set about capturing, say, all the Beatitudes (in Matthew 5:3-12, some 140 words) in a single picture--or even a dozen pictures? Even the Preamble to the U. S. Constitution, a mere fifty-two words, is hardly duplicatable in pictures. Concepts that are at all abstract are likely to elude replication by sheerly visual means, and that makes at least as large a difference between a novel and a film as any time differential. While it may not be perfectly true that the film is to the novel as the dumb-show was to the play, neither is it altogether untrue. Thus film has always managed greater success at stirring emotion than at capturing the conceptual. Anne Hollander observes again and again in Moving Pictures that the very "point" of movies is "not just that they move, but that they move us." From their beginning, Hollander contends, "what united all movies was the romanticism of their medium, its commitment not just to feeling but to the emotional foundations of living. . . ." She traces this tendency of cinematic art back through still photography to painting: "Like painting in the Northern tradition, the film aim is unmediated vision. . . ." [3]

Part of an important narratological difference between a novel and a film is the direct consequence of this difference between a verbal and visual medium. Very often in novels, there is a story-telling "presence" that remains unidentified but that has a function; that phenomenon is virtually impossible to duplicate in a film. A clear example is in the famous opening line of Pride and Prejudice: "It is a truth universally acknowledged, that a single man in possession of a good fortune, must be in want of a wife." Who says this? It is not, we will learn, the author's philosophy; some characters believe it, but some do not; it appears to be, rather than the expression of any one person's philosophy, a slice of public opinion. In a surprisingly short time, it will be clear to us that the sentence does not express a "truth universally acknowledged." It was never meant to be taken at face-value, but only in an oblique, ironic manner. How would one set about duplicating this in a film? Were the sentence inserted at the start, either in a graphic or a voice-over, it would almost certainly be not only taken seriously, but almost taken as a directive. It could be spoken by a character, early in the action, but then that character would merely turn out to be discredited to the extent that the statement proved unreliable. There would be no "choric" falling-short, no discrediting of "public opinion." In contrast to this incapability, one can see how both graphics and voice-overs work in Tony Richardson's film "Tom Jones." But there, as in the manner of Fielding's novel, the anticipations thus provided either prove true or blatantly, ludicrously untrue. They are seldom found just slightly, ironically untrue.

Differences are further exacerbated by the exigencies and the marketing decisions of contemporary film-making. Jay McInerney, author of Bright Lights, Big City, tells a funny story about the meetings he sat in on, when he was first brought to Hollywood to discuss the film to be based on his novel. The single most recurrent consideration seemed to be whether "treatments" of the story were properly "pitched" to "the seventeen-year-old." In vain did McInerney protest that his novel seemed to him innately adult in its appeal. His ignorance of cinematic marketing clearly left him out of the loop.[4]

Any film made today represents a sizeable investment. Almost invariably, the appeal must be to a mass audience if the investment is to be recouped. Consequently, almost any film, though it may also mean to be artistic, must give some consideration to popular appeal in the broadest sense. A novel does not represent quite the same magnitude of investment, and publishers are considerably more diversified than film-makers. A single big hit for a publisher will cover any number of books showing only small profit or even a loss.

The necessity of going for that mass audience was brought home the hard way to poet-novelist Robert Penn Warren. He watched Robert Rossen direct the filming of "All the King's Men," based on Warren's novel. At last, he was more-or-less consulted:

> "When the editing of the film was being done, Bob, out of courtesy, invited me in. He ran off several different endings, then asked me which I liked best. I said the second, or third, or whatever it was, but added that

none of the endings had a meaning like my
novel--this said in the friendliest way.
And Bob replied, 'Son, when you are dealing
with American movies you can forget, when
you get to the end, anything like what you
call irony--then it's cops and robbers,
cowboys and Indians.'" [5]

Typically, films that go for the mass market--and in
these days of megabuck cinema, that means almost all
films--follow the Rossen dictum in several ways. Not
only do they tend to simplify themes that novels pursue,
and draw generally less complex characters, but they
still, this long after the Legion of Decency, play safe
in regard to morals and politics. From "Grapes of
Wrath," through "Gentlemen's Agreement," to "Apocalypse
Now" this has been the case. That film is more akin to
the short-story than to the novel is one useful
distinction. Perhaps another might be borrowed from
Graham Greene, who labelled all of his own fictional
works, "Novel"--the more serious, purposeful efforts--
or "Entertainment"--the pot-boilers. Most films might
be thought of, in these terms, as "entertainment."

Even apart from these economic considerations, the
manner in which films are created is inherently different
from that of novels, and again there are consequent
differences in the products. Relative to a novel, film
is art-by-committee. Granted, a novel has not been
produced solely by an author; it has editor, publisher,

agent, etc., in its lineage. But in its substance it is much more the work of a single creator than is any film. The latter has evolved almost equally through the talents of one or more each of: scenarist, director, casting-director, cinematographer, and editor--not to mention numerous actors and attendant costumers, cosmeticians, and so forth. The combination of the committee factor and the economic considerations make a finished film a unique product. These exigencies must have been part of what Hollis Alpert had in mind when he once declared that a film could be artistic but probably never be a true work of art like a novel.[6]

Almost every novelist who has sold film-rights to a book has undergone approximately the same experience: the resulting film bears but little resemblance to what the novelist thought s/he had done, and what resemblance there is may not be flattering. Worse, the film may be that version of the story which most people will know and remember. Writer Gary Krist has found a homely analogy for the experience:

> The process can be a little like having
> your house featured in a slick decorating
> magazine. After the designers and style
> consultants have reworked your decor--
> moving furniture, replacing lamps to throw
> the right kind of light, editing out your
> defiant little lapses of taste and house-
> keeping--what emerges is a very different
> kind of place. But it is the place that
> most people will subsequently think of as
> your home.[7]

Despite all the differences already cited between novels and films, it may finally be the case that the film looks and sounds so different from the novel that birthed it because each makes or may make very different use of sequence. There is a temporality that a film is virtually stuck with, while the same is not true of a novel. Christopher Isherwood, speaking as a character in his own novel <u>Prater</u> <u>Violet</u>, explains:

> "The whole <u>beauty</u> of the film...is that it
> has a certain fixed <u>speed</u>. The way you see
> it is mechanically conditioned. I mean, take
> a painting--you can just glance at it, or you
> can stare at the left-hand top corner for
> half an hour. Same thing with a book. The
> author can't stop you from skimming it, or
> starting with the last chapter and reading
> backwards. The point is, you choose your
> approach. When you go into a cinema, it's
> different. There's the film, and you have
> to look at it as the director wants you to
> look at it. He makes his points, one after
> another, and he allows you a certain number
> of seconds or minutes to grasp each one.
> If you miss anything, he won't repeat him-
> self, and he won't stop to explain. He
> can't. He's started something, and he has
> to go through with it." [8]

Isherwood addresses this difference as "speed," or pace, while this introduction calls it "sequence," but for the purpose here, the distinction is minimal. Isherwood, notice, also speaks of a film's "points" being made "one after another." Pace and order are virtually inseparable in this context. One might have supposed that, in this age of VCRs, this difference between novel and film might disappear. We could, after all, watch a film on videocassette in such order and at whatever pace we choose. Still, I think most of us do not. We remain fastened, instead, to that sequence that the director (and/or editor) chose. The essay here on "Blue Velvet" will quote writer Seymour Epstein on this difference. The quotation is worth repeating here:

> There is a basic dichotomy between fiction writing and movie making. . . .It's this: ·novelists try to integrate person and event so that narrative grows with a felt inevita- bility. Moviemakers think in terms of "scenes," and a constant shuffling of person and event to fill these scenes eventuates a kind of dramatic scramble that is anything but inevitable.

This narratological difference will be prominent in several of the essays that follow, particularly those on "Blue Velvet," The French Lieutenant's Woman, and The Prime of Miss Jean Brodie.

There is but one reason to consider these differences, and that is in order to understand the ways in which a film can never be--nor should ever try to be- -a precise duplication of a novel. Each has its own way of telling a story. That is why a film can always be thought of as another interpretation of a novel. For us, here, the transformational process is just the vehicle; the goal is to understand and appreciate the "making" of novels. Whether one wishes to study them, teach something about them, or merely enjoy them, the use of other versions as a critical tool can be useful and informative.

1. Joseph Heller, "On Translating Catch-22 into a Movie," in Frederick Kiley and Walter McDonald (eds.), A Catch-22 Casebook (New York: Crowell, 1973), p. 362.

2. John Simon, Movies into Film: Film Criticism 1967-1970 (New York: Dell, 1971), p. 1.

3. Anne Hollander, Moving Pictures (New York: Alfred A. Knopf,1989), pp. 7, 446, and 447.
    Obviously, I cannot provide proof, but the reader should believe that the first time I looked at the last quoted passage, I read "unmeditated." The Freudian slip is as possible in reading as in speaking.

4. Another story of a young novelist watching what happens to his creation on its way to becoming a film is told in the essay here on The Sterile Cuckoo.

5. Quoted in Alan Casty, "The Films of Robert Rossen," Film Quarterly, Winter 1966-67, p. 91.

6. Simon, p. 2.

7. Gary Krist, "The Junior Wife's Story," Review of Raise the Red Lantern: Three Novellas, by Su Tong, The New York Times Book Review, July 25, 1993, p. 12.

8. Christopher Isherwood, Prater Violet (New York: Farrar, Straus and Giroux, 1945), p. 32.

"BLUE VELVET"

It is curious how many people, some of them usually acute, perceptive viewers of film, were taken in by David Lynch's "Blue Velvet." Although its acceptance was uneven, it did receive praise, both in the popular press (The Village Voice, among others) and in academic journals (Literature/Film Quarterly, e.g.). In some ways this is not altogether surprising, for the film does have the capability, especially at first sight, to intrigue a viewer, with its bizarre kind of visual realism and with its melange of symbols that, for a time, seem to be adding up to something, perhaps even something significant. But Lynch commits blunders (as scripter and as director) in sequence, causation, and consistency. These in turn leave gaps in plausibility, in sheer logic, that destroy all that the symbols and so forth seemed to be constructing. Although the film is not based upon any novel, it is worth considering here because it is a film that particularly alienates someone whose narrative values are literary. A close look at the failures of plotting in "Blue Velvet" will be insightful to much of the rest of this book.

Let it be understood early that the objections to "Blue Velvet" that will be made here are not the ones generally advanced. Most negative judgments of this film have been made on criteria that are primarily moral. Thus, some critics do not get beyond its being crudely violent, being pornographic, being sexist, and creating an atmosphere sleazy and sensationalized. To be sure, most of these are accurate. The film is obscene, it does shock and disturb and revolt almost any viewer, and it does want to posit a view of humankind that most of humankind desires to reprove. But none of this is what ultimately ruins the film

for some of us. What does that is a matter that reminds one of an Oscar Wilde witticism: Asked under cross-examination whether his literary magazine at Oxford had been an immoral publication, Wilde replied, "It was worse than that, sir; it was badly written."

More specifically, Lynch's film is not so much badly written as it is badly designed; or, perhaps, it has an adequate design, but that design is badly followed. In any case, an infamously wrong nineteenth-century literary judgment seems more accurately applied to Lynch's film. Someone (it is believed to have been George Brinley) wrote in the Spectator that Charles Dickens's Bleak House was

> chargeable with not simply faults, but absolute want
> of construction. . . .Mr. Dickens discards plot,
> while he persists in adapting a form for his
> thoughts to which plot is essential, and where the
> absence of a coherent story is fatal to continuous
> interest.

It is just this that constitutes the central weakness of

Blue Velvet. Lynch establishes a narrative frame, works

within it for a while, then drops it at any occasion when

something thematically "clever" appeals to him.

Ultimately, narrative logic is the criterion that renders

this film unsuccessful.

Let us first summarize what it is that critics have

found working well in "Blue Velvet." Lynch portrays a

duality of characters--the naive Jeffrey Beaumont vs. the

singularly demented Frank Booth--which serves to

counterpoint some duality within a character--i.e.,

Jeffrey. The consequent of this duality is Lynch's main

achievement thematically, namely his ability to show us

"two very separate worlds: the real world, that which we

can see and hear and touch; and a subconscious, dream

world. . . ." [1] This is the progression usually found by

those who praise the film: The duality of the characters

leads to our perception of the duality of a character,

which leads to our awareness of the theme of

"separateness within." Several writers have recognized

that Lynch seeks to find "the mystery and madness hidden

in the 'normal'," [2] and that the business of this film is

the "constant subversion of apple-pie normalcy."[3]   But
there's a large glitch here: Capturing that theme in any
genuine way would necessitate that Lynch first capture
something that is "real" or "normal." Indeed, that theme
would be better served if he could start from settings,
characters, and behaviors that are ordinary, then track
those ordinary items to their underlying (and
extraordinary) layers of unconscious mystery and madness.
But it is just there that Lynch's art collapses.

One clear indication of how willing, perhaps even
eager, Lynch is to depart from the realistic in order to
get at the weird is what he does with the "town" of
Lumberton, the setting for the entire film. It is clear
at the outset that this is a small town. Not only are
there rambling roses against white picket-fences, but a
fire-truck meanders through a residential neighborhood
and the firemen wave. In the background is heard the
epitome of a community-tied, small-town radio station:
"At the sound of the falling tree, the time is. . . ."
When a camera scans the town, nearly all the buildings
are single-story, several of them on the edge of a small
lake. Lumber trucks go right through the business
district, and all the streets are narrow and tree-lined.
So it is not surprising, at first, to find nearly all
reviewers speaking of Lumberton in this way: "a sunny
small town" (McGuigan & Huck, in Newsweek), "peaceful

Lumberton" (Corliss, _Time_), "the small logging town of Lumberton

. . . a bland American community" (Rafferty, _The Nation_), and "an archetypal small, sleepy city" (Kael, _The New Yorker_).[4] What is rather surprising is that none of these critical viewers seems to have noticed Lynch's cheating in this regard. It is a small town when that's convenient to his theme, and it is a big city when that serves his need. Starting with Jeffrey's discovery of the ear (and Detective Williams's straight-faced appraisal, "Yes, that's a human ear, all right"), Lumberton starts quickly becoming a large city, not because it has begun to grow, but because Lynch has apparently changed his mind. Suddenly, evidence of urban life is everywhere. The police department has a rather sophisticated crime lab. At the stakeout on the site of Jeffrey's finding the ear, there are no fewer than ten investigators. Crime lords like Frank and Ben have apparently been trafficking in drugs and violence (not to mention kidnapping, lip-synching, and kinky sex) for some extended time. The "town" soon has huge buildings, some of them with dozens of apartments. It eventually has wide streets, where high-speed car chases go virtually unnoticed. Sandy's high school--formerly Jeffrey's as well--is so large that students do not generally know one another ("You know, I remember you from high school" has never been said in a genuinely small town). Although Jeffrey's dad owns a local hardware store, he and Jeff are apparently not well-known to anyone. (Jeffrey has to introduce himself to Detective Williams though they live in the same neighborhood.) The police department has several plainclothesmen--at least one of them in cahoots with gangsters, unbeknownst to his partner. Drug-dealing, big-time dealing that is, is apparently commonplace here. ("A drug dealer was shot to death and a woman got her legs broken. Police found a huge amount of drugs. . ." And this did not, directly, involve Frank.) Near the film's end, there are no fewer than four police cars at Dorothy's apartment, while another raid is going on at Frank's. Whatever else it is, this is no normal small town. Nor is it a small town at all, except, that is, when Lynch wants it to be.

That Lynch changes the dimensions of his setting whenever the fancy strikes him is hardly the only problem of its kind in this film. The logic of characters' motivation also takes a beating. The most blatant example of this is Jeffrey's going to Dorothy Vallens's apartment. Why he does this is one of the film's genuine mysteries. What he says is that he will "hide and observe" in the apartment because he imagines that "Someone could learn a lot" by so doing. A lot about what? The point is never clarified. And at the Slow Club on the evening when he plans to do the hiding and observing, he toasts Sandy with "Here's to an interesting experience." He does not, of course, say, "Here's hoping we find what we're looking for," because he does not know what he will be looking for. Why he is really there, clearly, is because David Lynch needs for him to be there, in order to flesh out (so to speak) a Lynchean fantasy. Lynch has admitted[5] that when he wrote the screenplay, he began with no plot in mind but only a set of fantasies, one of which was his recollection that he himself "always wanted to sneak into a girl's room at night and just watch her."[6] The fantasy goes on: "I would be watching her and I would see a clue, whether I knew it then or later, an important clue to a mystery, like a murder." This is the answer to why Jeffrey must go to Dorothy's apartment.

The apartment provides any number of amusing illogicalities, from its louvered closet-doors to its inspiring one of the film's funniest lines, intentionally or otherwise, in Dorothy's "I looked for you in the closet tonight." It seems, for whatever host of reasons, to be the focal-point of Lynch's, and the film's, most prominent gaps in logic. In the story's waning moments, after Dorothy has been hospitalized, Jeffrey decides to go back to the apartment. When Sandy urges him not to,

he insists, "I've got to." Why he must go would be yet
another of the film's mysteries, were it not for the fact
that, again, Lynch has grotesque surprises waiting there
for Jeff--and us. Dorothy's husband Don is there, dead,
minus one ear, and with the ubiquitous and obligatory
chunk of blue velvet stuffed in his mouth; and Detective
Gordon (Williams's partner) is there, also shot to death
but inexplicably still standing. Jeffrey's attempt to
leave will be intercepted by the arrival of Frank, but
in the meanwhile his response to the bizarre corpses is,
"Well, I'm gonna' let them [presumably the police who,
he believes, are on their way] find you on their own."
So what did he expect to do in coming here at all? And
why is Frank coming (back?) here? Don't ask.

What is most wrong about Lynch's vacillations in his
own narrative logic is that they make his protagonist
look stupid when he is (apparently) supposed to look
merely innocent. The line betwen naivete and
befuddlement is a narrow enough one at any time, and
Lynch has litle margin to work with, in regard to
Jeffrey. That such a youthful character looks almost
silly at times is permissible. Consequently, Lynch can
get away with Jeffrey's banal but oh-so-serious homage
to Sandy. "You're a mystery," he tells her at one point,
though it is clear to any   audience that she is
absolutely ordinary at best and somewhat sappy at worst.

And when she is at her worst, in that foolish rhapsody about the world's being filled with "trouble 'till the robins come" (bringing the "blinding light of love"), the sappiness is lost, if not upon Lynch, at least upon poor Jeffrey, who responds: "You're a neat girl." But even this is not destructive of the character's serious value, until Lynch also makes him foolishly, randomly motivated --or, more accurately, unmotivated.

Nor is it only the characters that move through this film in sometimes random, unmotivated fashion. Occasionally the camera also moves to an image that is required to wage a theme but is totally extraneous to anything like plot. The most (in)famous of these is that "beneath-the-surface" shot right after Jeffrey's father has been felled by, aparently, a stroke.[7] The camera then penetrates among blades of grass on the Beaumont lawn, magnifying them hugely, to show the insect life beneath. Bugs are fighting, or feasting, or both.[8] But what should have been one of the most organic (in several senses) shots in the film instead appears obviously grafted on. There is just no reason--except the thematic excuse--for the camera to be showing us the middle of the sod at that point; nor does it pan there gradually from the fallen Mr. Beaumont, but instead cuts to the bugs directly. It all goes to make the point that "It's a strange world," which later the two main characters will tell each other--and us--repeatedly. Naturally, the fact that a middle-aged man can one moment be in apparently perfect health, watering his lawn, and the next moment be on his way to an intensive-care unit, will not make that point nearly so well as a colony of feeding, fighting bugs.

All of this sacrificing of narrative logic to the dictates of theme might be worthwhile if the theme were sufficiently significant. But in the long run Lynch has nothing to say that has not been better said innumerable times. Even when people who very much like "Blue Velvet" begin to talk about its content, they quickly settle into banalities. Thus, J. Hoberman, in The Village Voice[9] speaks of Lynch's purpose as being "to literally [sic!] rub your nose in the terrifying profusion of life." And the usually fluent Pauline Kael, on the same point, lapses into cliche: ". . .the darkness was always there, inside." She imagines Lynch tapping his head[10] while telling us: "It's a frightening world out there, and. . .in here." (The latter part one can well believe.)[11] Such insights would seem to suggest that we have put up with this grotesquerie, sleaze, and violence,[12] in order to "learn" that among life's profusions are dark mysteries within the human unconscious. If this sounds like Freud for fourth-graders, it doesn't get any more impressive when we hear Lynch's views on what the film is all about. In his longest interview on "Blue Velvet," Lynch, admitting a detestation of storyboards, and admitting also that he "didn't have any plot at all" when beginning, but "only impressions," nevertheless speaks freely upon the "ideas" that motivated him to do this film. They all have to do with the fact that "Sex can get into all sorts of strange areas," because "So much of sex is mental," and "the mind is such a fantastic thing." Partly, too, his methods were driven by suggestions from external sources: "Somewhere along the line I had a book on sexual aberrations...." And the consequence of all this can be seen in the final words of Lynch's summarizing of the "ideas that were like magnets" to everything else in the film: "There are people who analyze things, like psychiatrists, and that would be interesting for me, because we do stuff and it's solely based on feelings."[13] So when we hear the characters in the film infer that "It's a strange world," and repeat it several times as though it were novel and/or profound, we can be fairly certain that it is not meant as parody. It accurately represents the depth of Lynch's conclusions.

There remains one thing about this film that is not easily resolved--its extremely polarized reputation. At the same time that such an astute critic as Betsy Berry sees much in it to like, such a veteran reviewer as John

Simon labels it "a piece of mindless junk."[14] Yet, back
on the former side, other reviewers who have earned high
regard--Kael, e.g., and Terrence Rafferty[15]--mainly find
favor with it. Perhaps there is an explanation of this
in the following dichotomy: people who "read" a film much
as they do a novel will dislike "Blue Velvet" intensely;
people who "view" a film much as they do, say, an art
exhibit will find it more satisfactory. Thus Pauline
Kael begins her favorable review with a sheerly visual
emphasis:

> When you come out of the theatre after seeing. . .
> "Blue Velvet," you certainly know that you've seen
> something. You wouldn't mistake frames from [it]
> for frames from any other movie.[16]

And so, too, Berry presents her best defenses of "Blue
Velvet" when she describes its recurring images:

> the camera begins a downward, spiraling journey
> into a full-frame human ear. A single candle
> flame is blown by a strong wind. Dorothy's voice
> implores someone to hit her, and a lion roars
> wickedly. A sweating, terrified Jeffrey sits up
> in bed, and we know then that we have been in the
> middle of his nightmare. The wolfish jaws of some
> unidentifiable animal hang on the wall. . . .[17]

If one wants to justify "Blue Velvet," it is perfectly
appropriate to do so on the basis of such images, for
moments like this are when Lynch is at his best. Now he
can present symbols virtually at random; now his film can
be genuinely surrealistic rather than just non-
sequential. But sooner or later, he must--or at least
he does--return to that "form for his thoughts to which

plot is essential," and then the faults cited here become glaring.

Ultimately, this division of responses points up, especially to those who are staunch admirers of narrative sequence, a truism about cinema. It is the same one that writer Seymour Epstein talks about in explaining what happened to a story of his when it was transformed into the made-for-TV movie, "The Comeback":

> There is a basic dichotomy between fiction writing and movie making. . . .It's this: novelists try to integrate person and event so that narrative grows with a felt inevitability. Moviemakers think in terms of "scenes," and a constant shuffling of person and event to fill these scenes eventuates a kind of dramatic scramble that is anything but inevitable.[18]

A work that ends by bringing on a mechanical robin to demonstrate further that "it's a strange world" is not likely to achieve a felt inevitability.

1. Betsy Berry, "Forever, In My Dreams: Generic Conventions and the Subversive Imagination in Blue Velvet," Literature/Film Quarterly, v. 16, no. 2 (1988), p. 82.

2. Pauline Kael, The New Yorker, Sept. 22, 1986, p. 99.

3. J. Hoberman, The Village Voice, Sept. 23, 1986, p. 99.

4. Cathleen McGuigan with Janet Huck, Newsweek, Oct. 27, 1986, p. 103. Richard Corliss, Time, Sept. 22, 1986, p. 86. Terrence Rafferty, The Nation, Oct. 18, 1986, p. 383. Kael, p. 99.

5. Lizzie Borden, "The World According to Lynch," The Village Voice, Sept 23, 1986, pp. 62-3.

6. Borden, p. 62.

7. A stroke is apparently what he is later being treated for in the hospital, though some viewers, presumably because Mr. Beaumont clapped his hand to the base of his skull, persist in thinking him the victim of a bee sting.

8. It is one of Lynch's tendencies, in this film more than elsewhere, to complicate, mostly through the use of insufficient lighting, numerous images. Thus, people often disagree on just what it is they have seen in this film. The "bee sting" is one example. Another is the question of what Frank Booth inhales through his oxygen mask. Berry's essay suggests yet another, as it is clear to her that "the actual sexual act" between Frank and Dorothy Vallens is consummated, while I have never been sure there is any penetration. And I do not know how anyone could know for certain that Frank was "in tumescent readiness." Maybe the lighting is dimmer on my copy of the film.

9. Hoberman, p. 56.

10. Kael, p. 103; p. 99.

11. In the Borden interview, Lynch is quoted as saying: "There are some women that you want to hit because

you're getting a feeling from them that they want it...." Borden, p. 62.

12. "We," that is, with the exception of Kael, who thinks "the violent images aren't obtrusive in this film." Kael, p. 101.

13. Borden, p. 62.

14. John Simon, National Review, November 7, 1986, p. 54.

15. One might note, however, that Rafferty, like many another critic of this film, almost constantly hedges his bets, especially in paradoxical or even oxymoronic phrases. It is "all the more riveting for being a bit tacky" (p. 384); even its "potentially most alienating elements" work (p. 385); it forms a new genre, "the demented matinee" (p. 385); and it achieves "radiant seediness" (p. 384).

16. Kael, p. 99.

17. Berry, p. 87.

18. Seymour Epstein, The Denver Post, Sunday, 5 February 1989, p. 10D.

<u>THE STERILE CUCKOO</u>

In the Introduction, Gary Krist is quoted on the experience of a writer who sees her/his novel adapted to film, but can hardly recognize the finished product. This essay is the story of one such experience. The process by which John Nichols's novel The Sterile Cuckoo became a film is indicative of several of the difficulties which confront any literary artist who wishes to write for films or who wishes to see a work of fiction transferred to the screen. In just a few strategic moves, necessary moves from the point of view of the producers, a promising writer's first novel was transformed into a film that was equivalent to the novel in but very few ways, different in almost all possible ways, and inferior in all too many ways.

Film, in those days, was attractive to Nichols. In years since, it has still had some attraction for him, despite some rather bizarre experiences.[1] The attraction is not altogether surprising. Films reach a larger audience; they present the capability of achieving immediacy, spontaneity,[2] and synaesthetic power impossible to achieve in the novel; and films hold out the challenge of newness--not nearly as much innovation in style or technique has gone into screen-writing as has gone into the novel, partly because of the much shorter history of the former. Still, it is curious that Nichols was not forever repulsed by the "Sterile Cuckoo" experience.

In 1968, still awhirl from the sudden heady success of his first novel, Nichols charged off to Holywood, prepared to be of whatever assistance he could in writing a screenplay, helping select a cast, and even shooting some footage designed to help find a location for filming. Nichols was able to think of this novel with some justified pride; he had watched it come a long way from its earliest drafts. What was now one of its outstanding strengths had once been a glaring weakness. It had been, at one point, a novella which the main character, Pookie Adams, had dominated, while the other supposedly main character, Jerry Payne, had been nothing but a literary device. Part of the means by which Nichols altered this was by making Jerry the story's narrator, thus making his view of Pookie the only view which the reader gets. Then Jerry's own personality undergoes some changes, as does Pookie's. As his maturity increases, his perceptions change, though whether for better or worse is part of the ambiguity in which the novel concludes. So, in its final form, the novel had achieved an admirable balance: it was Jerry's story as much as it was Pookie's. Little could their creator know what the filmed version would do to this relationship.

When Nichols first granted rights to film <u>The</u> <u>Sterile</u> <u>Cuckoo</u>, he also agreed to write the screenplay. The director was to be Robert Mulligan, and the producer Alan Pakula. Possible locations were discussed at some length. Nichols advocated shooting the film as near as possible to Hamilton College, where he had been an undergraduate, from which experience he had derived much of the novel's substance. Finally, to improve his argument, he shot some 8mm footage of the college area, and it was chosen as the site. It was also agreed that the starring roles should go to actors relatively unknown, both for thematic and economic reasons.

Thereafter, however, several changes were made to the original plan. Primary among these was the decision that made Pakula both director and producer. Perhaps because Pakula was enthusiastic about this new undertaking--it would be his first directorial venture--several other changes followed. From somewhere or other came more money than had, apparently, been anticipated at the outset. The film originally planned would have had a budget of some five hundred thousand dollars; the final product is believed to have cost approximately two million. Also, the original plan, at the fervent insistence of Nichols, called for a black-and-white film. This would have minimized a number of visual possibilities, naturally, and would thereby force more concentration upon character. What was obviously going to be one of the difficult aspects of characterization for the film to capture was the impressive verbal capability of Pookie Adams. A black-and-white film with numerous cuts from and to exchanges of repartee between Pookie and others would have attempted to preserve this important facet of her attractiveness. Nevertheless, the final version of the film takes full advantage of color for its own sake: long, lingering passages of Pookie and Jerry wandering through seemingly endless meadows and forests, surrounded by spectacular--and silent--scenery. Partly, of course, these tedious passages were necessitated by another decision: Dory Previn had been hired to write a song for the film, and the Sandpipers to sing it. In order that this talent not be wasted, Pookie and Jerry had to fill time, while the song (eventually to win an Oscar) was given an inordinate proportion of the soundtrack.

All of these changes, however, and even that change whereby Nichols was eased out of the writing of the screenplay, and Alvin Sargent eased in, were upstaged by the decision which gave the role of Pookie Adams to Liza

Minnelli. According to the Hollywood grapevine, Minnelli had been knocking on producers' doors from the time she first read the novel. She clearly recognized, in the part of Pookie, a potential vehicle to stardom. How right whe was, incidentally, can be seen in the contemporaneous reviews of the film, practically every one of which hinted at an Oscar nomination for her.[3] It was this decision more than any other that made the most significant differences betwen the literary and the filmed versions of the story.

One of the problems which the filmed version had to face up to, and which the novel had been able to handle rather easily, was the creation of Pookie's basic insecurities. Looking at the youthfully vibrant, personable Minnelli, even when she is shown with chopped hair, baggy woolen sweaters, and out-sized, round-frame glasses, an audience would find it difficult to believe that this had ever been the girl who had, as the novel's Pookie had, "been one of the two elites in dancing class who sat out the 'Boy's Choice'," and who remembered herself upon the occasion as "a small gauzy heap of hope wearing smudged white gloves, a wilting taffeta dress, and oversized glasses, waiting with Cinderella smile to try on the glass slipper that never came."[4] On the contrary, Minnelli's Pookie would more likely have danced all night with the Prince.

There are several consequences of such a brightly emerging new star's having been cast as the supposedly plain, unattractive, and unconfident Pookie Adams; not the least of them is that the film must necessarily be more concerned with the theme of death than was the novel. The novel's Pookie is threatened, more than anything else, by the prospect of eventually having to go back home and become a nobody, another of the "Inanities personified" that she sees her parents as being. (17) One of the novel's central images portrays concisely this threat to Pookie: in her bedroom, she imagines that she can hear the small harp in the attic "slowly dying," symbolic to her of "the little hope that had been her mother's youth, and most likely her own also." (17) But Minnelli's Pookie is clearly too attractive a person to have to be concerned about fading into the obscurity of Merritt, Indiana. To this Pookie, it requires something larger, more catastrophic, to be a threat; and so the film's Pookie worries aobut the possibility of her imminent death. Sargent and Pakula invent for her a story of her having once confided to the family's mailman that she was dying, whereafter he watched her closely for years, waiting for the end to come. This being not quite enough to carry the idea of a threat, the filmmakers also felt compelled to do some downright hokey things with tombstones and graveyards.

Among the things lost in the transition to this more overt use of the death theme is one of the novel's best scenes. On one of their drunken week-ends at college, Pookie and Jerry end up, with two of their friends, dancing on a tombstone, only to have the dance stopped short by the entrance of Poppy Cobb, chairman of the English Department and resident poet. Only after Poppy has gone away, do the now-nearly-sober revellers realize that the grave they have been dancing on is that of Poppy's wife. The realization comes when they recognize one of his poems inscribed on the headstone:

> Thou has not gone
> So far from me;
> Thy memory rides always
> The horseman of my heart
> Into Eternity.   (157-8)

In its being less than great poetry, the poem is just right. It turns the scene into one of the novel's moments of genuine pathos; but it would have been too brief (perhaps even too subtle) for the film. Besides, it brings a rare moment of thoughtful insight to Jerry, just as much as it does to Pookie, and, in the film, that would have been wasted, because the film--again, partly owing to the glitter of Minnelli--belongs to Pookie.

If it was necessary that the film over-emphasize Minnelli-Pookie's fear of death, then it became no less necessary to cut out some of the other business of the novel, especially as that business contributed to the characterization of Pookie. Some of these, also, were unfortunate amputations. There is, for instance, early in the novel, a seemingly digressive story which Pookie divulges to Jerry on the occasion of their first meeting. It tells of one of the child Pookie's apparently few moments of peaceful security, when she and her grandfather sat at breakfast in the earliest hours of day, and he confided to her the little-known "fact" that "A cow has eleven stomachs." (26-7) This tale is trivial enough, but Pookie's choosing it as "one of her most memorable, most meaningful moments of life," makes it a good representation of the rare blend of wit and whimsy that constitutes Pookie Adams. (27) The scene is perhaps too poignant a celebration of life to fit into the somewhat maudlin character of the film's Pookie, and so it is omitted.

Also lost in transition is Pookie's traffic accident. One can argue that this would have had to be left out of the film for time-saving purposes, for Pookie's account of it is rather lengthy. However, it is also clear that this bit of "something" in Pookie's life (it is the only time her name gets into a newspaper), combined with the necessary morbidity of Minnelli's character, would have taken all the mingled sparkle and pathos away from the character and made her too heavily tragic.

There are a number of ommissions that are, initially at least, difficult to account for. Perhaps most conspicuously absent is the poem which Pookie makes up, near the end of the novel, which provides the title. (196-7) What non-readers of the novel supposed the combination of "sterile" and "cuckoo" meant in the film's title is anybody's guess.[5] The film was at least consistent in this regard, for Pookie's other ambitious, and even more facetious, attempt at poetry is also missing. That is the one that she writes during an idyllic spring vacation which she and Jerry spend in an otherwise abandoned frat-house. Suggesting something produced by cross-breeding the Jabberwock with the Grinch, the poem is entitled "The Lavendar Grella." (132-3) Foolish though it is, the poem becomes a significant part of the novel's drama, for it provides the issue for one of the confrontations between Pookie and Jerry--a minor confrontation, it seems, but one that signals a deep and unbridgeable gap. When she finds that Jerry has not been even slightly amused, Pookie asks, "Don't you get any fun out of words?" But Jerry explains his critical reserve by declaring: "I'm insensitive to absolutely hair-brained disjointed nonsense." (134)

Perhaps this whole matter of poetry and nonsense was avoided by the filmmakers because they felt that issues concerning words and their potential are best left to the literary medium, and that the business of film must be that which is visual. But if that were the case, then perhaps the single most surprising omission is that of the episode in which Pookie wages a vendetta against a flock of crows. (121-130) The crows intrude noisily upon Pookie and Jerry, near the end of their romantic spring vacation, waking Pookie from one of the wildest dreams even she has ever had. She decides that, in order to drive them away, she must shoot one. After she has found a target-shooting arsenal in the frat-house, she procures plenty of ammunition, and there ensues a zany series of misadventures, ending in Pookie's having her picture taken in a triumphant pose with her trophy, one of the noisy, bothersome crows. Both literally and symbolically, the episode serves--albeit not subtly--a definite function in the novel. It would, however, have been as bothersome an intrusion as the crows themselves if it had been allowed to be a part of the filmed version, for that ever-present aura of mortality with which Sargent and Pakula so contrivedly surrounded Minnelli's Pookie would have been almost instantly dispelled by her triumph over the symbolically ominous crows. And so, paradoxically, one of the novel's most effectively "visual" scenes was not recorded for the film.

Apart from her preoccupation with death, there are

other ways in which the Sargent-Pakula version of Pookie
Adams differs significantly from Nichols's character.
Primary among these is the verbal difference. In the
novel, the clumsy, unattractive, insecure little person
which is Pookie is balanced by a shocking uncontrolled,
but captivating, verbal ability. (Particularly is this
true in the constant contrasts betwen her and the no less
intelligent, but infinitely less verbal, Jerry Payne.)
The film also seeks some ambiguity in the character of
Pookie, but in a different fashion, on a much different
basis. To be sure, Minnelli's Pookie bubbles out a
number of engaging speeches (and Minnelli handles this
part of the role quite well), but there is none of the
striking flair for far-fetched simile, for wild
hyperbole, for vivid analogy, that graces the Pookie of
the novel. The movie's Pookie appeals to us much more
through physical appeal: that sympathetic gamin-like
quality that appears to have run in Liza's family. Thus
Pakula's concept of Pookie gives us the charm of looks
rather than wit, and then that character is moderated-
-not yet "balanced," but moderated--by her neurotic sense
of her own mortality. So the problem that must at this
point have confronted the screen-writers is this: the
film has not created the same kind of character that the
novel created (that is, a witty-but-unpretty Pookie whose
self-image, uncertain at best, leaves her fundamentally

insecure). Instead, it has established a charming but determinedly immature Pookie. That being the case, what was now needed in order to provide "checks and balances" to her character, to render her somewhat ambiguous, in order that the audience not be put off by the bittersweet, maturing disappointment that she will have to undergo at the story's end? It is here that the film's Pookie Adams becomes not just different, but disappointing, for the main way in which our sympathy for her is mitigated is by our necessary recognition of what an inveterate liar she is. True, Nichols's Pookie was given to embroidering the truth, but never does one have the impression of being in the midst of a deliberate fabrication in the novel as one does when the cinema Pookie weaves tales of her "visits" with her father. This is, of course, harmless enough, and even smoothed over by Pookie's later admission of having been lying in those tales; but not all of Pookie's lies are so harmless in the film. Her entirely self-devised "pregnancy," for instance, is a cause of considerable uneasiness on the part of Jerry. And this, while it too is certainly forgiveable, is compounded by other touches of viciousness which the screenplay has given Pookie: the frat-house expose of all the darkest secrets of her housemates might be the result of her having been booze-soaked, but there is no such excuse that will cover her almost totally unmotivated allegations of Jerry's homesexuality. This may result in an interestingly ambiguous (or ambivalent) character, but it is certainly not the same ambiguity that Nichols achieved--nor is it nearly as appealing.

As disappointing as the film's characterization of Pookie may be for its own sake, it is just as unfortunate in the other difficulties that it causes. Given Liza Minnelli as its star, "Sterile Cuckoo" was almost certain to become a one-person story. Given the amount of concentration that Pakula and Sargent gave to mitigating the natural charm and atrtactiveness of Minnelli, it most surely did become a one-person story. This meant that the film, at best, could not hope to have more than half of the novel's dimension, for in the novel Jerry Payne is a necessary, functioning character. He is the narrator in the novel, which means that we are dependent upon him for our perceptions of Pookie; and we are aware, along the way, that _his_ perceptions change. His maturation, to some extent his insensitization, is watched by us with at least as much interest and nearly as much emotion as that with which we perceive Pookie's. But all of that is lost from the screen version. It is interesting, by the way, that in the casting of Jerry's role, the original plan, of casting competent actors thus far unknown to movie-goers, was followed. Wendell Burton was "discovered" on stage in San Francisco where, as "good old wishy-washy Charlie Brown," he was being nightly upstaged by Snoopy. It is unfair to his abilities that in this film his main assignment seems to have been--with the exception of the excellent "seduction" scene--to stay out of the way.

Consequently, the consideration of Jerry Payne's changing perceptions becomes irrelevant to the film. Similarly, the matter of Jerry's temporary "dissipation" --vital to the novel--is irrelevant to the film. Thus Jerry, ironically, goes back to being what he was in some of the earliest drafts of the novel: nothing more than a foil for Pookie.

And so the novelist watched while the film bearing his novel's title became, as a result of changes dictated mainly by the logistics of filmmaking, something very different from that which he had intended. While Nichols had almost never thought of The Sterile Cuckoo as a "message" novel, yet he was aware that the published version had come a long way from the early drafts, particularly in the area of characterization. His Pookie Adams and his Jerry Payne each constituted that combination that a fledgling novelist rarely achieves --a "type," but with considerable uniqueness. They seemed, further, to have the kind of appeal that popular films strive for. A range of American personality-types could identify with one or the other. Yet by the time the movie appeared, one had been altered beyond recognition, the other emasculated.

1. In addition to all the disillusionment that was caused him by the filming of "The Sterile Cuckoo," Nichols has had other curious adventures in filmland. He has written treatments of his own novels and others, which never became films, and he received no screen-credit for having co-written, with Costa-Gavras, the screenplay for "Missing." Instead, he is mentioned in the credits as an advisor, the result of complicated negotiations.

    More recently, he has written (and received credit for) the screenplay of a more successful transformation of one of his novels, Redford's "The Milagro Beanfield War."

2. Admittedly, a disputable term. In an essay on Henry Roth, Leonard Michaels has said that Roth once looked for work as a screenwriter, because he felt that his short-story writing lacked spontaneity. Roth little knew, Michaels says, "that a screenwriter has less to do with spontaneity than, say, the mummies of ancient Egypt." (New York Times Book Review, Aug. 15, 1993, p. 20.) Still, from the perspective of an audience, there is sometimes a felt spontaneity to film, an "instant-ness," that is difficult for a short-story or a novel to achieve.

3. She was nominated for, but did not win, an Academy Award.

4. John Nichols, The Sterile Cuckoo (New York: Avon Books, 1965), p. 14. All references in the text are to this edition, with page numbers in parentheses.

5. In Great Britain, the title was changed to "Pookie."

CATCH-22

"Catch-22" provides the classic example of a film's having to sacrifice quantitatively, relative to a novel. One comes away from Director Mike Nichols's (and/or scriptwriter Buck Henry's) "Catch-22" with a sharp realization of how much of Joseph Heller's novel it was not possible (or practical) to keep in the film. Consider, for instance, the reaction the film creates in a viewer who has previously read the novel and finds missing the following characters: Chief White Halfoat (and his "choosing" to die of pneumonia, after he has arranged to kill Capt. Flume); Capt. Flume (see above); ex-PFC (later ex-Cpl., ultimately ex-Sgt.) Wintergreen; General Peckem; Lt.(later Col., then General) Scheisskopf; Scheisskopf's wife (with or without Dory Duz's dogtags); Dory Duz (see above); the maid in the lime-colored panties; Lt. Mudd (the dead man in Yossarian's tent); Appleby; Dunbar (who shoots skeet because he hates to, who doesn't drop his bombs on a little Italian village, and who gets disappeared); Huple, the 15-year-old pilot; Hungry Joe; Huples' cat; Major _____ de Coverley, etc., etc. Further, that novel-reading viewer finds that the following situations or events (or, in the old vaudevillean term, "bits") are also absent: Major Major's father's ability to give names and to <u>not</u> plant alfalfa; the "T.S.Eliot" telephone calls and memos; Capt. Black's Glorious Loyalty Oath Crusade; Yossarian's argument with Scheisskopf's wife over who doesn't believe in God more than the other doesn't; Cpl. Whitcomb's form-letter to survivors; Orr's putting horse chestnuts in his cheeks when he can't find crab apples; Nately's whore's saying "Uncle" for the generals; the censoring of letters from the patients in the hospital (usually by Irving Washington and/or Who's-in-the-John Milton) and its bringing of CID men in maroon bathrobes, and so on and so forth. Sooner or later, in this film, as perhaps in any film, Marx's theory about quantitative differences evolving into qualitative ones is upheld.

Throughout both the novel and film, there are, of course, contrasts between the comic and the somber. But the proportion of these contrasts seems to be reversed. The novel gets many bits of frantic nonsense and absurdity into its opening pages, then moves gradually into the more gruesome aspects of war. It becomes progresssively less funny as it goes along--but is never totally without a sense of humor and a sense of the ridiculous. An example is Yossarian's series of responses to the "soldier in white": the first time he sees the completely bandaged patient, he treats him as a joke; the second time, he frets over him; by the third time the soldier shows up (?), Yossarian denies that this is the same man.[1] The novel, then, is a work of black humor that turns into a serious anti-war story, and more --a revolutionary work of fiction that opposes much of what might be thought essential to a capitalistic bureaucracy.

The film, however, does not retain this same ratio of humor to purposeful seriousness, a fact that has been recognized by Heller himself. In the "Questions and Answers" section of a Heller essay--originally a talk --printed in A "Catch-22" Casebook, Heller says:

> I think there is...a lower proportion of humor in the film than there is in the book. But I think underlying the book from the very first chapter-- and I know this because I wrote it--there is an undercurrent of the morbid danger of war.[2]

The film does not have sufficient time to use comedy as relief--to soften the harshness of war, in order to hit us with the war theme again, the way the novel does. It doesn't have the time to be as funny as the novel is and still be as serious as the novel (also) is. Notice, for instance, that by far most of the missing bits and characters listed above are humorous bits and characters. Consequently, the film becomes almost the novel's opposite: a serious anti-war work with an undercurrent of humor. A case in point is that of Milo Minderbinder, head of M & M Enterprises. There may be something funny about Milo in the early going of the film, but there certainly is nothing funny about his last several appearances, particularly the last time, standing in the jeep conveying him triumphantly through shattered Rome, suggestive of a Nazi staff officer--complete with "M & M" arm-band. In the novel, he was funny for a long while and even then did not turn as unfunny as in the film. Furthermore, the novel's humor derived from Milo's innocence, his unquestioning acceptance of the sleaziest tenets of capitalism; that innocence departs from him in the film.

The film also cuts out some of the novel's depictions of terrors that are not the result--or at least not the direct result--of war. Thus, all of the novel's "inquisition" scenes are absent, those scenes that deal with trials and interrogations.[3] The main ones of the novel are Clevinger's "trial" by the Action Board,[4] the CID men's questioning of Major Major (96-100), and the interrogation of Chaplain Tappman (387-97). Others include Yossarian's being grilled by Cathcart and Korn, after Kraft has been killed over the bridge at Ferrara (141-4); his interviews with Maj. Sanderson, the psychiatrist (303-6, 306-8, and 311-12); and his negotiating session with Cathcart and Korn (430-8), included in a greatly shortened version in the film.

These provide some non-martial examples of man's inhumanity to man, as well as some other kinds of bureaucratic insanity, which are necessary to the novel. A particularly good instance is Yossarian's first enocunter with the "head-shrinker" (303), in which we see one of those potentially harmful, very negative misapplications--perhaps all too common a misapplication --of the psychoanalytic habit of thought. Yossarian refuses Sanderson's offer of a cigarette. When asked why he has "such a strong aversion to accepting" one, he explains that he has just put one out, which is still smoldering in the psychiatrist's ashtray. "Major Sanderson chuckled, 'That's a very ingenious explanation. But I suppose we'll soon discover the real reason'." That sounds like recent revelations concerning Sigmund Freud. Uncomfortably like.

It is more difficult for a film to tamper with chronological narrative than it is for a novel to do so. That is, the film that chooses to disrupt sheer chronology runs a greater risk of confusing us, perhaps of losing our concentration completely. Largely, this is due to the temporal nature of film, _vis-a-vis_ the spatial properties of a novel. When the novelist departs from a chronological relating of events, not merely by flashbacks, say, but more drastically than that--consider Joyce or Borges or Faulkner, especially in The Sound and the _Fury_--s/he does not force us to rely upon memory in order to keep events straight. If worse comes to worst, the reader can always flip back through the portion of book now held in the left hand, to check up on what was repeated, how it has been altered. But film is like stage-drama: there is no flipping back to what we have "read" previously.[5] The film moves inexorably forward, winding through time, and chronology can only be altered cautiously.

This puts a limitation upon Mike Nichols that Joseph Heller did not have to confront. Even though many viewers, and many reviewers, complained about this aspect of Nichols's film--that they got "lost" in a film that began with the story's climax, returned to its earliest details, then worked back toward repeating it--the fact is that the film in this case is considerably more straightforward than the novel. Nichols and Henry start, to be sure, with a scene that comes late in the plot, chronologically, that is, Yossarian's "interview" with Cathcart and Korn. Then he gets stabbed, and then we go back to the earliest point, apart from Snowden's death, that the film will deal with. From there, again with the exception of Snowden, the progression will be consistent. This is probably a wise decision on Nichols's part, given the nature of film; as we shall see, however, it may be thematically unfortunate. In Heller's work, on the other hand, at the time the story opens, with the love-at-first-sight meeting between Yossarian and Chaplain Tappman, most of the events that will make up the remainder of the novel have already taken place. Thereafter, we are given all of the other details by a back-and-fill process that almost never moves in a straight progression. Jumps in time, forward as well as backward, occur unexpectedly; almost everything is told us more than once, just as Yossarian, for a time, "sees everything twice." Very often, the method is more digressive than progressive: a chapter titled "Doc Daneeka" is partly about Daneeka, just as much about Capt. Black, and even more about ex-PFC Wintergreen, Dunbar, and Clevinger; the next chapter, titled "Chief White Halfoat," never mentions Chief White Halfoat in the last six-and-a-half of its twelve pages.

Yet one other kind of disruption of chronology goes on in the novel. Just as the narrative method is chaotic, so also the setting is unstabilized. While the story mainly takes place during World War II, it does not stay put there. Instead, we see Major Major promoted (to Major, naturally) by "an IBM machine with a sense of humor" (88); similarly, the cetologist from Harvard was "shanghaied ruthlessly into the Medical Corps by a faulty anode in an IBM machine. . . ." (15) And we discover that Nately's mother has told him that he is better than members of the tobacco-growing Reynolds or Duke families, "whose income was derived from the sale to the unsuspecting public of products containing cancer-causing resins and tars" (255), a concern that was not much prevalent in 1945. This instability, combined with the novel's habit of leaping from one event to another with no clear transition (a device that the film is able, mainly, to keep) and its putting these events in no chronological sequence, causes us to depart from any usual sense of time as an orderly progression. Heller has indicated that these departures are not accidental:

> Catch-22 is not really about World War II. It was written during the Korean War and during the period when Senator Joe McCarthy was riding high in the Senate and when John Foster Dulles was bringing us to the brink of war with Russia about every week.[6]

"Brinkmanship," the concept by which we all remember then-Secretary of State Dulles, was, of course, popularized by Dulles himself: "The ability to get to the verge without getting into the war is the necessary art. If you try to run away from it, if you are scared to go to the brink, you are lost."[7] That Heller's novel has points of correspondence with the heyday of Joe McCarthy might be borne out by the following brief segments from an actual hearing conducted by McCarthy's Permanent Subcommittee Investigation of the Senate Comittee on Government Operations. The witness at this point was Dashiell Hammett, who had recently emerged from prison, a fact that will be referred to here by chief

counsel to the committee, Roy Cohn:

> C: Mr. Hammett, is it a fact that you
> recently served a term in prison for
> contempt of court?
> H: Yes.
> C: And from what did that arise?
> H: From declining to answer whether or not I
> was a trustee of the bail bond fund
> of the Civil Rights Congress. . . .
> C: Now, you said it was for refusal to
> answer. The fact is: You were a trustee
> of the bail fund of the Civil fund of
> the Civil Rights Congress. Is that
> right?
> H: That is the question that I went to jail
> for not answering; yes.
> C: Well, let me ask you: Were you a trustee
> of the bail bond fund of the Civil
> Rights Congress?

Not surprisingly, at least to most of us, Hammett once

again declined to answer--as anyone with a schoolboy's

capacity for logic might have foreseen that he would,

since he had previously done so even in the face of a

jail sentence. But the "real meaning" (compare Major

Sanderson) to this kind of invoking of a constitutional

right was provided, in the same hearing, by Senator

McCarthy:

> Well, now, you have told us that you will not
> tell us whether you are a member of the
> Communist Party today or not, on the ground
> that if you told us the answer might
> incriminate you. That is normally taken by
> this committee and the country as a whole to
> mean that you are a member of the party,
> because if you were not you would simply say,
> "No," and it would not incriminate you. An
> answer that you were not a Communist, if you
> were not a Communist, could not incriminate
> you. Therefore, you should know considerable

about the Communist movement, I assume.[8]
"Clevinger was guilty, of course, or he would not have been accused, and since the only way to prove it was to find him guilty, it was their patriotic duty to do so." (82) There was little reason for Heller to be completely inventive in matters such as this. He had only to adopt the method of Will Rogers: "I don't make jokes. I just watch the government and report the facts."

Not everything contrary to logic in our society had been straightened out between 1961 when Heller published the book and 1970 when the film appeared. In a world in which our generals could speak of destroying a village in order to save it, and our president could assure us that he was accelerating a war only in the interest of peace, Heller's "logic" still rang true. In the words of John Calley, the film's co-producer: "Unfortunately. . . you can always count on the country to do things to keep a picture like this timely."[9]

The disruptions of chronology, then, fit into Heller's overall texture of illogic, insanity, and paradox. This is a novel in which Lt. Mudd is officially "alive," although he is actually dead, while Doc Daneeka is officially "dead" although actually alive. Some of the contradictions, even when they come within a single sentence, strike us as being perfectly true, at least of some kinds of people: "Colonel Cathcart was conceited because he was a full colonel with a combat command at the age of only thirty-six; and Colonel Cathcart was dejected because although he was already thirty-six he was still only a full colonel." (192) But the more distubing paradoxes are those that involve abridgements of freedom and dignity. Yossarian becomes an object of resentment to many others because "he was jeopardizing his traditional rights of freedom and independence by daring to exercise them." (404) Perhaps this puts him in the same boat with Dashiell Hammett.

Yossarian's recognition that we all accept much too passively the hideousness of war (along with other inanities, inside or outside of the military-industrial complex, that get the same unquestioning acceptance) is a turning-point in both film and novel, but especially in the novel. Yossarian has all along needed to recognize how easy it is, as Korn says (or does Cathcart say it? Does it matter? Note, too, that the film leaves the line precisely intact): "How easy you'll find it to like us once you begin." (436) Such passivity, "Yo-Yo" realizes finally, becomes habitual:

> Someone had to do something sometime. Every victim was a culprit, every culprit a victim, and somebody had to stand up sometime to try to break the lousy chain of inherited habit that was imperiling them all. (414)

It is worth noting that these lines immediately precede Yossarian's wandering through the seamy life of Rome

(420-7; the chapter is entitled "The Eternal City"), called by some the "Descent-into-Hell scene." One must remember that in typical mythic recurrences of this scene, the wanderer/hero is chastened and strengthened in the crucible of the "underworld" that he visits. Yossarian, following his wandering, is able to return to Pianosa and confront what he now recognizes as his real duty. Thus, at the end of the novel, he informs Chaplain Tappman and Major Danby: "I'm not running _away_ from my responsibilities. I'm running _to_ them." (461) For his conscience has now been rendered capable. When the Chaplain suggests that that conscience will now give Yossarian no rest, he replies "'God bless it. . . .I wouldn't want to live without strong misgivings'." (462)

Finally, the film is less interested in being symbolic than is the novel. Someone has said about the filming of One Flew Over the Cuckoo's Nest that Milos Forman took almost as great pains to keep McMurphy from seeming a Christ-symbol as Ken Kesey had taken to make him one. Something of the same seems appropriate to Nichols's film; while watching it, there is little reason for us to keep in mind that "Yossarian" means "son of Joseph." In the novel, the name is perfectly appropriate (although one must remember that Joseph is also Heller's name) to a character so persecuted and, ultimately, so redemptive. When he finally leaves Pianosa, he leaves behind Chaplain Tappman, now prepared to persevere as a more effective disciple. Indeed, "persevere" is the Chaplain's own word for what he'll do in Yossarian's absence; and "'we'll meet again when the fighting stops'." (463) When Yossarian sits, naked, in a tree, he informs Milo that it is the tree of life, "and of knowledge of good and evil, too." (The innocent Milo, incidentally, insists that it is only a chestnut tree. [269]) Yossarian is, at this point, a new Adam, as was Jesus Christ. In the "Descent into Hell" scene, while we remember that Christ, according to tradition, spent the days prior to the Resurrection "harrowing Hell," Yossarian wanders through "the Eternal City," thinking "he knew how Christ must have felt as he walked through the world." (424) And when Cathcart, in one of his most paranoid moods, sits in his office and writes Yossarian's name,

> the very sight of the name made him shudder. There were so many esses in it. It just had to be subversive. It was like the word subversive itself. It was like seditious, and insidious too, and like socialist, suspicious, fascist, and Communist. (215)

Given all of the foregoing symbolism, the reader half expects that Cathcart will add "and like Jesus." Probably Cathcart would consider Jesus dangerous too-- and certainly subversive.

By no means all of Heller's themes were lost by
Nichols and Henry. Enough of the original was retained
to make a meaningful anti-war film. But, as has been
pointed out by Heller himself, and emphasized here, there
was more to the novel than an anti-war theme. The
novel's sweep--better yet, its attack--was both more deep
and more broad. The loss of all the novel's extra-
military satire is certainly an example of quantitative
change making a difference in quality.

1. See Fred H. Marcus and Paul Zall, "Catch-22: Is Film
    Fidelity an Asset?" in Marcus (ed.), Film and
    Literature: Contrasts in Media (Scranton, Pa:
    Chandler, 1971), p. 130.

2. Joseph Heller, "On Translating Catch-22 into a
    Movie," in Frederick Kiley and Walter McDonald
    (eds.), A "Catch-22" Casebook (New York: Crowell,
    1973), p. 361.

3. This point was also clear to Heller. See Kiley &
    McDonald, p. 356.

4. Joseph Heller, Catch-22 (New York: Dell, 1961), p.
    73 and pp. 76-83. Subsequent references will be to
    this paperback edition, with page numbers in
    parentheses in the text.

5. Even in this era of videocasettes and remote-control
    clickers, the mechanics for this kind of retrospec-
    tion make it awkward, relative to travelling
    backward in a book.

6. Kiley & McDonald, p. 357.

7. Life, Jan. 16, 1956.

8. Richard Layman, Shadow Man: The Life of Dashiell
    Hammett (New York/London: Harcourt Brace, 1981), pp.
    227-8.

9. Quoted in Time, June 15, 1970. The anonymous article
    is reprinted in Kiley & McDonald. See p. 344.

ONE FLEW OVER THE CUCKOO'S NEST

One way to perceive essential differences between Ken Kesey's novel _One Flew Over the Cuckoo's Nest_ and Milos Forman's film based on that novel is in terms that Friedrich Nietzsche coined in order to discuss and analyze Greek tragedy: "Apollonian" and "Dionysian." Essentially, Nietzsche argued in _The Birth of Tragedy_ that Greek tragedy depends for its effects upon the tensions between these two modes of perception or discourse. With the Apollonian, Nietzsche associates all elements rational and analytic, things that contribute to structure and clarity, as appropriate to Apollo, the sun-god. To the province of Dionysus, the wine-god, falls that which is ecstatic, energetic, drunken, irrational. This chapter will attempt to show how the difference in the use of Apollonian and Dionysian elements makes for significant differences in the impact of this novel and this film, and how, as a result, it is the novel that is more "tragic." There is no intent here to demonstrate that Kesey's novel is better than Forman's film merely because it is more tragic. That it _is_ better may be an opinion that underlies the whole chapter, but for a different reason. If we consider _Cuckoo's Nest_ in the Nietzschean fashion--as a tension but ultimately a marriage of Dionysian energies, those ecstatic and intoxicated realities, and Apollonian consciousness, that measured restraint which Nietzsche said provides for detached rational contemplation--then we shall see that the film relies more completely upon Dionysian properties, while the novel achieves a balance, a thoroughness, by a greater inclusion of the Apollonian.

To some extent, this results merely from the obvious differences between the two media: verbal rather than visual metaphors, and a ten- or twelve-hour reading rather than a two-hour viewing will, naturally, provide a greater possibility of "rational contemplation." Furthermore, the pace at which the work will be assimilated, the sequences and the continuity (or discontinuity) into which that pace will fall, these are much more in the control of the novel-reader than they are of the film-viewer. But if Nietzsche wishes to demonstrate, as he certainly seems to do, that part of the Apollonian function is to serve as the interpreter of our dreams and fantasies, then we can see that function operating in Kesey's use of Chief Bromden as the narrator of his novel. For it is from the narrative point-of-view that we see, in the McMurphy of the novel, a more complete tragic hero than the McMurphy portrayed by the film.

Before looking at the ways in which our perceptions

are shaped by Chief Bromden's narrative, let us examine some specific differences between the novel and the film that are the necessary consequents of differences between the two media. Because the novel has world enough and time to dwell upon intricate dimensions of character, it can present more ambiguities within a given individual; it can establish and resolve more paradoxes. Consequently, the R. P. McMurphy of the novel is, morally speaking, both a better person and a worse person than the film's hero.

In both versions of the story, McMurphy is an attention-getter from the moment he enters the ward. In each version, he is brash, aggressive, confrontative in ways that none of the others is; he quickly establishes himself as the next "bull-goose loony." And in each he is somewhat ambiguous: he is a gambler, a con-artist, a pitchman. "Chief Broom" says of him early in the novel:

> The way he talks, his wink, his loud talk, his swagger, all remind me of a car salesman or a stock auctioneer--or one of those pitchmen you see on a sideshow stage, out in front of his flapping banners, standing there in a striped shirt with yellow buttons, drawing the faces off the sawdust like a magnet.[1]

At the same time, however, he is a positive influence on the other patients; they learn that he is not afraid of "Big Nurse" (nor, apparently, of anyone or anything else), they learn from him the value of maintaining one's laugh (for "when you lose your laugh, you lose your footing" [68]), and they anticipate his potential for forcing some changes. The Chief observes, by the end of McMurphy's first week, that "they haven't really fogged the place. . .since McMurphy came in." (75)   To this point, the two versions of McMurphy do not substantially differ.   Then, however, the novel includes a series of six important incidents, each of which is either missing from the film, or significantly altered, or not emphasized enough to seem important.   In the novel, these incidents all serve to place McMurphy in a new light: the previously casual trouble-maker starts to become a purposeful reformer; the hell-raiser may just be becoming a hero.

The incidents follow an important revelation to McMurphy--that, having been committed involuntarily, he is more at the mercy of Nurse Ratched and her crew than he had previously realized.   He is on the verge of resigning his trouble-making ways in order to become a docile and obedient (and self-serving) patient who will thus have some chance of being released.   The compelling incidents follow.

#1--<u>Cheswick's suicide</u>.   This is appropriately placed as the first in the series of events which brings McMurphy out of his "retirement," as it is Cheswick's response to that withdrawal.   He has apparently become despondent over his part in the deception of McMurphy, that is, over not having told Mack what all it means to be in committed status. Upon arrival at the pool on the first day after he has reached an understanding of McMurphy's attitude, Cheswick "said he did wish something mighta been done, though, and dove into the water." (166) He grabs the grate at the bottom, and, by the time anyone can undo the grate and bring him up, he has drowned.

#2--Sefelt's seizure. An epileptic, Sefelt has been avoiding his daily dosage of Dilantin, convinced that it is causing his gums to soften and his hair to fall out. Consequently, he falls into a seizure, virtually at McMurphy's feet, in the breakfast line one morning. Although McMurphy has "never seen such a thing," (167) the irony of Sefelt's situation, and that of his friend and fellow-epileptic, Fredrickson, is clear to Mack: the choices for Sefelt and Fredrickson are seizures or rotting gums. There is a bit of an allegory, too, that is not lost on McMurphy. When Fredrickson observes, while they watch Sefelt come to, "'Hell of a life. Damned if you do and damned if you don't. Puts a man in one confounded bind, I'd say'," McMurphy acknowledges, "'Yeah, I see what you mean'," and "His face has commenced to take on that same haggard, puzzled look of pressure that the face on the floor has." (170)

#3--The visit from Harding's wife. Although she is spoken of in the film, Vera Harding never appears. In the novel, she comes for a visit, but spends all of it flirting with McMurphy and swapping insults, mostly sexual ones, with her husband. Harding's attitude during and immediately after this visit draws from McMurphy his first real expression of hostility toward the other patients:

> "Hell's bells, Harding!...What do you want out of me? A marriage counsellor?...I've got worries of my own without getting hooked with yours. So just quit!" He glares around the library at the other patients. "Alla you! Quit bugging me, goddammit!" (174)

But, more important, it also leads to his first apology and the revelation of his "bad dreams." (175) Here, it first appears

that Mack is beginning to "lose his laugh." Immediately thereafter, back in the ward, he attempts to cut the cards and "the cards splash everywhere like the deck exploded between his two trembling hands." (176)

#4--The discussion of EST. In the film, McMurphy apparently knows nothing of electro-shock therapy until his first trip to the "Shock Shop." In the novel, all of the "Acutes," led by Harding, engage in an explanation of what Harding calls the "grand old Faulknerian tradition. . .Brain Burning." (178) This allows the novel to make another of the associations between life on Big Nurse's ward and life in the outside world, an association which is missing from the film: When Mack exclaims "'Jesus, didn't they think it might do some damage? Didn't the public raise Cain about it?'" Harding responds "'I don't think you fully understand the public, my friend; in this country, when something is out of order, then the quickest way to get it fixed is the best way'." (179)

#5--The revelation of the "Voluntary" status of the other patients. This is revealed in the film, but not dwelt upon; in the novel, the fact that nearly all of the patients except McMurphy are there of their own volition is revealed in a longer, more significant scene, during which McMurphy insists to Sefelt that he, Sefelt, and presumably several of the others "'could get along outside if you had the guts--'." This brings a tearful, screamed response from Billy Bibbit:

> "Sure!...If we had the g-guts! I could go outside to-today, if I had the guts....But did you ever have people l-laughing at you? No, because you're so b-big and so <u>tough</u>! Well, I'm not big and tough. Neither is Harding. Neither is F-Fredrickson. Neither is Suh-Sefelt." (184)

Billy becomes hysterical and the scene ends with McMurphy, a more thoughtful McMurphy than we have yet observed, staring at the door to the Shock Shop and muttering "'I don't seem able to get it straight in my mind. . . .'" (185)

#6--The taking of the tub-room. In the novel, this provides the final bit of motivation for McMurphy to come out of his self-inflicted retirement. Actually, he has probably made his decision beforehand, but the scene in which Big Nurse decides to take away the Acutes' privilege of playing cards in the tub-room provides the immediate impetus he needed. Having stopped at the canteen on his way back from getting a chest X-ray, and having loaded up on extra cigarettes, Mack has apparently already decided that he will retrieve them and renew the poker games in the tub-room, where the cigarettes are used in lieu of cash. Now Big Nurse makes her announcement, then, emboldened by the apparent lack of opposition she receives, provides an explanation that is perhaps her most derogatorily patronizing moment:

> "At some time--perhaps in your childhood--you may
> have been allowed to get away with flouting the
> rules of society. When you broke a rule you knew
> it. You wanted to be dealt with, needed it, but
> the punishment did not come. That foolish lenience
> on the part of your parents may have been the germ
> that grew into your present illness. I tell you
> this hoping you will understand that it is entirely
> for your own good that we enforce discipline and
> order." (188)

McMurphy then walks over to the Nurses' Station, smashes the glass, and gets his cigarettes. He has come out of retirement.

It is right about at this point that the film "rejoins" the novel. That is, the two plot-lines, following these six events that have been omitted from the film, are again parallel after McMurphy reactivates his campaign against Nurse Ratched. Clearly, part of the difference in effect generated by the novel from that generated by the film lies in these half-dozen steps which the film did not include. In the novel, Mack's withdrawal is perfectly understandable, thoroughly motivated, even rational. In the film, he never seems quite so--one should pardon the expression--committed to his course of action, or inaction, as he does in the novel. Instead, as we shall see, his motives and his behavior always are a little vague.

However, an even greater difference in the impact of the two versions of this story is provided by Kesey's inclusion in the novel of an odd sort of "control": the narrative point-of-view resident in the character of Chief Bromden, a controller-in-spite-of-himself. This it is which provides the novel with the difference which Nietzsche called "Apollonian," the element, in art, of "true dreams' interpretation." In The Birth of Tragedy, he elaborated upon this dream-modifying concept:

> This joyous necessity of the dream experience has been embodied by the Greeks in their Apollo: Apollo, the god of all plastic energies, is at the same time the soothsaying god. He, who (as the etymology of the name indicates) is the "shining one," the deity of light, is also ruler over the beautiful illusion of the inner world of fantasy. The higher truth, the perfection of these states in contrast to the incompletely intelligible everyday world, this deep consciousness of nature, healing and helping in sleep and dreams, is at the same time the symbolical analogue of the soothsaying faculty and of the arts generally, which make life possible and worth

> living. But we must also include in our image of
> Apollo that delicate boundary which the dream image
> must not overstep lest it have a pathological effect
> (in which case mere appearance would deceive us as
> if it were crude reality). We must keep in mind
> that measured restraint, that freedom from the
> wilder emotions, that calm of the sculptor god.[2]

Kesey's use of Bromden as his narrator provides us with
several dimensions which the film cannot, or at least
does not, provide. Among these are the relating of life
in Nurse Ratched's Ward to life on the outside, and a
means of comparing the mental institution to other
institutions established by our society. But mainly
Bromden as narrator gives us two benefits which the film
cannot duplicate. The first of these is the Chief's
flair for verbal flights of fancy--turns of phrase,
metaphors, similes, analogies, etc. The second, and more
essential to the tragic effect, is Bromden's capability
of transmitting to us directly and immediately the effect
which McMurphy's presence, and his eventual absence, has
upon all the other patients. This capability grants us
the means to arrive at a true sense of McMurphy's
importance to the others and, also, the means to come to
an "Apollonian" appreciation of the novel's tragic
dimensions. Let us consider these two benefits of
Bromden's point-of-view, in order.

Bromden delivers several memorable lines, the most
famous of which is his distinction between what is true

(or True)and what is only factual: in anticipation of our
judgments upon his story, he avers--"But it's the truth
even if it didn't happen." (8) He is at his verbal best,
however, in rendering descriptions, especially of people;
part of his first description of Harding is
representative:

> He's got wide, thin shoulders and he curves them in
> around his chest when he's trying to hide inside
> himself. He's got hands so long and white and
> dainty I think they carved each other out of soap,
> and sometimes they get loose and glide around in
> front of him free as two white birds until he
> notices them and traps them between his knees; it
> bothers him that he's got pretty hands. (18-19)

Now, Kesey could, of course, have included that
description in the novel with or without any identified
narrator; but notice how much of the quoted passage is
part of, is virtually dependent on, Bromden's unique
imagination. Some of it, indeed, is dependent upon his
own persecution complex. Still, it is engaging prose.
More important, it rings true of Harding and it causes
the reader to come to know him (and Bromden) in a manner
that might not have worked as well for Kesey had he tried
to do it without Bromden.

Later, Bromden describes the effort Harding makes
as "he does his best to laugh. A sound comes out of his
mouth like a nail being crowbarred out of a plank of
green pine. . . ." (60)
At another point he recalls a visiting doctor whom he

sees as "covered with grey cobwebs on his yellow skull.
. . ." (121)

Sometimes, Bromden's figurative explanations are
arresting because of the unrestrained hyperbole which is
another of his habits of mind:

> Catheters are second-hand condoms the ends clipped
> off and rubber-banded to tubes that run down
> pantlegs to a plastic sack marked DISPOSABLE
> NOT TO BE RE-USED.... (31)

And, at still other times, they are engaging figures
sheerly because the Chief is not, apparently, aware that
they _are_ figures. That is, his hallucinatory habit is
part of what makes the metaphors work; such is the case
when Bromden recalls the members of "the Combine" who
visited his parents' home when he was about ten years
old:

> . . .the sun, on these three strangers, is all
> of a sudden way the hell brighter than usual and
> I can see the. . .<u>seams</u> where they're put together.
> And, almost, see the apparatus inside them take
> the words I just said and try to fit the words
> in here and there, this place and that, and when
> they find the words don't have any place ready-
> made where they'll fit, the machinery disposes
> of the words like they weren't even spoken. (201)

But the main value that Kesey derives from the use
of Chief Bromden as narrator lies in the Chief's
perceptions of R. P. McMurphy and in the changes he
undergoes under Mack's influence. In Bromden's first
reporting to us on the arrival of McMurphy, it is clear
that this new "guest" is potentially, at least, a con-

man, as we have already seen here. Later, of course, Mack will become admired by not only Bromden but virtually all the patients in the ward for his bravery (or bravado?), which is established mainly through his "wager" in regard to Big Nurse--that he can drive her to distraction within a week, or, as the film has him say: "...put a bug up her ass so far she won't know whether to shit or go blind." (This scene, with slight differences in the language, is present in both the novel and the film.) In the meanwhile, though, McMurphy becomes important to the other patients largely because he teaches them the significance of laughter. Of this influence, Bromden is well aware, and is one of the beneficiaries. We have already seen here Harding's inability to laugh, an inability that is representative of the whole ward. The phenomenon presents a puzzle to McMurphy (whose first out-loud response upon entering the ward was a laugh), especially the first time he sits in on one of the "therapy" sessions, and gets no reaction to what he thought was a very funny aside to Ruckly. He "can't quite put his finger on" what's wrong here, but he is heading toward the realization that "The air is pressed in by the walls, too tight for laughing. There's something strange about a place where the men won't let themselves loose and laugh. . . ."(46) What he knows is, as we have seen, that one's laugh is necessary to maintaining perspective. And so he sets out, consciously, to make his own laugh contagious--"all the time he was dealing he was joking and talking and trying to get the players to laugh along with him. But they were all afraid to loosen up; it'd been too long." (78) To Bromden, all the while, McMurphy is reminiscent of "Papa." After one of Mack's efforts to relieve tensions by making fun of people in power, Bromden recalls his father having once done much the same thing to government agents. As he remembers, "It sure did get their goat; they turned without saying a word and walked off toward the highway, red-necked, us laughing behind them. I forget sometimes what laughter can do." (92) But McMurphy never loses sight of what it can do, and he keeps campaigning among all of the non-laughing patients, to the extent that Bromden wonders if anything is serious to Mack:

> Maybe he couldn't understand why we weren't able to laugh yet, but he knew you can't really be strong until you can see a funny side to things. In fact, he worked so hard at pointing out the funny side of things that I was wondering a little if maybe he was blind to the other side, if maybe he wasn't able to see what it was that parched laughter deep inside your stomach. (227)

But elsewhere Bromden realizes that, indeed, Mack does know both "sides," but chooses to live by the laugh. And laugh he does throughout much of the hilarious fishing expedition (during which Bromden expresses the above concern), "Because he knows you have to laugh at the things that hurt you just to keep yourself in balance, just to keep the world from running you plumb crazy. He knows there's a painful side. . .but he won't let the pain blot out the humor no more'n he'll let the humor blot out the pain." (237-8)

But while McMurphy is useful to the other patients, even perhaps a savior to many of them, including Bromden, he is still a con-man as well. This aspect of him is emphasized more in the novel--where, being a fuller, more developed, more keenly perceived character, he is both better and worse than he is in the film. The main example in the novel of his being, among other things certainly, a chiseler is an example which again involves the Chief. McMurphy has Bromden lift the utility panel in the tub room (255-6) before he gets bets down on whether or not Bromden can lift it. This scene is not in the film.

Ultimately, the impelling factor in McMurphy's ambiguity is the effect which we perceive upon Bromden, whether or not Bromden perceives it himself. That is, Kesey employs the Apollonian device of allowing us to look through the Chief's semi-hallucinating narrative and to detect changes in his person--some of which Bromden is aware of and some of which, apparently, he is not. Those changes are positive, whether or not McMurphy's motives were pure.

That part of McMurphy's influence that bears most directly upon Bromden gets underway almost immediately. On Mack's first day in the ward, the Chief starts to come out of "the fog":

> Before noontime they're at the fog machine again but they haven't got it turned up full; it's not so thick but what I can see if I strain real hard. One of these days I'll quit straining and let myself go completely, lose myself in the fog the way some of the other Chronics have, but for the time being I'm interested in this new man—I want to see how he takes to the Group Meeting coming up. (39)

And thereafter the Chief, because he is intrigued by McMurphy's strength and (apparent) freedom, stays alert: "They haven't really fogged the place full force all day today, not since McMurphy came in. I bet he'd yell like a bull if they fogged it." (75)

McMurphy has further significance to Bromden because, unlike the Chief and his father before him, Mack has escaped "the Combine." This is his main difference from "Papa," who was destroyed by it. But Mack escaped its clutches, perhaps because "he growed up so wild all over the country, batting around from one place to another, never around one town longer'n a few months when he was a kid so a school never got much a hold on him . . .keeping on the move so much that the Combine never had a chance to get anything installed." (89) Also, this kept him free from familial ties, consequently he has had

"No one to <u>care</u> about, which is what makes him free enough to be a good con man." (89)

When McMurphy has gone into keeping a low profile around the ward, has temporarily abandoned his rebellion against Nurse Ratched and the system, Bromden can sense the "pull" on him. He expresses this through the metaphor of the "sniffing dog":

> ...I wanted to tell him not to fret about it, that nothing could be done, because I could see that there was some thought he was worrying over in his mind like a dog worries at a hole he don't know what's down, one voice saying, Dog, that hole is none of your affair--it's too big and too black and there's a spoor all over the place says bears or something just as bad. And some other voice coming like a sharp whisper out of way back in his breed, not a smart voice, nothing cagey about it, saying, <u>Sic</u> 'im, dog, <u>sic</u> 'im! (186)

It is interesting that Bromden uses the metaphor of the dog to characterize Mack's worries and how they are conflicting with his drives; earlier, this was just what the Chief watched in a "vision" (perhaps literally, but with Bromden who can be sure?). And that vision was important not just for what it symbolized concerning freedom, etc., but for the fact that it was the first exploration of the world around him that he had made in a long time--"one night I was even able to see out the windows..." (154) It represented the Chief's newly discovered ability at "seeing lots of things different"; (154) and that was a difference that McMurphy's influence had brought about--because he hadn't let "the Combine

mill him into fitting where they wanted him to fit."
(153) Something "way back in the breed" motivates
McMurphy also. He, too, is stirred by that "not smart"
voice. Were he to remain "cagey," he would also remain
"free enough to be the good con man"; but, in the world
of Bromden and McMurphy, one does not get to be an
individual without being a fighter. If Mack were not the
kind who hears that voice, then he would not be the
Combine-busting force that he is. Therein is the paradox
of R. P. McMurphy: the pressure within him, to be a
fighter, is bigger and stronger than any pressure from
without; and it is that internal pressure to which he
will respond--and succumb. He must be a Combine-fighter,
and that will be both his triumph and his destruction.

Meanwhile, we evaluate his success _via_ the
perceptions of Bromden--that is, our perceptions of the
Chief, as well as his own perceptions of everything,
including McMurphy. The ringing in his head stops (190)
and he notices "vaguely that I was getting so's I could
see some good in the life around me. McMurphy was
teaching me." (243) Even when coming out of shock-
treatment, he will not succumb to the "machinery": "It's
fogging a little, but I won't slip off and hide in it.
No...never again..." (275) Even after McMurphy has been
taken away, the Chief is still the gauge of tensions and
pressures in the ward. And he observes, simply:

"Everything was changing." (305) Big Nurse is no longer a terrifying machine: "She couldn't rule with her old power any more...She was losing her patients one after the other." (307) Sefelt and Frederickson check out (together); Harding signs out (and is picked up by his wife), just as he had predicted when urging McMurphy to escape; three other "acutes" leave; George Sorenson and six others transfer to other wards. Of the crew that went fishing, only Bromden, Martini, and Scanlon remain to receive what's left of McMurphy back in the ward. Realizing that Mack himself

> wouldn't have left something like that sit there in the day room with his name tacked on it for twenty or thirty years so the Big Nurse could use it as an example of what can happen if you buck the system...
> (308)

the Chief finishes the job, taking what little is left of McMurphy's life.

Leaving Mack's cap with Scanlon, Chief goes out in the way McMurphy showed him long before, by shoving the control panel through a window in the tub room. He catches a ride with a truck-driver and gives him "a good story about me being a professional Indian wrestler [McMurphy's invention] the syndicate had tried to lock up in a nuthouse...." (311) The story is good enough that the driver drops him off, gives him a jacket to cover the institutional clothes, and loans him ten bucks. Bromden has him write down his address so that the money can be repaid.

We see, clearly, all that Bromden has learned, most
of it from (or through) R. P. McMurphy:

> --to take care of himself;
>
> --to enlist support of others in that care;
>
> --to appreciate the value of confronting;
>
> --to distinguish between foe and friend;
>
> --to be responsible to and for the latter.

He has, as he says in the novel's last sentence, "been
away a long time"; but he may well be on his way back.

The Nietzschean dichotomy has worked well here. The
film, in its engaging robustness, in its spectacle, and
in its frenetic comedy, is almost sheerly Dionysian; the
novel, with those Apollonian elements that the film
lacks, has a more effective balance. Part of the
difference is in sheer quantity. We have seen elsewhere[3]
how that alone can make a significant difference. But
the greater cause of the differing effects is the
necessary absence from the film of Bromden-as-narrator.
Not only does that make the usual differences that loss
of a first-person point-of-view will make,[4] but it also
represents the loss of a "controlling" character in
something like Nietzsche's sense. We can see a more
reasonable development of plot and of characters in the
novel than we can in the film, because the novel's
Bromden is, in whatever metaphor one prefers, our gauge,

our mirror, our agent. Through him, in a direct way that a film or play probably can not duplicate, we see the changes that McMurphy effects and, thus, see the importance of McMurphy's tragic presence.

1. Ken Kesey, <u>One</u> <u>Flew</u> <u>Over</u> <u>the</u> <u>Cuckoo's</u> <u>Nest</u> (New York: Penguin, 1973). This is the "Viking Critical Edition," edited by John C. Pratt. Future references will be to this edition, with page numbers in parentheses in the text.

2. Friedrich Nietzsche, <u>The</u> <u>Birth</u> <u>of</u> <u>Tragedy</u>, in <u>Basic</u> <u>Writings</u> <u>of</u> <u>Nietzsche</u>, Walter Kaufmann, ed. (New York: Modern Library, 1968), p. 35. The translation is Kaufmann's.

3. See particularly the preceding essay, on <u>Catch</u>-<u>22</u>.

4. This will be discussed in more fundamental detail in an up-coming chapter on <u>Bang</u> <u>the</u> <u>Drum</u> <u>Slowly</u>.

THE CAINE MUTINY

The film "The Caine Mutiny" is perhaps more memorable than is Herman Wouk's novel that was its genesis. In some ways, the film is a better work, a less flawed work, than is the novel. However, it presents a case in which the film could have been considerably better than the novel, had it not retained most of the very items that marred the novel's success.

Wouk creates, in this novel, a number of opportunities for a screenplay writer. First, he tells a fascinating story. At the same time, he does not provide great depth of character. As we shall see, that is ultimately one of the novel's failings--his characters are up-front, black-and-white, basic types, with one exception, and the one exception could have been excised with no loss resulting to the novel's quality.

Consequently, characterization in this case should have been no problem to a film-maker. In addition, Wouk consistently over-writes. He goes on at too great length, he states things that need no statement, and he forces conclusions that should either have been left implicit or been omitted. All of these traits mean that The Caine Mutiny, which made a nearly great stage-play, could also have been transformed into a first-rate film. However, the film, while it has some fine moments, is considerably less than first-rate. Ironically, it lost its chance at greatness not, as many films-derived-from-novels do, by cutting and altering too much; rather, this one falls short by what it chooses to retain.

What we have discovered time and again by looking at the transformational process is that film does well, normally, with plot. It typically does less well with characterization, with depth and breadth of theme, with narrative point-of-view, and with those several aspects of style, especially irony, that will not readily translate into the pictorial. Consequently, Producer Stanley Kramer, Director Edward Dmytryk, and Screenplay Writer Stanley Roberts had ample opportunity to improve upon Wouk's novel. Whether or not Wouk was conscious of it at the time--there is some reason to believe he was not--by far the greatest strength of The Caine Mutiny is its plot. Wouk is a fine story-teller. Practically everyone who writes about him agrees upon that point, even those critics and reviewers who do not like much else about his work.[1] He may perform less admirably in other aspects of the novelist's art, but virtually everyone who reads The Caine Mutiny gets caught up in the Queeg portion of the story.

One indication of how good this film could and should have been is that the novel was converted into a stage-play that was both a critical and a popular success. The play, The Caine Mutiny Court-Martial, focused only on that part of the original story that takes place in court. Part of the inherent difficulty in producing it lay in what would have to be omitted. Charles Laughton, who directed, complained when first considering the script that the reader of the novel came to that scene with three hundred pages of background in mind: "Without that information the trial scene on the stage would be a mere confusing mass of words."[2] Yet, the play, while it has some faults, is, for the most part, good theatre. And a film could be a greater improvement upon the original material, for it could present whatever was essential in that first three hundred pages.

The film is not, by any means, a complete failure. But it fell far short of being the improved version of the story that it could have been, mainly because it chose, for some reasons that are explicable and some that are not, to repeat every one of the novel's main blunders. In particular, there are three "bulges" that swell Wouk's novel. They are obvious enough that the film-makers might have been expected to spot them; more than that, one might have expected anyone transforming this novel to cut these items, because they are time-consuming without being thematically, or otherwise, functional.

First, Wouk feels compelled to embroider upon his plot. He does not just tell the story of Commander Queeg, his officers, and the crew of the _Caine_. Rather, he makes the novel the story of Willie Keith, a Princeton graduate, who, unable to decide between becoming a comparative-literature professor or a honky-tonk pianist, joins the Navy and goes through Midshipman school. Willie's story surrounds the _Caine_ portion of the plot. We are sixty-five pages into the novel before this young protagonist sets foot on the ship, we are one hundred fifteen pages along before Queeg comes aboard, and--what few readers remember--the novel goes on for more than fifty pages after the court-martial has ended. By almost anyone's judgment, the Willie Keith portion could have been omitted. It does not work well as a _Bildungsroman_ to begin with--Keith seems hardly less adolescent at the end of the story than he'd been at the start--and even if there had been some clear development, his story might not have been worth the space and energy, for he is a jejune character at best. Nor is his presence necessary as a narrative device, for Wouk does not make much use of narrative point-of-view. Indeed, if he had done so, he might have succeeded in giving the Queeg story some of the ambiguity he seems, at the end, to want it to have, and he might not have had to force ambivalence upon his story, as he does.

In part, Wouk probably stumbled upon Willie Keith as an authorial persona. Keith shares many of the details of Wouk's own life. Both studied comparative literature, one at Columbia, the other at Princeton. Each attended Midshipman School at Columbia, then became communications officer on a mine-sweeper (Wouk's first ship was the _Zane_). As Willie's father dies during Willie's first year in the Navy, so did Wouk's father die when Wouk had been in about the same length of time. Coincidentally or not, Keith's initials form an abbreviation of Wouk's last name.

But Willie becomes a character separable from the author, albeit an unattractive character, and one who is not even especially interesting. A momma's boy, even though he keeps telling himself he will no longer be one, he joins the Navy mainly to avoid the Army. He is snobbish, racist, and--even for 1951--sexist. "He

. . .flirted with girls of his own class, and pressed matters further with girls of lower station."[3] We never see him fully outgrow this. Not only a nasty little twerp, he is also a gutless one, and constantly fears how his mother will feel about Marie Minotti, who goes by "May Wynn," her stage name. Once he has slept with May, he realizes the very next morning that the event has "sunk the girl [sic] in his esteem though it had heightened her as an object of desire." (196) Of course, it does not much matter to May how she is treated, for she is an all-too-typical woman (or "girl") in Wouk's fiction. So the entire Willie Keith sub-plot could be cut with little negative effect upon the novel.

The second bulge of the novel is not such a major structural matter, but is, by comparison, a seemingly trivial inclusion. This bulge involves a legal error, committed by prosecutor Jack Challee and defense lawyer Barney Greenwald in Steve Maryk's court-martial. Both are insistent upon proving Commander Queeg's sanity or insanity, respectively. This not only makes for intrigue, and a chance for Greenwald to be immensely clever in cross-examining psychiatrists, but it creates a convenience for Wouk: he can write a trial-ending scene in which Queeg becomes an incoherent babbler on the witness-stand and thus proves Greenwald's case, and Maryk's innocence. Now, the presence of this is understandable, in a way, as it does make for some good courtroom melodrama, and it clearly grew out of Wouk's "study of psychoneurotic case histories"[4] prior to his writing the novel. But it needlessly complicates the novel's court proceedings and it harms the verisimilitude of the plot. Worse than that, it makes Greenwald look like a careless lawyer, for he lets himself get sucked into an irrelevant consideration, and one extremely difficult for him to contest, since the prosecution has brought in three psychiatrists to testify to Queeg's sanity. It also makes the novel longer than necessary--again, presumably, making it more adaptable to film, as it cries out to be lessened.

One of Wouk's several prefaces to this novel cites the three articles from Navy Regulations that allow-- but set stringent conditions upon--such an action as that which Maryk performed. The most directly relevant is Article 184:

> It is conceivable that most unusual and extraordinary circumstances may arise in which the relief from duty of a commanding officer by a subordinate becomes necessary, either by placing him under arrest or on the sick list; but such action shall never be taken without the approval of the Navy Department or other appropriate higher authority, except when reference to such higher authority is undoubtedly impracticable because of the delay involved or for other clearly obvious reason. Such reference must set forth all facts in the case, and the reasons for the recommendation, with particular regard to the degree of urgency involved.

Now notice how simplistically Lieutenant Challee plans
his prosecution:

> The defense could not possibly deny that the
> event had occurred; Maryk had signed logs
> describing it. The key words [in the
> specification of charges] were <u>without</u>
> <u>proper</u> <u>authority</u> <u>and</u> <u>without justifiable</u>
> <u>cause</u>. To establish their truth, Challee
> simply had to prove that Queeg was not and
> never had been a madman. (376)

His case might be that simple if the charges specified
"without justifiable reason for believing the commanding
officer to be mad," but they do not. Surely one can
imagine justifiable causes that do not necessitate the
commanding officer's being insane. If, given certain
stressful conditions, he is merely incompetent as a ship-
handler, then his ship and its men would have been
sufficiently endangered for Maryk to have been justified
in taking control.

This error is repeated constantly throughout the
court-martial. During a break in testifying, Willie
Keith begins to rethink his testimony and, by extension,
his actions during the typhoon:

> In plain truth, he had obeyed Maryk for two
> reasons, first, because he thought the exec
> was more likely to save the ship, and second,
> because he hated Queeg. It had never
> occurred to him, until Maryk took command,
> that Queeg might be really insane. And he
> knew, deep down, that he never had believed
> the captain was crazy. Stupid, mean,
> vicious, cowardly, incompetent, yes--but
> sane. The insanity of Queeg was Maryk's only
> possible plea. . .and it was a false plea
> . . . . (399)

Clearly, the captain's insanity is not the solely relevant factor, if in fact it is relevant at all. When one considers the characteristics that could render a captain a danger, in time of stress, to his ship and its crew, stupidity, cowardice, and incompetence are more than adequate; there is little reason to insist upon finding him insane into the bargain. Furthermore, Article 184 does not, in any terms, make mention of insanity.

Yet this same notion is pursued still further in this exchange between Challee and Maryk:

> "You got a headful of [psychiatric] terms you didn't understand, and on that basis you had the temerity to depose a commanding officer   no the grounds of mental illness. Is that correct?"
>   "I didn't relieve him because of what the books said. The ship was in danger--"
>   "Never mind the ship. We're discussing your grasp of psychiatry, Lieutenant. . . ."
>   (418)

This would replace the key point with an irrelevance.

The capper to this line of reasoning is in Challee's closing argument:

> "The one issue in this trial was the insanity of Commander Queeg--the insanity, not the mistakes or misdeeds or poor judgment. The language of Articles 184, 185, and 186 excludes every possibility except the complete, utter, and unmistakeable madness of the captain."   (436)

This is nonsense on stilts. Let it be cited once more: The reader looks in vain for any mention, in the

applicable regulations, of "madness," "insanity," "mental
disturbance," "mental illness," or any similar term.

Before we come to the third superfluity, a blunder
of major proportions that is virtually fatal to the
novel, it is necessary to review how thoroughly and
sequentially Wouk presents to the reader his portrait of
Lieutenant Commander Philip Francis Queeg. That portrait
is drawn elaborately if not subtly; it is considerably
more blatant than it is ambiguous, and that fact becomes
vitally important in the concluding section of the
novel.

When Queeg first comes aboard the _Caine_, he seems
confident and self-assured. Indeed, he relieves the
previous skipper, Lt. Cdr. DeVriess, earlier than
DeVriess had thought he would. In just one momentary
flash does he give any hint of the Queeg that is to be:
In one of his first speeches to any officer, he tells
Tom Keefer, "'In this Navy, a commanding officer gets a
chance to make one mistake--just one mistake, that's all.
They're just waiting for me to make that one mistake'."
(132) But as soon as command is his, Queeg begins to
disintegrate. The first time, under his guidance, that
the ship gets underway, it is on a perfectly routine move
to a fueling dock. However, it quickly becomes anything
but routine. Queeg backs the ship down so rapidly that
he rips its forecastle against the ship moored alongside,

causing structural as well as superficial damage. Then
he issues "a tangle of wheel and engine orders. . ."
(140) and backs the ship aground. Seemingly unflustered,
Queeg chooses not to file a grounding report with his
squadron commander, as regulations require, but to
signal, by light, a passing tug to tow him out of the
mud. When the squadron command learns of the grounding
anyway, and orders a report, Queeg invents a reason for
the grounding: ". . .failure of the engine room to
respond in time to engine orders telegraphed from the
bridge." (142) Then he sends his Executive Officer, Burt
Gorton, ashore to find out if he, Queeg, is in trouble.
This earns the exec a chewing-out from the Squadron
Operations Officer, Captain Grace: "You go tell Queeg
that if he has any inquiries about operations he's to
come here in person, and not send subordinates. Is that
clear?" (144) The new skipper follows that by informing
all his officers that "a naval officer is supposed to
execute his orders, not speculate about them. . ." (147)

He gets the ship underway on a target-towing
operation, on which he insists, while backing out into
the channel, that he be given the operation's course-
heading; clearly, he has forgotten that the ship is still
backing. (150) While the ship is in fog, Queeg runs from
wing to wing. "His jaw was slack; his lips trembled."
(149) Informed that he is bearing down on a battleship,

"Queeg opened and closed his mouth three times without uttering a sound, then he choked out, 'All engines back full--bah--bah--belay that--All stop'." (151) The battleship passes, barely, "hooting angrily." It then becomes clear that the Caine is on the wrong side of the channel. (151) Shortly after that, while Queeg is reprimanding a sailor for not having his shirttail tucked in, the "Caine majestically steamed over its own tow cable," (155) severing it, then continues in at least a half-circle more before the captain notices. When he does notice, he files another false report to his superior. (156) Although retrieving a target-sled is no great project, Queeg does not do so; the implication is that he does not know how to do so. Later, he blames Gorton for not telling him that it would have been easy to do.

For all this, Queeg is ordered to make a report in person to Capt. Grace. The order comes in an official mailgram, which, in unusually strong language, demands the report "on latest fiasco." (158) Queeg goes to Grace and, after assuring him "'I am not so stupid as to lie to a superior officer'," proceeds to evade the truth, blatantly. Asked directly if he turned in a circle and cut the towline, Queeg says "'with all submission'" that he must "'resent that question, and regard it as a personal insult'." When the question of whether or not

it happened is repeated, Queeg replies: "'If it did, sir,
I think I ought to have recommended my own general court-
martial.'" (163) Before their interview ends,[5] Captain
Grace offers Queeg a state-side job, "with no reflection
whatever" upon his performance on the Caine. (165)
Eventually, he relents and lets Queeg return to his
command, cautioning him that he should be less concerned
about making mistakes and should just concentrate on
doing what is useful and sensible. (166) Queeg has, at
this point, been in command less than four weeks.

From this point, Queeg gets no better. His
competence as a ship-handler, his emotional stability,
his ability to interact with other people, his capacity
for enduring stress, his honesty and fair-mindedness--
all of these are shown to be lacking over the next couple
of hundred pages. Soon, the officers of the Caine speak
of him, to one another, with unveiled derision. After
Keefer suggests to Maryk what has long since occurred to
the reader, that Queeg may be mentally disturbed and a
danger to the ship, Maryk begins keeping a "log" of the
captain's aberrant behavior. In the meantime, the reader
also compiles a case against Queeg's competence to
command a ship. It is necessary to review, here, some
of the items that go into making up that case (actually,
fewer than half of those that the novel describes), in
order to show the degree to which, and the overwhelming

quantity with which, Wouk establishes Queeg's incompetence. The incidents, which are in addition to those already cited, are arranged here in basically chronological order; one must remember that some of them are not known to Maryk, and almost all are unknown to any of Queeg's superior officers. Only the reader knows all the details of all the incidents first-hand.

Liquor. Queeg has all the officers sell him their liquor rations. He has the ship's carpenter make him a crate for thirty-one bottles of booze, which he means to bring into the states, illegally. (His response to its being a violation of law and regulations: "Rank hath its privileges. . . ." [179]) When the boat crew cannot handle the heavy crate, and it sinks, he blames Keith. He seems about to deny him a chance to go ashore in the states, until Willie "volunteers" to pay him one hundred and ten dollars for the lost alcohol. Later, Queeg attempts to lie about this at the court-martial, claiming that the crate sank with "uniforms, books, navigating equipment." (423) When Greenwald suggests that the carpenter's mate who built it could be subpoenaed, Queeg begins to remember more accurately. (424-425)

Combat. Once the Caine has been ordered to Kwajalein, Queeg falls into "a curious lassitude." (224) He stays in his cabin, clad only in underwear, doing jigsaw puzzles. He does not take his meals with the other officers in the wardroom, but orders to his cabin "almost nothing but enormous quantities of ice cream with maple syrup. . . ." (225) Lest we miss these signs, Wouk has Willie Keith notice that Queeg acts "like a man trying to forget a terrible sorrow." Thereupon, Wouk sets us straight: "It never crossed the ensign's mind that the bad news might have been the operation order." (225) It is important to notice here that we are not confused, nor are perceptions made ambiguous, by any trick of point-of-view. On the contrary, the third-person narrative voice corrects the mistaken impressions of Willie Keith.

Yellowstain. When Queeg comes to the bridge for this operation, he is "hunched almost to a crouch, his head moving ceaselessly to and fro. . . ." (232) He does not take the conn, but leaves it to Willie. When Ensign Keith, in his first combat situation, asks once what he should do, this is the response: "'Whatever you please,' said the captain, and giggled." (232) It is during this operation that his officers realize that Queeg is never seen on the side of the bridge exposed to enemy fire. When the ship gets close to the landing-boats to be escorted, Queeg gives the conn to Maryk. (236-237) At the court-martial, he also lies about this incident. (429-430)

U.S.S. Stanfield. After Kwajalein, the next time

the _Caine_ goes near combat is during the invasion of

Saipan.   That leads to "one of the briefest and most

important entries" in Maryk's "medical log" of Queeg:

> . . .this vessel was investigating the scene
> of an air crash with a destroyer. The
> destroyer, 1000 yards on our beam, was taken
> under fire by a shore battery. Captain
> reversed course and left scene without firing
> a shot, though battery was well within our
> range and our guns were manned and ready.
> (270)

Again, there is no problem with reliability of point-

of-view, here. We have witnessed enough previously to

know that Maryk's log entry is accurate. Significantly,

this incident is not mentioned at the court-martial.

Nor is it used at all in the play or in the film.

Strawberries.   This famous incident is perhaps

Queeg's zaniest episode.   In a quest for some fresh

strawberries that had remained after dinner, but which

turn up missing during the night (when Queeg has called

for some), he seizes every personal key on board,

convinced that, somehow, someone fabricated a duplicate

key to the wardroom icebox. The case necessitates strip-

searches of all the crew. When he is told (twice) that

the steward's mates were seen eating the left-over

berries, he refuses to believe either report. Along the

way, he threatens dishonorable discharges to anyone who

lies to him about the incident.

The typhoon.   Early on in this climactic scene,

Queeg shows signs of cracking. His voice is "shrill" at one point, and a "squeak" at another. (326) When upset to discover that the depth charges have been set on safe without his having ordered them to be--although to do so was a reasonable precaution--he turns upon the sailor who did so: "'You speak when you're spoken to, you goddamned imbecile, and not otherwise,' [he shrieks], '. . .Now Steve, I want you to get another helmsman and keep this stupid idiot's ugly face out of my sight from now on--'" (328) When, a short time later, Maryk tries to suggest backing the starboard engine, the captain seems first not to hear. When Maryk raises his voice, then "Queeg, clinging to the telegraph with his knees and arms, threw him a frightened glance, his skin greenish, and obediently slid the handle backward." (329) His voice thereafter is "a muffled croak." When the backing tactic starts to work, and the rudder begins to respond, it is Maryk who has to instruct the helmsman to ease the rudder: "Without so much as a glance at the captain, Stilwell obeyed. Willie noticed the omission, for all that he was terror-stricken; and he noticed, too, that Queeg, frozen to the telegraph stand, seemed oblivious." (329) He continues in this trance-like state while Maryk has to suggest to him every order to the helmsman and the engine-room, at one point having to wrest the engine-room telegraph's handles "from Queeg's spasmodic grip."

(333) At last, when the ship is righted, and about the time that Keith has "lost all awareness of the captain's presence," because he is rapt in admiration of Maryk's navigating, Queeg, "blinking and shaking his head as though he had just awakened," attempts--after the fact--to countermand Maryk's orders. It is then that Maryk relieves him of command. (334) The film, it should be noted, keeps all of this last "business" in about the same order: Queeg clinging, frozen, to the telegraph stand, oblivious to what's going on, and then shaking his head as though he has just snapped out of a trance.

That the foregoing catalogue of incidents demonstrates beyond doubt Queeg's incompetence as a commanding officer should be clear to anyone. Yet, after having presented all of this, and after having taken us through Lieutenant Maryk's court-martial, at which he is acquitted, Wouk then commits the novel's devastating blunder: He attempts to reverse direction, to moderate (however retroactively) Queeg's character, to convince the reader that it was wrong for Maryk to have taken over command from Queeg, and erroneous of Maryk's court-martial to have acquitted him. This attempted reversal begins immediately after the court-martial has ended, when Barney Greenwald comes to the party thrown by Keefer (a combinative celebration of Maryk's acquittal and

Keefer's having sold his novel) and informs Maryk and Keith how wrong they were. He then indulges in some drunken [6] and not very relevant rhapsodizing about (a) how necessary this war is; and (b) how glad we should all be that, during peacetime, while most folk were enjoying whatever lucrative careers they were pursuing, "these birds we call regulars" were "'standing guard on this fat dumb and happy country of ours.'" (441)

Granting, even, that both of Greenwald's claims are true, they are quite irrelevant to the Queeg whom we have come to know. Surely there can be no reader who thinks Queeg is a good or even acceptable commanding officer? When one reads the catalogue of his abuses set forth here--and everything about him here has come straight from the novel--it is impossible not to perceive a bad officer, one who thoroughly deserved to be relieved of command. Better yet, if one imagines the novel as a depiction of "real life," there can be no intelligent reader who, imagining being aboard the Caine during the typhoon, would not feel exactly as Keith did about Maryk's taking over from the panicked, frozen Queeg.

This much of an attempt at reversing the main direction his story had taken throughout would be bad enough; but Wouk goes further. Willie Keith's story is resumed after the court-martial, with his going back to the Caine as executive officer. Tom Keefer is now the captain. How anybody could have appointed him to command, or why he would have accepted, is not quite clear. It all gets less credible when we are told that the Navy's "Bureau of Personnel had evidently decided that scattering the Caine's officers and crew was the best way to dissolve the bitterness of the Queeg days." (446) But of course Keefer and Keith had to stay, because Wouk is not finished with them. His purpose in "promoting" Keefer is, apparently, to moderate the reader's view of Queeg by making Keefer just about equally incompetent to command. This endeavor to create ambiguity-after-the-fact is doomed before it begins, as Wouk has made the case against Queeg too clearly, too blatantly, for us to let it be moderated at this late point. Curiously, he seems to feel that he diminishes any harsh judgments against the U. S. Navy by this reversal. No less oddly, critics and reviewers never seem to notice that, with this added-on portion of the novel, Wouk--albeit inadvertently--makes his harshest criticism of the Navy. To have allowed one Queeg to rise to command level would be a forgiveable error; to compound a Queeg with a Tom Keefer suggests the work of a truly bungling organization.

Finally, Wouk has Willie indicate, in a letter to May, that all of Queeg's troubles were only the result of the way his underlings treated him:

> I now see pretty clearly that the "mutiny"
> was mostly Keefer's doing--though I have to
> take a lot of the blame and so does Maryk--
> and I see that we were in the wrong. We
> transferred to Queeg the hatred we should
> have felt for Hitler and the Japs . . . .Our
> disloyalty made things twice as tough for
> Queeg and for ourselves; drove him to his
> worst outrages and made him a complete
> psychological mess. (463)

This is bad for two reasons. First, it contradicts the evidence that Wouk himself has so abundantly supplied. On almost his first day aboard the Caine, as we have seen, Queeg was talking about how "They" were just waiting for him to make a mistake. On his very first outing at the conn, he nearly wrecked his own ship, did damage to another, evaded his responsibility to report the incident, lied in the report when he was forced to make it, and later lied to a superior about having evaded the report in the first place. Clearly, he was something of a "mess" when the Caine got him. Second, this bit of pop psychology that Wouk attributes to Keith is too simplistic, even for such a naif as Willie still is. Are we to believe that if his officers had but given him tea and sympathy Queeg would have been perfectly competent in a typhoon? To his first executive officer, Gorton, Queeg behaved threateningly, meanly, and probably illegally, although Gorton was one of the most doggedly loyal officers he had.

This bit of absurdity soon leads to a central

inanity. Willie's conclusion from the foregoing is that
"once you get an incompetent ass of a skipper. . .there's
nothing to do but serve him as though he were the wisest
and the best, cover his mistakes, keep the ship going,
and bear up." (464) Credibility is the issue. Almost any
competent reader of this novel, considering what s/he
would have wanted done, if required to be present on the
Caine during the typhoon, would choose to have Maryk do
precisely what he did.   It is clear to all of us that
Queeg was not in control, in any sense of that phrase.
Nor can any of us who reads as far as the disapproval,
by the reviewing authority, of Maryk's court-martial's
decision, believe that the American people would be
better served by the return to duty of a Queeg and the
easing-out of a Maryk.   And a novel that makes itself
unbelievable, no matter how well it may have done some
things, has failed a rather fundamental requirement.

Independent of Wouk's treatment of the film's
source-material, the film-makers had reasons of their
own to be cautious. History shows it to be part of the
nature of censorship to come down even harder on theatre
than on printed matter; and this was the age of Joe
McCarthy and his henchmen, who had already singled out
Hollywood for particular abuse.   On top of that, the
rights to the film came into the hands of some

notoriously careful people--not surprisingly, for no one
unwilling to sacrifice art to caution would touch it.
At least four purchasers of the film-rights dropped their
options because of public resistance to the film from the
U. S. Navy.[7] Consequently, Stanley Kramer was able to
buy the rights "for a song."[8] Kramer would often be
involved, as producer and/or director, with films that
seemed to be dealing with "difficult" themes, but
invariably would find easy evasions.[9] The Navy even
objected to the use of "mutiny" in the title and
suggested it be replaced by "Incident."[10] Yet, following
negotiations, Kramer won more than normal co-operation
from the Navy. It would provide a ship for location,
ships for background, and official war film (in color)
for battle scenes.[11] Kramer himself would say he felt
"practically in command of Pearl Harbor for five weeks."[12]
To direct the film, Kramer chose Edward Dmytryk, who had
learned caution the hard way. One of the "Hollywood
Ten," Dmytryk had spent a year in jail, gone to England
for three years, then come back to the U.S. just in time
to be a star witness for the next round of HUAC hearings.
Consequently, he was removed from the blacklist.[13]

Given the inherent caution of the producer, and
the director's acquired caution, one might have guessed
that this would not be a film that would dare to be bold.
Additionally, one supposes that there must have been some

assurances given the Navy, for it to have changed course
so drastically, from opposition to almost unprecedented
co-operation. The concessions that Kramer made have been
primary in keeping the film from exceeding the quality
of the novel; they seem fairly obvious when one examines
the film.

As soon as the credits have run, and before there
is any picture, this message fills the screen: "There
has never been a mutiny in a ship of the United States
Navy. The truths of this film lie not in its incidents
but in the way a few men meet the crisis of their lives."
This is not particularly bothersome; in fact, it is not
so profusely apologetic as the prefatory "Note" in the
published version of the stage-play,[14] which is in turn
less elaborate than Wouk's disclaimer in the novel. So
far, then, the film was headed, perhaps, toward an
improvement.

However, any optimism raised by this beginning is
eventually let down. The film retains virtually
everything that was disappointing in the novel, and then
some. It keeps the Willie Keith portions, including his
romance with May Wynn. Obviously, that part of the film
goes by a bit more quickly than does the equivalent part
of the novel; on the other hand, the proportion of this
film given to Willie-and-May is a major flaw,
particularly the inordinately long time given to their

Yosemite trip. As in the novel, there is little we see in the film, even near the end, to suggest that maturity has made much inroad upon Willie. Not the least of the negative effects of the film's keeping all this is that it leaves too little time to capitalize upon what Wouk has done well.

As in the play and the novel, the legal considerations take a wrong direction in the film, concentrating upon Queeg's sanity. Here again, the film-makers missed an opportunity to improve upon the play. Some of the incidents that motivate Maryk to replace Queeg could have been made more ambiguous. More incidents that make Queeg look at least occasionally competent could have been added, providing a balance to his character. Some of the instances of his incompetence, cowardice, instability, etc., could have come to us indirectly--perhaps from unreliable reporters, such as Keefer--rather than being shown, just as Wouk could have altered point-of-view in the novel, so that we would have had to see events through the perceptions of, say, Keith. Instead, we get the same wrongly designed "dilemma" as in the other versions of this story: Do all these (clearly incompetent, endangering) actions of Queeg's constitute schizophrenia or paranoia or some other defineable mental illness?

Finally, the film retains, perhaps predictably, the

novel's major flaw: It too tries to reverse what we know long after we are sure we know it. In fact, the film takes an unfortunate turn of its own. In an effort, presumably, to make the reversal not quite so difficult for an audience to accept, the film adds a scene. After the "Yellowstain" episode, Queeg calls a meeting of all the officers. Starting with his admission that he is "not feeling well," it is a pathetic scene. He makes a self-pitying speech, in which he observes that, because "command is a lonely job," therefore the "captain of a ship needs. . .constructive loyalty." He desperately tries to joke about not being such a bad fellow, as evidenced by the fact that his dog likes him. He concludes by trying to draw an analogy of shipboard officers to a family. When he pauses for comments, the other officers embarrassedly try to look elsewhere. Nobody responds. Queeg retires to his cabin, asking that the pharmacist's mate send him more aspirin, as his "headache is much worse." Following this scene, Keefer makes his first allegations of the captain's possible mental illness. "He's a Freudian delight," Keefer asserts. "He crawls with clues." He does, of course, because Wouk, on the basis of his "study of psychoneurotic case histories,"[15] planted them.

When Maryk suggests, following this meeting, that perhaps the officers should have offered Queeg some show of support, Keith asks the salient, and never-answered, question: "What could we have said?" What, indeed?

After Maryk's court-martial, the film follows up on this added scene. The somewhat-intoxicated Greenwald informs Maryk and Keith that he is "sick about" having had to "torpedo" Queeg on their behalf. To Keith's demurral that Queeg "endangered the ship and the lives of the men," Greenwald responds: "He didn't endanger anybody's life. You did, all of you. You're a fine bunch of officers." This contradiction of logic and the audience's perceptions is then aggravated. "You know," Greenwald recalls, "I left out one detail [from testimony]. . .Tell me, Steve, after the Yellowstain business, Queeg came to you for help and you turned him down, didn't you?" When Maryk confirms that they did, there comes this stunner:

> "You didn't approve of his conduct as an
> officer. He wasn't worthy of your loyalty.
> So you turned on him. You ragged him. You
> made up songs about him. If you'd have given
> Queeg the loyalty he needed, do you suppose
> the whole issue would've come up in the
> typhoon? . . .Do you think it would've
> been necessary for you to take over?"

Astoundingly, Maryk agrees that it "probably wouldn't have been necessary," which leads Greenwald to conclude that indeed Maryk and Keith were guilty.[16] However, when he then turns on Keefer--accusing him, with less unsound logic, at least, of being the real villain in this piece

--he notes a contrast between the others and the captain, namely, "Queeg was sick; he couldn't help himself."

Where the novel is simplistic and illogical, the film is no less so. Its ambiguities are even less earned than were Wouk's.

This is doubly unfortunate, for the film, in this case, had every opportunity to exceed its source material. There was a terrific story at the center of the novel,[17] there were some movingly dramatic scenes (the typhoon, cutting the towing cable, Queeg's testimony, etc.), and there were portions from which cuts were obviously needed. Instead, the cautious trio of Kramer, Dmytryk, and Roberts stuck with almost everything Wouk had done wrong, and thus left themselves all too little time and space to capitalize upon what he had done well.

1. Thus we see, not surprisingly, an essay in _Time_ that calls Wouk "first and last a topnotch storyteller" (_Time_, September 5, 1955, p. 48). But we also see, more surprisingly, William Whyte admit that "Much of [the novel's] success...was due to the fact that it is a rattling good tale." (William H. Whyte, Jr., _The Organization Man_ [New York: Simon & Schuster, 1956], p. 269.) Chapter 19, "Love that System," pp. 269-75, is devoted to this novel. And even Harvey Swados, who is not fond of much that Wouk does, observes "that Mr. Wouk is an exceptionally good story-teller." (Harvey Swados, "Popular Taste and _The Caine Mutiny_," _Partisan Review_, 20 [Mar.-Apr. 1953], p. 252.)

2. _The New York Times_, January 17, 1954, Sec. II, p. 1.

3. Herman Wouk, _The Caine Mutiny_ (New York: Doubleday, 1951), p. 11. All references will be to this edition, with page numbers in parentheses in text.

4. This quotation is from a "Note" which prefaces the novel, on a page un-numbered but presumably p. _vi_. The novel has a quantity of prefatory material, about which more will follow here shortly.

5. Curiously, neither Greenwald nor anyone else, as best the reader can tell, talks to Capt. Grace before Maryk's court-martial.

6. How drunk Wouk means Greenwald to be is never clear. In a single sentence, at one point, he slurs the name of Keith's _alma mater_ as "Prinshton," then makes reference, flawlessly, to "stuffy, stupid Prussians." (441)

7. _Time_, June 28, 1954, p. 90.

8. _Newsweek_, June 28, 1954, p. 72.

9. _The Oxford Companion to Film_ (Liz-Anne Bowden, ed.) describes Kramer's films as those "that exploit the inherent dramatic value of moral conflict without disturbing too many preconceptions. (New York/London: Oxford U. Press, 1976, p. 397.) Among them are "On the Beach," "Inherit the Wind," and "Guess Who's

Coming to Dinner." This last is remembered by some
people as a "daring" film, though in fact the Black
man brought home by daughter-of-White-liberal-
parents is a highly reputed M.D.

10.   William H. Brown, Jr., "The Caine Mutiny," in
Magill's Survey of Cinema, English Language Films,
First Series, vol. 1 (Englewood Cliffs, NJ: Salem
Press, 1980), p. 275.

11.   Jessie Zunser, Cue, June 26, 1954, p. 16.

12.   Time, June 28, 1954, p. 90.

13.   Ephraim Katz, The Film Encyclopedia (New York:
Crowell, 1979), p. 344.

14.   Herman Wouk, The Caine Mutiny Court-Martial (New
York:Doubleday, 1954).

15.   One is reminded of David Lynch and his "book of
sexual aberrations." See the essay here on "Blue
Velvet."

16.   I am convinced that the following is factual, though
I have made no scientific survey on the point:
Almost everyone who has seen this movie, even--
perhaps especially--those who liked it, has
forgotten or never really noticed the first time
that Greenwald tells Keith and Maryk that they were
guilty. What viewers remember instead, apart from
the strawberries, is two things: Queeg's becoming
totally non-functional during the typhoon, and his
falling apart on the witness-stand.

17.   Lee Rogow stated in a review of the novel that the
best parts of the plot "fill two hundred and fifty
of the most exciting pages you'll find in any novel
of World War II...," but cautioned also that the
whole novel "fills about five hundred pages."
(Saturday Review, March 31,1951, p. 17.)

BANG THE DRUM SLOWLY

This venture into a novel-film transformation will
begin by seeming to wander--one should pardon the
expression--rather far afield. The reader must trust
that it will work back toward a main point. But first,
by way of prelude, the following dialogue. This came up
in an interview with John Nichols, whose earliest
experience with film is chronicled in another essay in
this book. Since The Sterile Cuckoo, Nichols has done
other writing for film, and he and the interviewer had
been discussing his script for the filming of another of
his novels, The Milagro Beanfield War, which at the time
was in production on location in New Mexico. The
relevance of this interview will soon become clear.

> INT: What you say [about the difficulty of anyone's
> adapting some of his fiction to film] seems
> logical to me too. I can't imagine trying to

make a film of, say, <u>The Magic Journey</u>.

JN: Oh, I figured out a neat ploy for that one.
I boiled down the first three hundred pages
of the book into two pages of screen-time.
It was wonderful. I opened the script up
with just a scene in a living room in Las
Vegas with Rody McQueen and some lieutenant
with him there, just trying to sell these
gangsters, these organized-crime figures, on
investing in Chamisaville and building this
racing track in the Pueblo. But the way the
scene is done, it's very clipped. You just
open up on all these figures in a darkened
room with a slide-projector. Rody and his
people are just pitching this town. And in
about six or eight slides they show the whole
set-up.

INT: ....and then there'e some flashback after
that? Or not?

JN: No. No flashback. That's it; in just eight
slides, they tell the whole forty-year
history of Chamisaville. Eight slides--
boom! It's done.

INT: No explosion at the Dynamite Shrine?

JN: No, you don't worry about that [stuff].
That's too complicated. You need to tell the
story of the last year, in that town.
Otherwise, you're doing some <u>magnum</u> <u>opus</u> that
never ends. . . .

INT: . . . .No April's childhood then, either?

JN: No, not the way I set it up. Those things
you can tell easily, with McQueen sitting in
his room, looking at photographs, or
something like that. But that's what's
true about films, and what you have to
realize: Movies are not novels; movies are
short-stories. What you have to do is to
select--you say, Okay, where's the story we
want to tell? And you tell it. And [forget]
the other stuff; you don't worry about that.
And if you start throwing the other stuff in,
cluttering it with a whole bunch of asides
and stuff like that, then you ruin it, you
ruin your movie.

INT: But, see, that's my point--I think we're
talking about the same thing, after all.
When I say I can't imagine anyone filming The
Magic Journey, this is the sort of thing I
mean. Because to my way of thinking, you're
talking about filming a slice of The Magic
Journey.

JN: Ah, but you wouldn't believe what one can do
if he does it well. The trick, of course, is
doing it well.

It is precisely because Nichols is "normally" a
novelist, but one who finds writing for film exciting
and attractive, that he is quoted here. What he has to
say about the differences in writing for the two media
establishes a large part of what will be contended in
this essay: movies are not novels; movies are short-
stories. Consequently, one of the most consistent areas
of difference when a film is "made from" (or "based
upon") a novel is a quantitative area. No matter how
well a film tells virtually the same story as a novel,
it will never tell the whole story of the novel. This
is, to be sure, an obvious enough point. Yet it can
hardly be said too often, for almost all other changes
follow from it, and looking at precisely what parts of
the novel get lost in transformation is instructive about
that particular novel.

What will be demonstrated here is that the Mark
Harris novel Bang the Drum Slowly[1] and John Hancock's
film of the same name (for which Harris wrote the

screenplay) are such differing versions of the same story that they might better be thought of as different stories. In fact, anyone who wished to learn, or to teach, the fundamental differences between novel and film might do well to examine this particular transformation, for it provides a textbook example of the qualities gained and lost when such a transformation happens. Looking at both versions of the story also provides some insights to baseball previously unrecognized even by devout followers of the game. But we will come to that demonstration shortly. First, it will be necessary to summarize the novel's plot, rather more elaborately than would be necessary to refresh a reader's memory, for it will become important here for the reader to realize that the novel's story is not only longer, but fuller (and, literature-oriented folk may want to add, "therefore, better") than that of the film.

Henry Wiggen, the novel's narrator, is an outstanding left-handed pitcher for the New York Mammoths. When the novel opens, in January of 1955, Henry has not yet signed his contract for the coming year, and he will eventually hold out for better terms until almost literally the last minute of spring training. Henry's immediately preceding season was his poorest in the majors, although he has been a star since his 1952 rookie season, described by Mark Harris (and

Henry the narrator) in the earlier novel The Southpaw.

Henry has been the roommate of catcher Bruce Pearson, partly because none of the other Mammoths wants to be, for Bruce is--socially and otherwise--something of a klutz. In hotel rooms on the road, Bruce is inclined to spend his time spitting out the window and keeping Henry posted on whether the saliva falls in an in- or out-curve. As a ballplayer Bruce is described by Henry thus:

> . . .here was a boy that could belt a ball a mile and run like a dear [sic] and throw like a rifle, one of the nicest arms in baseball, bar none, if he only didn't have to stop and think, never a natural but always a powerful promise. (32)

Bruce has never lived up to his powerful promise, because he gives the game no concentration, he brings to it no intensity. Consequently, he has remained, since his first full Mammoths season in 1949, a marginal major-leaguer.

The novel opens, then, with Henry and his wife, Holly, who is pregnant with their first child, being awakened by a collect call to their Perkinsville, New York, home from Bruce in Rochester, Minnesota. All Bruce will say on the telephone is, "'You have got to come and see me, Arthur.'" (The other players call Henry "Author" after he has "written" The Southpaw, and Bruce mis-hears it as "Arthur." Why he thinks everyone would call a man "Arthur" whose name is Henry is known only to Bruce.

This piece of business is not in the film.) Holly tells
Henry that if Bruce needs him he must go, so Henry does.
When he arrives at the hospital (not named, but clearly
intended to be the Mayo Clinic), Henry is told by a team
of doctors that Bruce has Hodgkin's Disease which will
certainly be fatal--or, as Bruce explains, "'It means I
am doomeded. . .' " (12).

Henry leaves Minnesota with Bruce, and they drive
to Bruce's family home in Georgia. Henry calls Holly
and tells her of Bruce's condition. She joins them in
Georgia, and, when it is time for spring training, she
goes back to New York as the two ballplayers leave for
Florida. In the meanwhile, Bruce tells his family's
minister, Reverend Robinson, of his illness, but does
not tell his family. Henry, however, has reason to
believe that Robinson has told Bruce's father.

In the Mammoths' training camp at Aqua Clara (at
least that's how Henry spells it; almost certainly its
"real" name should be "Agua Clara"--"clear water") the
big news is a new young catcher named Piney Woods. Henry
continues his hold-out, but watches the team play nearly
every day, becoming sure that his bargaining position is
strong, since the Mammoths have no other outstanding
left-handed pitchers. During this lay-off, however,
Henry is made to realize another possible crisis. When
he wants Joe Jaros, one of the Mammoths' coaches, to

include Bruce in all future games of "Tegwar" (a pretended card-game), Joe protests: "'Bruce. . .is too damn dumb. Anyhow, the way Piney Woods been hitting Bruce might not last the year'." (79). This prospect, of course, is not acceptable to Henry. Bruce has enough to bear already, without suddenly being cut from the Mammoths' squad; furthermore, Henry has all the instructions, from the Minnesota doctors, of what to do in case Bruce's disease should flare up at any time during the season. So Henry comes to terms with the ballclub regarding salary, but announces that he wishes to add a clause to his contract: he and Pearson will be a "package"--neither can be released from his contract or sold, traded, etc., without the other's going also. The club reluctantly consents, largely because they need Henry desperately; he signs his contract, re-joins the team, and the season gets underway.

The Mammoths do well throughout, yet they are never able to pull away from the rest of the league. Theirs is a team more given than most to needling, to "ragging" one another in various humorous-but-sarcastic fashions. And in the 1955 season, the ragging--for whatever host of reasons--has taken such a sharp turn that unhappiness, dissatisfaction with one another, seems to be inhibiting the Mammoths' ability to put away the pennant early. Much of the ugly teasing focuses on Henry and Bruce, particularly on Bruce because he is too slow-witted to make retorts to jibes and thus is an easy target. Additionally, Bruce is planning to marry a successful prostitute, Katie, who now owns her own "chain" of brothels. Not only does this bring more ragging upon him, but it creates an ethical dilemma for Henry. Wiggen works as an agent for the Arcturus Insurance Company in the off-season and he had previously sold Bruce a sizeable life-insurance policy. Katie begins to suspect, from things that Bruce has let slip, that he may have a serious ailment, so she begins pressuring Henry to change Bruce's beneficiary from his father to herself--a change that she has persuaded Bruce to seek also. At last, after Henry has successfully stalled for some time, she attempts to bribe him. And although Henry has become, in many ways, a money-oriented young man since coming to the major leagues (throughout Holly's pregnancy, he refers to the coming child as "600 Dollars," the amount s/he will signify on Henry's income tax), still he refuses Katie's offer and never does make the requested change.

Henry would be able to achieve at least a little relief from the tensions that grip him if he could effect two changes: to be able to stop the divisive ragging among his teammates, and/or be able to tell one of his daily companions the awful secret that he has to bear.

At last, in one of the novel's key scenes, he sees an opportunity to achieve both. In the Mammoths' bullpen, Henry is getting ready to begin warming up to start the second half of a doubleheader. The bullpen catcher is "Goose" Williams, a financially defunct alcoholic who, at thirty-five, is nearing the end of a less-than-noteworthy career. He is also one of Pearson's chief tormentors. Henry offers, in his role as Arcturus agent, to straighten out Goose's finances. In exchange, he demands, "'You must do me a favor. You must lay off Pearson.'" When Goose protests that "'A man has got to have a little fun,'" Henry informs him point-blank, "'He is dying'" (133). Williams promises that he will tell nobody, but Henry suspects almost immediately that the promise will not be kept; after all, he has broken the same promise himself. But the moment will turn out to be the novel's turning-point, for as more and more of the Mammoths find out the truth, they begin to react to it much as Henry has. It becomes a maturing factor in their lives, a presence that reminds them to make the most of the gifts they possess, to extend some respect to all of those around them who are also dying, and a reminder to them to do with intensity whatever it is that they do best. With this spirit, naturally, they win the pennant going away and they sweep the World Series. Bruce Pearson lives to see it, but barely; within a week following the last game, Henry gets the telephone call from Mr. Pearson informing him of Bruce's death.

Two things especially nag at Henry as he concludes his narrative: despite Bruce's having been the team's rallying-point and, if not one of its stars, at least one of its most consistent performers during his last season, no one from the club is at the funeral; and Henry himself did not honor Bruce's last wish, which was for Henry to mail him a World Series scorecard from Detroit. (Bruce suited-up for the first two games in New York, but did not make the final trip.) "Goddam it, anyhow," says Henry, "I am just like the rest. . . .How long would it of took? Could I not afford the stamps?" (242) Yet he has not been untouched by the experience, and he makes one more vow, albeit in light of his scorecard promise, perhaps an ambiguous one--

> He was not a bad fellow; no worse than most and probably better than some, and not a bad ballplayer neither when they give him a chance, when they laid off him long enough. From here on in I rag nobody. (243)

That, in compressed form, is the story as Harris tells it in the novel. The film also tells it in compressed form, although not every change that is made in the transformation is a loss. At times Hancock and his staff managed that "trick" John Nichols speaks of, "of doing it well." Let us examine the gains and the losses, in order to see what meaningful differences there are in this specific instance.

As one would expect, one of the more obvious differences, in addition to length, is the way in which the film captures the visual beauty of baseball. It emphasizes the pastoral quality (rolling green fields), as well as the "geometric" attractiveness (the symmetry of basepaths, on-deck circles, foul-lines, and so forth). This allows the film to generate an important dramatic paradox: the "open-ness" of baseball's pastures contrasted with the "restraint" of foul-lines, coaches' boxes, batters' boxes, etc. This is, of course, a story filled with contrasts, for on the one hand it is about being exuberantly, playfully alive, about a game that seems to perpetuate youth, about the vitality of athletes; on the other hand, it is about dying, about the rigid limits that time and fate impose upon our youth and upon our lives. In an ultimate sense, it is a story about freedom and its contrary. Baseball is, in this regard, especially suited to the ambiguous themes of the story, for baseball is unique among games in having a playing area that is precisely defined in its interior areas and almost totally variable in its periphery. Normally, ambiguity is one of the aspects of a novel that gets lost when it is transformed to film, but in this case the film sharpens some ambiguities.

The second prominent quality of the film that

distinguishes it from the novel is its ability to alter the pace of the work. More quickly and easily than the novel could have done so, the film can summarize the progress of a single game--by showing a succession of ringing base-hits, for instance. By contrast, an infield pop-up can be made to hang in the air for what seems (appropriately) like forever. Such changes in pace enhance the theme of "temporal relativity," the somewhat Lockean concept that is essential to both novel and film. Again, incidentally, one sees here the appropriateness of baseball as background to this story, as baseball has its own "temporal relativity." Since it has been for decades the only major, team-played, spectator sport in America that is not governed by a clock, it is the only one in which time is "suspended."

There are, however, characteristics of the novel that the film cannot adequately capture, let alone improve upon; not surprisingly, these are matters of verbal device, of narrative point-of-view, and--as indicated above--of sheer quantity.

The first example of quantitative difference--that is, of scenes that are in the novel but, for reasons of time, are missing from the film--comes in the story's opening.[2] It will be useful, here, to review the events of the novel's first eight or ten pages, starting with Bruce's telephone call. Henry is about to refuse the call; his former habit of accepting collect calls is one of the things he ceased, he informs us, once "I got wise to myself," (3) a phrase he is fond of. When he discovers that it is Bruce calling, he accepts it, although his first assumption is that, since Bruce is somewhere far from home, he must be in jail. Once he has learned that Bruce is in a hospital and wants to see him, he discloses this to Holly, whose response is immediate: "'Then you have got to go...'" (5). It is in this opening sequence that we first hear of Henry's insurance dealings: Bruce, we are informed, has "North Pole coverage" through Henry as agent (Henry's standing joke is that this covers everything but sunstroke at the North Pole), and the policy--mentioned herein earlier--is worth fifty thousand dollars. On the very day that Henry completed his insurance-seller's course, he sold the policy to Bruce while practising what he had learned. Bruce's only response had been "Arthur, just show me where I sign." (5) While he is in the midst of his reveries, most of them financially oriented, Henry tells us, in another typical Wiggen simile, that "I used to pee away money like wine until I got wise to myself." (6)

Henry leaves for Rochester and comes near to setting up a one-night stand with an airline stewardess in Chicago. Three things combine to keep him from consummating this opportunity: First, his recollections

of Holly. Second, a telephone conversation with the wife
of Goose Williams. (Henry makes insurance calls on this
trip so that he will be able to deduct the trip from his
taxes.) Mrs. Williams informs Henry that her husband has
cashed in his insurance; she worries that Goose is "all
through" at age thirty-five, with nothing but "'his wife
and his debts and his children, and all of them a pain
and a burden to him.'" (8) Third, another phone call,
this time to Joe Jaros. Again, Henry speaks only to the
wife, as Joe is baby-sitting with his grandchildren.
Henry then contemplates the dramatic differences in the
lives of Goose Williams and Joe Jaros, and chides himself
for ever having considered jeopardizing his own familial
future. For, ". . .look at Joe. He did not flub his life
away chasing after every pair of big white teeth he run
across. . . ." (9)

It is worth recounting the things we have learned
from these scenes that will be vital in the novel:

--Henry's verbal traits are wonderfully,
    intricately foolish--but engaging. (They are
    more than that, too, as we shall see
    shortly.)
--Holly is Henry's ethical counsellor--and a good
    one.
--Morally, Henry is less than mature, despite
    being a person who is repeatedly convinced
    that he is "getting wise" to himself.
--Henry, at this stage of his life, is frequently
    concerned about, perhaps even obsessed by,
    financial considerations.
--Bruce is naive, gullible, not altogether capable
    of taking care of himself, but is also
    gentle, co-operative, and always amiable.

And we are prepared, by these scenes, for two later developments that will also be vital to the novel. The first is Henry's moral education; for while he is not immune to the temptations of greed and/or lechery in these scenes, Henry is morally educable. And the second is the thematic function of such relatively minor characters as Goose Williams and Joe Jaros. But because the film begins with Henry and Bruce at the "big hospital" in Rochester (in fact, in the film it is identified, by a sign, as the "Mayo Clinic"), none of this thematic groundwork is present.

The film cannot, of course, include all of the novel's characters. And it must necessarily minimize the importance of some minor characters. That gives the novel another unmatchable quality, for Harris gets substantial significance from some of the novel's subordinate characters. Particularly this is true of "Pop" Wiggen and Mike Mulrooney (both missing from the film), and most especially of Holly Wiggen and Red Traphagen (each little more than a "walk-on" character in the film).

The original Holly, as we have already seen, aids Henry in making proper moral choices. In fact, it is she who makes the toughest moral choice in the novel. When Katie is at her most insistent that Henry change

Bruce's life-insurance beneficiary, Henry asks Holly if
he has the right to deceive Bruce about this, and she
assures him that he does. Indeed, she decides, "'I am
just now elected the new Change of Beneficiary Department
of the Arcturus Company.'" (129) And thereafter she
sends back "responses" to Henry's letters "to" the
company concerning the matter. (147) That sets up one
of the book's good juxtapositions of characters, for when
Henry congratulates Holly for her idea, she says, "'I am
thinking for 2. . .'" and Henry responds, "'I personally
been doing the same for some months now. . . .It is a
strain.'" (129) This contrastive analogy runs throughout
the novel: Henry is to Bruce as Holly is to the unborn
baby; the life that Holly nurtures is one that is
arriving, while Henry nurtures one that is about to
depart. Shortly after the scene just described, this
contrast becomes most prominent. In the middle of a
night, at about mid-season, Bruce awakens Henry, thinking
he has had an attack, but it turns out to be a false
alarm. Just a couple of weeks later, Michele Wiggen is
born, named after Mike Mulrooney, Henry's minor-league
manager. (Mike, in this novel, will be summoned to New
York, presumably at the conclusion of his minor-league
season, to add stability to the Mammoths' personnel after
everyone has learned the truth about Bruce.) Because the
league is on break for the All-Star game, Henry goes to

Perkinsville. He holds his child for the first time:

> . . .sitting on the bed with Holly and the sun was
> first coming in the window like it was that morning
> when Bruce had the attack, or thought he   did,
> and I was about ready to bawl again...sitting
> there with this little bit of a human person in my
> hand. (166-7)

Henry then goes to visit his father, and, as they have

breakfast together, "Pop" Wiggen asks for the address of

Bruce Pearson's father, so that he can write him a

letter, because as he says:

> "I sure think a lot about the old man. . . .Goddam
> it, you raise up a kid from 7 pounds to 205 and
> then some doctor comes along and tells you he has
> got a fatal disease. Nobody is supposed to die
> that young in these modern times. . . ." (168)

Motivated by all this emotion, and by what he has advised

his father about writing his feelings in a letter, Henry

begins that very night to write his book about Bruce

Pearson--this book.

Similarly, Henry gets good advice from Red

Traphagen. Red, who also appeared in The Southpaw, was

the finest catcher in Mammoths' history. Since his

retirement from baseball, he has been teaching college

literature classes in San Francisco. He too is summoned

by the Mammoths' brass, late in this 1955 season, to

provide extra coaching for the catchers--especially Piney

Woods, who has accompanied Mike Mulrooney from the Queen

City farm club--in case anything further happens to

Bruce. Meanwhile, Red coaches Bruce--and, in a sense,

Henry. He tells Henry that the new novel must concentrate on Bruce. Otherwise, readers might think it is about baseball, "'a game rigged by rich idiots to keep poor idiots from wising up to how poor they are.'" (207) People, Red avows, must be encouraged to act as though they all know they are dying. (207) Thoughtful and cynical, Red is contrasted with the sweet, kindly Mike Mulrooney. When Bruce has suffered the attack that will end his career, they keep the late-night hospital watch with Henry, and they provide him, and us, with two distinct ways of looking at death--and life:

> "It is sad," said Mike. "It makes you wish to cry."
> "It _is_ sad," said Red. "It makes you wish to laugh." (239)

Almost invariably, as we have seen, when novel begets film, the most exclusively verbal aspects of the novel are not passed along. Bang the Drum Slowly is no exception. Henry Wiggen as a narrator is reminiscent of some of the great characters of Ring Lardner. Or, in terms of real-life analogies, he possesses the verbal/logical skills of some of baseball's best--Yogi Berra ("I wanna thank all you fans who made 'Yogi Berra Day' necessary"), Dizzy Dean ("the runners are returnin' to their respectable bases"), or Casey Stengel ("I managed good but they played bad"). Henry's most humorous (and occasionally almost profound) bits of verbal gymnastics fall generally into three categories: Malapropisms, zeugma or other instances of mixed syntax and/or logic, and garbled cliche. Among the first group are: "I went up to Dutch's sweet and knocked..." (192) and "I...only went about my business shucking my shoulders." (193) And when you have heavy bags, Henry notes, you either carry them yourself or "pay a redskin to help you." (176) In the second category are similar howlers: "...it was now my ball game to win or lose which we did"; (163) "...it was me vs. Scudder, always a great ball game usually." (200) And of a late-season game in which he has pitched badly, Henry says, "It was just one of those days nobody got out of bed with any sense to start with." (230)

But it is in the third category of odd verbal traits that Harris makes a memorable narrator of Henry Wiggen. Henry is as given to reliance upon cliches as any "author" one could hope to find, but he tends to remember them imprecisely. And so he twists triteness to these uses: "I know the boys like the back of my book." (87) "[Sports other than baseball] were never my dish of meat." (47) Of the players who came up to the majors with him, Henry recalls "The 4 of us used to be as thick as flies. . . ." (154) When former Mammoths begin re-joining the club, the press grows alert: "The paper just got through wondering all over the place why Mike was

there, and now Red give them new food for their fire."
(198) But meanwhile, Dutch Schnell has taken some gambles
"and it worked, for we stood above water." (185) And when
it is clear that the Mammoths will win the pennant again,
then everybody in New York "started falling all over
themself handing you the town on a silver spoon." (227)
Two of the best Wiggenisms deserve a place in the Runyon-
Lardner Hall of Fame: When he talks to Bruce on the
phone, Henry knows Holly is not ignoring him, for "I seen
her listening out of the corner of her eye." (3) And
later he recognizes how Bruce's secret became known to
Mammoths' management: Joe Jaros's wife "was the one left
the cat out of the barn. . . ." (180) All of these verbal
matters are virtually impossible for the film to
duplicate. Likewise, there is no way that the film can
capture the novel's metafictive, "Tristram Shandy"
touches. Consequently, the film has nothing quite the
equivalent of those moments late in the novel when the
reader is invited to watch Henry "write" the early
chapters of the novel, and another bit of intimacy
between Henry and his audience is thus lost, for we know
in the novel that a large part of what helps Henry bear
up under his heavy responsibility is "telling paper."
(176)

   This diminishing of Henry's verbal importance to us
leads to a more significant difference between novel and

film. The film, because it can show us what Henry sees,
will seldom bother to have him also tell it to us. Henry
is a part-time narrator in the film, giving us occasional
voice-over observations. Having him as this kind of
narrator cannot, of course, be the same as having him
interpret everything--as having him create in us a
dependence upon him--as he does in the novel. Thus, to
a large extent, our perception of Henry's growth, his
moral development, or lack of same, is lost. As has been
suggested here earlier, the novel's Henry Wiggen begins
the season as a young man with considerable concern for
money. Four pages into the novel, he is thinking in
financial terms almost exclusively. When he discovers
Bruce is in the hospital, he recalls what kind of policy
Bruce has with Arcturus; Holly chides him, "'Surely his
coverage is not all you can think of'. . . .'No,' said
I, 'naturally not,' though it was. First you think about
money." (6) But later he rejects the bribe attempts of
Katie, and he also tells us that, even when he gets close
to his fifteenth win, which would put his bonus clause
into effect,

> I actually never give it much of a thought nor
> stopped to think how close I was to the bonus
> clause. . . .When your roomie is libel to die
> any day on you you do not think about bonus
> clauses, and that is the truth whether anybody
> happens to think so or not. (152)

However, he does seem to insist on this point, perhaps

overmuch, and he does react ambiguously at novel's end, as we have seen. But the film loses this nice moral ambiguity by omitting Henry's financial concerns almost completely. There are several other results of Henry's not being in the role of narrator: the film becomes Bruce Pearson's story, whereas the novel was clearly Henry Wiggen's; and the film, thematically, has not quite the breadth or the depth of the novel.

But perhaps the most important loss, to the filmed version, of Henry's function as narrator is his occasional capability, in the novel, of being downright poetic. That same folksy style--earthy, frank, sometimes clumsy, but by no means always foolish, nor always merely humorous--can, at times, be eloquently, movingly lyrical. On their way from Rochester to the Pearson family home in Georgia, Bruce reminisces to Henry about his days of playing ball on a field of peanut hay. And Henry recalls it for us:

> and little by little he told it, the smell of it
> when it was wet in the morning, and the smell of ti
> when it dried, how it stuck to your feet wet
> and then crumbed off, and how a baseball picked up
> the color of the field until soon you could not
> hardly see the ball against the ground, and you
> took it and taped it in white tape until the tape,
> too, was the color of the field, and you taped it
> again, and then maybe again until the ball was too
> big and you all got a hold of nickels and dimes
> that you hid in the mill and went over to
> Bainbridge, 6 or 8 of you because you never
> trusted any one kid with the money and bought a
> new white baseball and tried for a long time to
> keep it off the ground. (22)

The "breathlessness" of Henry's reporting this all in one sentence adds to its rhythms and its natural drama. Much later in the novel, Henry's recollection of a speech by Bruce is similarly earthy-but-lyrical. The other players on the Mammoths are wishing the pennant race were over, but Bruce is not:

> "It could go on. . . .I even do not mind catching too goddam much any more. . . . .I like sweating...I like hitting. Sometimes I even like popping out, looking up there and seeing how high you drove it . . .I love stinking. . .and coming in and ripping off your clothes and getting under the shower and thinking about eating," and he sat thinking over what he said, and the more he thought about it the better it sounded, and he went and showered, and the boys all done the same. (187-8)

In a story ostensibly about dying, these are rather remarkable celebrations of life.

And so the differences between these two versions are those we come to expect between novel and film: The film has immediacy, and gives us the sense of having personally known Bruce Pearson and lived through his ordeal with him; but the novel gives us a wealth of theme and character and contrast not attainable in the film. Because "movies are not novels," but "are short-stories," each version tells the story well--but, as Henry Wiggen himself might say, the novel tells it more.

1. Mark Harris, _Bang the Drum Slowly_ (Lincoln: U.of Nebraska Press, 1984). This "Bison Book" reprint of the 1956 novel is the best edition currently in print. References hereafter are to this edition, with page numbers in parentheses in the text.

2. Recall the point made in the Introduction here: one gives the reading of this novel some six or eight hours, well more than twice what one would allow to viewing the film.

SHOELESS JOE AND "FIELD OF DREAMS"

> "I like the marvelous only
> inside the real."
> Alain Fournier,
> quoted, often, by
> John Fowles.

This chapter will be an elaboration of the argument made in the earlier essay on "Blue Velvet." There, we see how a film went wrong in regard to the logic of plotting. Here, we shall see the contrast between such lapses and a novel that got it right.

"Field of Dreams" raises a number of interesting transformational issues. It points up, first, the observations made elsewhere here about the differences in time allotted to each, and so forth. It also reminds one that movies seldom get details right when they deal with baseball. But, above and beyond these, it brings up some issues not so trite or so nearly self-evident. Among such are mainly these two: Fantasy does not work as well in film as it does in fiction; and, since both novels and films depend at least somewhat upon narrative sequence, consequently both are partly dependent upon logic, common sense, and fidelity to fact, where plot is concerned.[1] "Field of Dreams," scripted and directed by Phil Alden Robinson, does not capture fantasy in the same way that W. P Kinsella's Shoeless Joe does. Nor does Robinson's film build the same sequence of credible motivations and logical follow-ups as does Kinsella's book. To the extent that it does not, the film falls short of being satisfactory as a work of art.

In an essay titled "On the Tragedies of Shakespeare,"[2] Charles Lamb contended that many plays, and particularly those of Shakespeare, are better read than seen, because fantasy, or powerful imagination, works better in print than in a visual medium. When we read the plays, Lamb argued, we are intrigued by the characters in their meditations, their spirit, their impulses. "But when we see these things represented, the acts which they do are comparatively everything, their impulses nothing." As we watch the staging of the plays--inevitably and inexorably realistic--"we have given up that vantage ground of abstraction which reading possesses over seeing" (Vallance & Hampden, p. 31), and we cannot have things both ways. What Lamb was saying about the stage is much more true of film when compared to fiction. Ordinary cinema, barring special effects or surrealistic devices, generates little habit of pretending or exercise of imagination. What it wants an audience to know, it shows. Printed fiction, on the other hand, does get to have things both ways. Thus, as we read Shoeless Joe, the ballfield can exist and not exist simultaneously; Ray Kinsella can be at once loony and penetratingly, perceptively sane. But in "Field of Dreams" the ballfield is undeniably there--and so are the ballplayers. We can see them, and we are likely to question the percipience of anyone who cannot. There is not the same sense, then, of Ray Kinsella's living in (and living out) a fantasy, psychologically induced or otherwise. This is a detraction from Kinsella's work, for the novel is, as one critic put it, "strikingly innovative in its elimination of the barriers betwen fact and imagination; the dream, magically, _is_ the reality in Shoeless Joe."[3]

Looking at the final version of the film, one can conjecture a number of choices that Robinson made as he began production. The apparent first one was typical, and from it followed virtually everything that makes the film--while a success by some measurements--a disappointment to one who very much liked the novel. That decision, it would seem to any outside observer, was to go for a film of the broadest audience appeal: a popular (as differed from, say, "artsy"), straightforward (not symbolic, not "Bergmanesque"), feel-good, family film. There is not anything innately wrong with this decision; but it led, in this case, to consequences that distorted and diminished the movie's source material.

First, Robinson threw away the psychological aspects of Kinsella's story. In the early stages of the novel, Ray's father is much on his mind. Their relationship had been less than ideal, and Ray never got to make up to his father for several things left deficient between them.

(Some of this is included in the film, but it does not enter until much later.) When Ray hears "the voice," it is not any whisper of mysticism; it is instead "the scratchy Middle American" of "a ballpark announcer."[4] And that it may represent a sheerly internal, psychological phenomenon is as instantly clear to us as it is to Ray:

> Was it really a voice I heard? Or was it perhaps something inside me making a statement that I did not hear with my ears but with my heart? Why should I want to follow this command? (6; emphasis is the novel's.)

Immediately, he answers his own question in terms of the loves in his life: "Annie, Karin, Iowa. . .[and] the great god Baseball." (6) Since it was from his father that Ray learned to love baseball, the two are virtually inseparable in his mind; and his need to build the ballfield is directly related to his need to make restoration to his dad. Furthermore, in the novel, but not in the film, Ray's agreement to finish the ballfield is a contract with Joe Jackson that will guarantee Ray's father's return. "You give us a place to play," says Shoeless Joe, "and we'll look at your catcher." (16) So Ray endures the ordeal of building the whole ballpark by himself, because, as he says, "I want that catcher to appear." (23)

In eliminating Ray Kinsella's psychological

motivation for building a ballfield--and perhaps for hearing "the voice" in the first place--Robinson's screenplay also eliminates the important socio-political dimension of Kinsella's novel. That Joe Jackson is the ballplayer who returns from "the other side" to play on Ray's field is not accidental, nor is it separable from Ray's wish, coming far too late, to appease his father. In the Kinsella household, Joe Jackson had not just been admired as a great baseball player; his iconographic importance went further. He was, Ray says, "a symbol of the tyranny of the powerful over the powerless." In that house, too, the name of Judge Kenesaw Mountain Landis, the first Major League Baseball Commissioner, who banned Jackson and his team-mates from Organized Baseball forever, "became synonymous with the devil." (7) These responses came to Ray directly from the elder Kinsella, as does much of Ray's attitude toward baseball (and other things): "My father loved underdogs. . .[and consequently] loathed the Yankees--an inherited trait, I believe." (6) His view of the banned ballplayers is also an inherited trait. He never refers to them in the common judgmental terms (i.e., "Black Sox") but calls them instead "the Unlucky Eight. . .banished forever for supposedly betraying the game they loved." It is probable, Ray acknowledges, that they took money from gamblers.

> But throw the Series? Never. . .It was the
> circumstances. The circumstances. The players
> were paid peasant salaries while the owners
> became rich. The infamous Ten Day Clause,
> which voided contracts, could end any player's
> career without compensation, pension, or even
> a ticket home. (8)

This is not, incidentally, an unsupportable view of the

1919 World Series "scandal." Charles Comiskey, the White

Sox owner, was indeed a petty tyrant, and the players

entertained the possibility of a fix partly as a means

of getting even--personally, philosophically, and

financially. Jackson's case in particular was never

clear-cut. If he could bat .375 for the eight games of

the Series, lead both teams in hits, and lead his own

team in runs scored and runs-batted-in while tanking the

Series, one wonders what he might have done when trying!

But the importance to Kinsella's novel, an importance

almost completely absent from the film, is that Ray

Kinsella feels that Shoeless Joe needs to be exonerated,

just as he feels that he still owes something to his

father, the proto-typical advocate of Jackson.

Therefore, he is psychologically and politically pre-

disposed to desire a miraculous resurrection. But both

these strands of motivation are abandoned in the film.

"Miracle" is present in the novel, but in an

entirely different way from the film's use of it. All

that is miraculous in the novel is founded in nature and/or baseball, and it is waged in poetic fashion by Kinsella's use of narrative point-of-view. Ray frequently waxes poetic in the novel, but almost never does in the film.[5] The first time, in the novel, that he tells us how he feels about his farm, he is immediately led into a poetic recollection of his having experienced, in his term, an "epiphany":

> It was near noon on a gentle Sunday when I walked out to that garden. The soil was soft and my shoes disappeared as I plodded until I was near the center. There I knelt, the soil cool on my knees. I looked up at the low gray sky; the rain had stopped and the only sound was the surrounding trees dripping fragrantly. Suddenly I thrust my hands wrist-deep into the snuffy-black earth. The air was pure. All around me the clean smell of earth and water. Keeping my hands buried, I stirred the earth with my fingers and knew I loved Iowa as much as a man could love a piece of earth. (14)

The epiphany he describes was experienced by Ray well before he ever built his ballfield. The connection that it draws between him and his land is yet another bit of preparation for the magical experiences he will later undergo, but it is another dimension of Ray's character that the film chooses to omit. Later, Ray speaks even more poetically of nature and the land:

> A breath of clover travels on the summer wind. Behind me, just yards away, brook water plashes softly in the darkness, a frog shrills, fireflies dazzle the night like red pepper. A petal falls. (16)

Even if the echoes of Yeats ("plashes") and Pound (that falling petal) are not intentional here, one of the important things seen in these passages, besides Ray's attitude toward the land, is his--and the novel's-- tendency to view things through imagination. We see this poetic tendency at least one more time in the novel, when Ray is at Fenway Park with J. D. Salinger. The equivalent scene is in the film, but this excerpt, being reliant on words, is not included. Right at the moment that the lifetime record of "Moonlight Graham" is on the scoreboard, there is a spectacular play on the field: a rookie pitcher forgets to cover first base on a hot shot to the first baseman, but the out is saved by the hyper-alert second baseman who gets over to cover first, makes an almost miraculous catch of the first baseman's throw, then even more nearly miraculously avoids colliding with the runner. Ray tells us that

> The play reaffirms what I already know--that
> baseball is the most perfect of games, solid,
> true, pure and precious as diamonds. If only
> life were so simple. I have often thought,
> If only there was a framework to life, rules
> to live by. But suddenly I see, like a
> silver flash of lightning on the horizon, a meaning
> I have never grasped before. . . .Within the
> baselines anything can happen. Tides can
> reverse; oceans can open. That's why they say,
> "The game is never over until the last man is
> out." Colors can change, lives can alter,
> anything is possible in this gentle, flawless,
> loving game. (78; emphasis is the novel's.)

This "miracle," Ray's epiphany, and all of his poetic

idealizing of "the land" combine to create a sort of "natural magical realism." The film more nearly attempts magical realism with the magic removed.

Consciously or unconsciously, then, Phil Alden Robinson, presumably in his quest for a simple, straightforward film of broad appeal, threw away the novel's poetry (or most of it), along with its psychological and political motifs. But in losing these, the film lost all of the strands of motivation for its main character's behavior, for what happens to him and what he does about it. Whereas Kinsella made the novel earn its indulgence in sentiment, by laying down a carefully sequential plot made up of natural magical realism and psychologically credible incident, Robinson chooses an easy route to Ray's building of a ballfield: God orders it. The novel's hearty agrarianism gets translated into New Right fundamentalism--"Pride of the Yankees" meets "Song of Bernadette."

Somewhere in this decision-making process, Robinson stumbled upon what probably seemed a happy discovery, a way to put some political motivation back into the story. He had to make some kind of swap, in any case, for the novel's use, as a character, of J. D. Salinger.[6] So Robinson invents a Black writer named Terence Mann, formerly a Radical Chic novelist, now virtually a hermit. In order that there may be credible incentive for the interest that Ray and Annie, his wife, have in T. Mann, they are made over into sixties-Berkeleyites. Then, to fire them up about Mann and his works as a cause, Robinson writes into the story a town-meeting scene, in which Mann and his works are under seige for being seditious and/or salacious. And right about there, any logical development that the plot had enjoyed begins to fall apart.

In the first place, the town-meeting scene is badly conceived and badly written. The townspeople are cardboard figures, which might have been acceptable for satirical purposes, except that Annie Kinsella is no more real than they. Her main speech is no less hysterical, no less simplistic, and no less stupidly generalizing than the ravings of the woman she refers to as "Eva Braun here." That all the local fascists would be instantly won over by that speech to a love for constitutional principles does not seem to be what would likely take place at any censorship meeting. The scene is one of the two least honest and least credible scenes in the film.

The other one, however, is even worse, for it mars the logic of the film's plot more severely. That is the final long speech by Terence Mann, in what should be the film's climactic moment and is, instead, its largest failure. James Earl Jones declaims the lines perfectly well. Vocally, the moment works fine. The basso profundo of Jones is in fine form, and it adds to a series of good "operatic" moments in the film, beginning with Kevin Costner's voice-over narration and continuing through a couple of good set-speeches by Burt Lancaster, playing Moonlight Graham. But the illogic of the situation undermines everything positive about the scene. "People will come," Terence Mann says, "as innocent as children, searching for the past. . . ." He stands with the field as backdrop and proclaims, "the one constant through all the years has been baseball." With all those exclusively white ballplayers' faces behind him, he can say this? "It reminds us of all that's good. . . ." This from a Black radical novelist, an activist in the sixties? The character is middle-aged. He must remember Jackie Robinson. He must know that Josh Gibson and Cool Papa Bell never got to play in the major leagues at all, and Satchel Paige not until he was--who knows what?-- fifty maybe? And that even then The Sporting News said Bill Veeck had "demeaned the standards" of major-league baseball in signing him.[7] He must know all this. Yet he stands there celebrating baseball for its maintaining of innocence and "purity" (in this kind of context, one of the most consistently racist terms). It is not a convincing moment.

So, Phil Robinson's decisions leave the film without the psychological dimensions of the novel, without most of its poetry, and with only a truncated and sadly distorted version of its social and political themes. What's left, besides a cheap-and-easy pop theology, is a heavy dose of sentimentality. Philosophers and critics from Aristotle to Anne Hollander have pointed out that visual objects enhance an emotional appeal.[8] Consequently, an excess of unmitigated sentimentality is a more constant threat to a film than to a novel. Shoeless Joe is about as sentimental a work as one should want to find. Indeed, it occasionally veers to the downright saccharine. Still, it maintains, throughout, a synchronizing of fantasy and realism that makes the sentiment palatable and causes one to appreciate the novel's serious artistry. To retain that capability should have been one of the main choices for the makers of "Field of Dreams."

1. Among the practical matters botched by this film is the glaring one of its having Shoeless Joe Jackson both bat and throw wrong-handed. I am indebted to Ann Kinsella for pointing out to me that some have theorized that this kind of reversal could be deliberate, to show a mirroring which has resulted from Jackson's return from "the other side." But if that were the intent, then all of the "returned" ballplayers should be similarly reversed, which they are not.

2. Reprinted in, among other places, Rosalind Vallance and John Hampden, eds., _Charles_ _Lamb_: _Essays_ (London: The Folio Society, 1963).

3. William Plummer, "Pride of the Sox," in _Books_ _in_ _Canada_, April 1983, pp. 8-9.

4. W. P. Kinsella, _Shoeless_ _Joe_ (New York: Ballantine, 1982), pp. 3-4. References hereafter will be to this paperback edition, with page numbers in parentheses in the text.

5. This is hardly surprising. As we have seen often here, films often shy away from verbal emphases and this one is no different, except for its "operatic" segments, to be noted here later.

6. Both Kinsella and James Earl Jones have indicated in public interviews that Salinger's attorneys were making menacing noises even before the film went into production.

7. Paige won six games and lost one that year, with an ERA of 2.47. He would later say, "I demeaned them standards somethin' fierce."

8. Aristotle makes this argument in the _Poetics_. For a summary and some applications of it, see Edward P. J. Corbett, _Classical_ _Rhetoric_ _for_ _the_ _Modern_ _Student_ (New York: Oxford U. Press, 1965), pp. 86-94. For the application of approximately the same point to film, see Anne Hollander, _Moving_ _Pictures_ (New York: Knopf, 1989).

<u>A</u> <u>ROOM</u> <u>WITH</u> <u>A</u> <u>VIEW</u>

A Room with a View presents that rare example of a good novel that was transformed into a good film. It provides some key lessons in elements of fiction that will not transfer directly, but which have effects that might be approximated by equivalent devices. The film's director, James Ivory, and screenplay-writer, Ruth Prawer Jhabvala, made some wise choices in terms of simplification and compression. Consequently, while the film does not retain all of the novel's nuances of tone nor its wit, it does retain some, and it adds a few devices of its own that make the loss considerably more palatable than might have been the case had the film been less carefully, lovingly, conscientiously adapted. A close look at this adaptation illustrates almost perfectly how "transformation-as-criticism" should work, for the techniques and tactics one finds in the film point up how much the novel relies upon the literary predecessors of those devices.

Among the things which this adaptation has done well is its capturing of one of Forster's most functional characters, Charlotte Bartlett. Although functional, she is not, to borrow the convenient terminology that Forster invented, a "flat" character. She easily fits some stereotypes, certainly, but she renders the reader/viewer a number of surprises near the end of the film.

Ultimately, in film or novel, she proves most useful to the young would-be lovers, Lucy Honeychurch and George Emerson. In the novel, George expresses an awareness of this near the conclusion;[1] in the film, one can trace, even more clearly than in the novel, the stages in Charlotte's reversal--in her decision, that is, to help alter the natural course of events so as to favor George's suit. It all begins with her seeing the moving-company people emptying the Emersons' villa. She shortly thereafter discovers that George, contrary to Charlotte's expectations, has apparently never told anyone about having kissed Lucy; he did not even tell his father, although their relationship would certainly have allowed him to do so, had he so chosen. She also realizes that Lucy had foretold this accurately. Charlotte then informs Mr. Emerson that Lucy's engagement is off; this is the first, of course, that he has heard of that, and she must know that he will tell George. Finally, she departs from the rectory, hurriedly, just as Lucy enters, leaving Lucy and Mr. Emerson alone together. What she must know now, given what she just told Mr. E., is that he will plead George's case with Lucy. It is interesting that the film can make such an ambivalent character of Charlotte, since our seeing and hearing her in action, in the early going, makes us perceive even more sharply the extreme prudery, snobbishness, and conventionality

of this character. This ambivalence is also in keeping
with Forster's development of the character.

This film, like many another adaptation, is hard put
to make the same use of literary allusion that the novel
does. But the film substitutes allusions of its own that
work in approximately the same way that allusion does in
Forster's (or anyone's) fiction. The film's main
allusions are operatic. Particularly, it uses the music
of Puccini. Over the opening credit lines, terminating
just at the start of the film proper, and repeated over
the ending, is the beautiful aria from "Gianni Schicci,"
"O Mio Babbino Caro." The single-act opera, one of many
focusing upon a trickster, is not especially relevant to
Forster's work, or to his heroine. In this aria,
however, the mood and the fears expressed, that the
heroine may suffer torments for love, are somewhat more
appropriate to the life of Lucy Honeychurch. Lauretta,
Gianni Schicci's daughter, urges him to intervene in the
matter of a will, as a favorable reading of it would
allow her to marry Rinuccio, one of the deceased's kin.
She cannot live without the young man, she tells her
father:

> O, dear daddy,
> I like him he's so handsome;
> I want to go to Porta Rossa
> To buy the ring!
> Yes, yes, I do want to go!
> And if I were to love him in vain,
> I'd go to the Ponte Vecchio

> And throw myself in the Arno!
> I fret and suffer torments!
> O, God, I wish I could die!
> Daddy, have pity, have pity!

The other Puccini aria, "Che il bel sogno di Doretta," is used in the scene in which Lucy and George Emerson have their first passionate encounter, on the outing to Fiesole. The story of Doretta is told in Act I of "La Rondine." In this case, both the aria's words and its original context are relevant to Lucy and to Forster's story. In the opera, Prunier, the poet, has been sharing his latest lyric with a number of friends, including the two main characters, Magda and Rambaldo. When Prunier comes to a halt in his song (about how a young woman named Doretta dreamed one day that the king had looked upon her), explaining that he has not yet devised an ending, Magda finishes it for him, in this aria. It is a tale most revealing of the teller, as Magda longs for "happiness to reappear" in the form of an encounter that she had long ago with a young man whose name she never learned. This sets the tone for the remainder of Magda's story in the opera. The words to the aria are of special relevance to Lucy in this scene, as she is kissed by George:

> Who can explain Doretta's beautiful dream?
> How does the mystery end?
> Alas! One day a student kissed her lips
> And that kiss was a revelation.
> It was passion itself!
> Wild love! Wild intoxication!

> Who could ever explain the subtleties
> Of such an ardent caress?
> Ah, my dream! Ah, my life!
> How important are riches
> If happiness should reappear?
> Oh, golden dream, to love like that!

More will be said here, later, about Forster's use of allusion. But Jhabvala and Ivory get approximately the same benefits: a viewer who perceives all the parallels between Puccini's work and Forster's is informed by the analogies. But even if they do not register upon us fully, the arias are admirable in and of themselves; both are beautiful, and they are perfect "backdrops."

One of the alterations that the film makes to Forster's story is a reversal of sorts. In the scene that corresponds to Chapter Nine ("Lucy as a Work of Art") in the novel, Cecil clumsily botches an attempt to kiss Lucy, after having first obtained her permission to kiss her. The film then includes a moment in which Lucy's mind flashes back to her having been kissed, enthusiastically and without permission, by George. In the novel, after the awkward kiss, it is Cecil who reflects. Recognizing that the "embrace" had been a failure, he concludes that it failed because he was so tentative, so "refined." And so, in his mind, he revises history:

> He recast the scene. Lucy was standing
> flower-like by the water, he rushed up and
> took her in his arms; she rebuked him,
> permitted him and revered him ever after

for his manliness. (124)

However, Forster did give Jhabvala a hint for the film's alteration, for in the novel there is a clue that Lucy, too, has "flashed back": She says, when finally she says anything after the awkward embrace, "'Emerson was the name, not Harris'...." thus setting straight a "lie" she had previously told about events in Florence, although Cecil does not understand the reference. (125) The flashback reminiscence is a brilliant bit of transforming. Yet it is a change of meaning too. One of the strengths of this adaptation is in Jhabvala's (and/or Ivory's) not being afraid to add or to alter.

The film gives a viewer a sense of that genius of place that Forster, borrowing perhaps from Virgil and Pope, was fond of. All of the Italian scenes demonstrate the artistic nourishment that the souls of Forster's characters--well, some of his characters--ingest while there. The statuary, the architecture, the religious icons of Florence are in ample supply, and lend much to the story's atmosphere. On the trip to Fiesole, to "see a view," the characters are shown over and again before backgrounds right out of art galleries. But it is important to show that England is not bereft of such scenery; so there are excellent landscape shots in that part of the film also, particularly those of the "Sacred Lake."

Not the least of the ways in which Ivory's film has, once again, captured the spirit of Forster's work is in its capacity for being funny at some of the moments when we least expect it to be. One sequence in which this is most observable is immediately before, during, and shortly after one of the most tense scenes in the novel, that in which Lucy informs George Emerson that he is not to come near her again. When she sends Charlotte to fetch "him," Charlotte asks, "Cecil?" "No, no," Lucy replies, "the other one." While George makes what is his best speech in the story, and--in the long run--a very convincing argument to Lucy, we see Cecil in the background, awkwardly swatting at flies with a book. As the scene ends, Charlotte insists that she will never forgive herself for her part in having created the most recent tension (by telling Eleanor Lavish about the passionate encounter between Lucy and George in Italy). Lucy observes that she invariably says this, but "You always do forgive yourself, Charlotte." There follows next the scene in which Lucy breaks off her engagement to Cecil, all the while citing to him lines she has plagiarized from George ("You're the sort who can't know anyone intimately"), until he finally is led to observe that she seems to be "Speaking with a new voice." But this scene is almost precisely and fully as Forster wrote it; the comic bits prior to it are mainly the film's own.

Still, although this is both a competent and
faithful transformation, there are relevant differences
between what Forster did and what Ivory-Jhabvala have
done. As usual, those differences tell us much about the
novel.

One of the main ways by which Forster makes meaning
in all of his fiction is by use of what he calls, in
Aspects of the Novel, "rhythm." Most simply defined,
rhythm--as Forster means the term--is "repetition plus
variation." Its most elaborate use can be seen by
analogy to music. When the orchestra comes to the end
of, say, Beethoven's Fifth Symphony, "we hear something
that has never actually been played...." That
"something" is the symphony as a whole, as an entity;
this entity "has been achieved mainly. . .by the relation
between the three big blocks of sound...." [2] It is this
relation that Forster calls "rhythmic." In music or in
literature, a theme, a motif, can be there now, and not
so prominently there later:

> There are times when it means nothing and
> is forgotten, and this seems to me to be
> the function of rhythm in fiction; not to
> be there all the time like a pattern, but
> by its lovely waxing and waning to fill us
> with surprise and freshness and hope.
> (Aspects, 239)

Both this definition and this function come into
play in A Room with a View. Forster's main rhythmic

device in this novel is contrast, particularly of characters. Contrasts are first established, then explored, then minimized. This last feature is the "variation"; in some cases what appeared to be contrasts early are, by the end, no longer contrastive at all. If one might begin with an over-simplification, and the promise to qualify it later, the characters in A Room with a View are contrasted acording to the extent of their conventionality. Those who will allow convention, or notions of "delicacy," to force all their decisions are those who have enlisted, or been inducted, in the "army of darkness," who will "march to their destiny by catch-words." (204) Lucy Honeychurch is both compared and contrasted to her mother's cousin, Charlotte Bartlett, throughout the novel. Underscoring this motif of similarity-plus-difference are the observations of her mother, that Lucy reminds her of Charlotte, and the statement by Charlotte, that Lucy reminds her of Mrs. Honeychurch. (11 and 227) This interchange is part of Forster's deployment of a "light-dark" rhythm.

The most important associations of light in the novel are with George Emerson, particularly when he comes into the midst of the Honeychurches. To Lucy's mother, he explains how he relates light to kindness: "'Choose a place...where you won't do very much harm, and stand in it for all you are worth, facing the sunshine.'" (176)

Lucy is aware that her mother is impressed by George, and
shortly thereafter, she watches him extend to his father
an affectionate touch: "The kindness that Mr. Beebe and
Lucy had always known to exist in him came out suddenly,
like sunlight touching a vast landscape--a touch of the
morning sun?" (177) Immediately thereafter, Lucy's party
returns to Windy Corner, where she greets Cecil "with
unusual radiance."(179) George's visit follows, and,
during it, Lucy realizes that he has begun "to stand for
all he was worth in the sun." (184) This leads directly
to an epiphanic moment, the importance of which Lucy only
half-consciously apprehends:

> Ah, how beautiful the Weald looked! The hills
> stood out above its radiance, as Fiesole stands
> above the Tuscan Plain, and the South Downs, if
> one chose, were the mountains of Carrara. She
> might be forgetting her Italy, but she was notic-
> ing more things in her England. One could play
> a new game with the view, and try to find in
> its innumerable folds some town or village that
> would do for Florence. Ah, how beautiful the
> Weald looked! (181-2)

The repetition of the enclosing sentence helps make this
one of Forster's more poetic paragraphs. It also is one
that touches upon almost all of the novel's contrastive
elements: light/dark, Italy/England, and--one we shall
return to later--the matter of a "view." It is also
worth noting that this chapter ends with George's kissing
Lucy for the second time.

After that chapter ("The Disaster Within"), there

begins a succession of four chapters entitled "Lying to [various persons]." Lucy's conventionality will not succumb easily, and she imagines she must restore the pristine status of her engagement (and her life). This necessitates her lying to almost everyone, not least of all herself, about not being in love with George Emerson. At the outset of the first chapter in this sequence ("Lying to George"), Forster establishes the contrast between Lucy's being in this situation, and condition, and George's standing in the sunlight: "The armour of falsehood is subtly wrought out of darkness, and hides a man not only from others, but from his own soul. In a few moments Lucy was equipped for battle." (189) At the end of the next chapter ("Lying to Cecil"), Forster elaborates upon the make-up of the army of the "benighted," and he works in, again, the comparison--of Lucy to Charlotte--that is essential to this novel's method of characterization as well as to much of its theme. The army is composed, he tells us, of "pleasant and pious folk," but they "follow neither the heart nor the brain." Following someone else's dictates instead, they do not attain self-understanding. They have "sinned against passion and truth" and will pay for that sin by producing discomfort for themselves and others, always. Or, to put the matter, as Forster does, classically:

They have sinned against Eros and against

> Pallas Athene, and not by any heavenly inter-
> vention, but by the ordinary course of nature,
> those allied deities will be avenged.

In entering this army, Lucy once more joins familiar company: "The night received her, as it had received Miss Bartlett thirty years before." (204)

Lucy continues, for a while, to practice self-deception, to indulge in "a ruse...to justify her despondency--a ruse of which she was not herself conscious, for she was marching in the armies of darkness." (212) Through this period, she does not confide in anyone, as she has learned to dislike confidences, "for they might lead to self-knowledge and to that king of terrors--Light." (225) At last, in the chapter titled "Lying to Mr. Emerson" (which might more accurately be called "Trying to Lie to Mr. Emerson"), she is led to understand that "the function of Love" (236) is essential to life, that "love is eternal," (237) and that her relationship with George is "one of the moments for which the world was made." Then, "the darkness was withdrawn, veil after veil, and she saw to the bottom of her soul." (238)

The contrasts of light and darkness are directly related, of course, to the ubiquitous metaphor seen in the title of this novel: that of "a view." Literally and/or metaphorically, a room with a view is prominently mentioned three times. The first is at the very start of the novel, implicit in its opening sentence, when Lucy and Charlotte do not have a view. (Mr. Emerson and George do, as Mr. Emerson has announced by the second page.) The last time is when Lucy and George, honeymooning, are back in one of the same rooms that the Emersons had been assigned in the first chapter. (The film, as we shall see, underscores the recurrent metaphor, at this point, more blatantly than Forster does.) In between, indeed almost exactly halfway between, these two literal uses of the motif, there occurs its main figurative appearance. Cecil and Lucy go for a walk in the woods near Windy Corner, and he complains that she does not seem to think of him as being much connected to nature: "'I had got an idea--I dare say wrongly--that you feel more at home with me in a room.'" He, on the other hand, always thinks of her, he says, as connected with, "'a view--a certain type of view.'" After reflecting on this a bit, Lucy admits that he is right: "'When I think of you it's always as in a room.'" When he asks if that room is a drawing-room, with no view, she affirms that is without a view. (122) That Lucy unconsciously apprehends--as we see clearly--a contrast betwen Cecil and George on this point becomes clear shortly, in an exchange that we have looked at previously. Cecil asks if he might kiss her, for the first time, and receiving permission, does so as half-

heartedly as he does clumsily. "As he touched her, his
gold pince-nez became dislodged and was flattened between
them." (124) They leave the area, in silence. Cecil
wishes that Lucy would say something that might "show him
her inmost thoughts." At last, she does: flashing back
upon misinformation she had previously given him about
the Pension Bertolini, she says, "'Emerson was the name,
not Harris.'" Although she goes on to indicate that she
means (or means to mean?) the elder Emerson, the reader
knows that Lucy, too, has developed an awareness of
contrasts, not least of all in honesty of passion. Thus,
the chapter ends with an emphasis on the befuddlement of
Cecil: "He could not know that this was the most intimate
conversation they had ever had." (125) These contrasts
in images, then, of light-vs.-darkness, view-vs.-
sightlessness, and beauty-vs.-delicacy, are essential to
one's understanding of contrasts in characterization, as
all of the major ones fall into one or more of these
pairs. It is the "beautiful indelicacy" paradox that
begins Forster's contrastive methods of characterization.
When one of the Alan sisters (in the novel it is
apparently Catherine; it is certainly she in the film)
remarks that some people--she clearly has in mind Mr.
Emerson's offer to swap his and George's rooms for Lucy's
and Charlotte's--are capable of actions simultaneously
"indelicate" and "beautiful," Charlotte is puzzled by the

very concept. "'Are not beauty and delicacy the same?'" she asks. (13) Lucy almost immediately starts to observe examples of this contrastive pairing on her own. Thus she wonders, about the exchange of rooms, "whether the acceptance might not have been less delicate and more beautiful." (15) When next one sees the Emersons, she is prepared to be to them "beautiful rather than delicate . . . ."(25)

The main area of character-contrast has thus been established; it pits the Emersons directly against the conventional delicacies of Charlotte Bartlett, with Lucy in the middle but inclining toward Emersonian beauty. Thereafter, the contrast is advanced by the behavior and the opinions of Mr. Emerson and Mr. Eager. It is somewhat typical of Forster that secondary characters represent the two "sides," the two possibilities that will later create tension for the novel and for its main character, Lucy. The clash between Emerson and Eager comes in the novel's sixth chapter, that with the inordinately long title, "The Reverend Arthur Beebe, the Reverend Cuthbert Eager, Mr. Emerson, Mr. George Emerson, Miss Eleanor Lavish, Miss Charlotte Bartlett, and Miss Lucy Honeychurch Drive Out to See a View; Italians Drive Them." (It is worth noting the presence in this title of the "view" metaphor, its being associated with the necessary presence of "Italians," and its being submerged in the verbiage of the title.) When their driver attempts to get romantic with his female companion (Mr. Beebe thinks of them in the novel, and speaks of them in the film, as "Phaethon and Persephone"), Mr. Eager insists that the young woman be put off the carriage to walk. Mr. Emerson strenuously objects, urging the Rev. Eager, "of whom he stood in no awe," to let the couple be, as we find happiness so seldom that it seems to him like sacrilege to suppress it. (73) Each of the young lovers appeals to Lucy to intervene, the young woman in fact pointing "to the other carriage" as she does so. But Eager is not to be restrained in his cause, and at last Persephone gets down from the box, as Eager proclaims "'Victory at last!'" Mr. Emerson argues that "'It is defeat. You have parted two people who were happy.'" (74) And the party continues its tour, divided, "their anxiety to keep together being only equalled by their desire to go different directions." (76) The Reverend Eager anticipated--as well as created--division; at the very start of the tour, he was appalled at its make-up: "Lucy and Miss Bartlett had a certain style about them, and Mr. Beebe, though unreliable, was a man of parts. But a shoddy lady writer and a journalist. . .They should enter no villa at his introduction." (69) But Mr. Beebe tries to take a centrist, moderate position on the censuring of Phaethon and Persephone; he calls out that "after this warning the couple would be sure to behave themselves properly." (73) And Lucy has clearly not allied herself with Eager. When the driver and his girlfriend are first noticed making amorous overtures, Lucy suffers a "spasm of envy," and realizes that the two Italians are "probably the only people enjoying the expedition." (72) After the dismissal of Persephone, when the party has arrived at its stopping-place, Charlotte and Miss Lavish urge Lucy to remain near Mr. Eager, but she refuses, because she would be "only at ease amongst those to whom she felt indifferent." (77)

The carriage trip is the climax rather than the beginning of Lucy's disaffection for Mr. Eager. Earlier, in Fiesole, when Lucy and Charlotte were with him, he was not only rude to a street-vendor, but was little short of violent with the man. Lucy was led then to suspect that the chaplain was no positive model of his calling. "She doubted that Mr. Eager was as full of spirituality and culture as she had been led to suppose." (62) No sooner has she thus begun to mistrust him than he lives up (down?) to her suspicions by attempting to derogate Mr. Emerson--in his absence, of course. Immediately, Lucy's hackles are up: "For the first time Lucy's rebellious thoughts swept out in words--for the first time in her life." (63) The attempted derogation takes a reverse effect; not only is this the first instance of anything like conscious rebellion with Lucy, and the start of her education, but it is also the beginning of her being kindly disposed toward the Emersons. Shortly thereafter, there are "questions rioting" in Lucy's brain, and she realizes that the "well-known world had broken up. . . ." (65)

Jhabvala's screenplay operates in approximately the same way, regarding the use of contrasts, as does Forster's novel. The clash between Mr. Emerson and Mr. Eager is an eye-opener to Lucy in each case, and is part of what starts her process of maturation. But Forster's pattern of contrasts is considerably more complex, especially in its use of Mr. Beebe. In the novel the little clergyman adds to the contrastive mix of characters but greatly complicates it also. Before Mr. Eager has ever been brought into the novel, Forster has set up a contrast betwen him and Mr. Beebe, of whom Lucy observes, "He seems to see good in every one. No one would take him for a clergyman." (11) Additionally, Beebe almost simultaneously becomes part of the character-contrasts on another front. When Charlotte is told by George Emerson that she cannot see his father because that elderly gentleman is in his bath, she is shocked out of all the indignation she has been feeling over the swapping of rooms. Her "barbed civilities" are all blunted; young Emerson has "scored a notable triumph to the delight of Mr. Beebe and to the secret delight of Lucy." (14) Elsewhere, Beebe is useful to Forster as a sounding-board, or a barometer; by the time we are told (130) that Beebe's "opinion of [Lucy] rose daily," we realize that ours has too, perhaps partly as a result of his.

Late in the novel, however, Beebe becomes a considerably more complicated character, as Forster's methods of contrast likewise become more complex. Beebe continues to be the good, charitable cleric; when he hears that Mr. Emerson is moving, he fetches him to the rectory, where there is a cheery, warm fire by which Emerson can be comfortable. (233) But his behavior in response to Lucy's romantic entanglements seems, initially at least, contradictory. He is clearly pleased when Lucy breaks her engagement to Cecil--as he was clearly less than pleased when she first became engaged. (Both of these reactions are even more overtly clear in the novel than in the film.) The reader supposes that both reactions were the result of Beebe's fondness for George Emerson. Yet, when he discovers that Lucy means to marry George, he is not, ostensibly, the least bit supportive. To her confession that she has "misled" everyone, he responds "Oh, rubbish, Miss Honeychurch!" He then goes on to declare that he is "'more grieved'" than he can express. "'It is lamentable, lamentable--

incredible.'" At this point, Mr. Emerson demands to know what Mr. Beebe thinks is wrong with George, presumably as a prospective husband for Lucy. "'Nothing, Mr. Emerson [Beebe responds], except that he no longer interests me. Marry George, Miss Honeychurch. He will do admirably.'" It would seem that Beebe has done a double-reverse here; he might have been expected, by us as well as by Lucy, to be more humane and less severely clerical in this situation. However, there are extenuating details. When Mr. Emerson reacted "hotly" to Beebe's "rubbish" exclamation, the rector "laid his hand on the old man's shoulder pleasantly." (239) It is fairly clear from this act, done "pleasantly," that he does not want to hurt any feelings, means no animosity toward George, and does not want to be any major obstacle to Lucy's future; nevertheless, he cannot, whether for religious or personal reasons, bring himself to condone Lucy's choices. This reluctance was accounted for, if not fully explained, earlier, when his "belief in celibacy" was expressed by himself as: "'They that marry do well, but they that refrain do better.'" (216) Thus, Mr. Beebe, earlier a figure contrasted to Charlotte Bartlett and Mr. Eager, now becomes no less useful to Forster as a demarcation. His limits allow him to be contrastive up to a point, and no further. One of the last ways in which he serves Forster's methods of characterization is when Lucy is not quite able to perceive "that Mr. Emerson was profoundly religious, and differed from Mr. Beebe chiefly by his acknowledgement of passion. . . ." (234)

As will happen elsewhere in this particular transformation, our viewing of the Ivory-Merchant film enriches our reading of Forster's novel. The novelist's elaborate devices of characterization-by-contrast are used in reduced fashion in the film. The simplicities of the latter underscore the novel's complexities. This is not meant to disparage the film at all. Reduction, we must never forget, is necessary to the film-maker who wishes to adapt a novel. So, while this film has a rhythm of its own, it could not hope to duplicate the layers of repetition-plus-variation that the novelist is able to afford.

Other aspects of Forster's novel are so singularly verbal as to be induplicatable, or virtually so, in any other medium. They are those aspects of style, of management of words, that make this novel what it so uniquely is. Among them are wit, allusion, aphorisms, metaphor--especially extended metaphor, or analogy--and irony. These are by no means exclusive categories; as the reader will see, they overlap considerably. Still, it will be useful, for discussion purposes, to try to deal with them under separate headings.

Wit is the primary component of tone in Forster's novel, and tone is essential to everything else. Throughout his fiction, but especially in A Room with a View, there is a constant paradox: a view of the world that is skeptical and satirical exists side-by-side with events and circumstances that are endearingly sentimental. Characters are mocked--usually gently, sometimes not so--at the same time that they are treated most humanely. Consistently, tone is both a goad and a balance to content and to theme. Frequently, tone is conveyed through characters and the treatment they are accorded by the narrative voice. Thus, Cecil is always treated ironically, but almost never harshly. When, for instance, Lucy's Italian travels have begun to improve --or, to use his word, to "develop"--her, Cecil starts to re-evaluate her as a prospect. "So it happened that from patronizing civility he had slowly passed if not to passion, at least to a profound uneasiness." (102) Later, when Lucy breaks off their engagement, Cecil seems to take it all rather too well. But on the chapter's last page, the narrator sets it right: "For all his culture, Cecil was an ascetic at heart, and nothing in his love became him like the leaving of it." (204) At other times, tone is established by the narrative voice commenting on meanings rather than on characters. One such instance is the narrator's warning us what Lucy is up against:

> . . .there was presented to the girl the
> complete picture of a cheerless, loveless
> world in which the young rush to destruction
> until they learn better--a shamefaced world of
> precautions and barriers which may avert evil,
> but which do not seem to bring good, if we may
> judge from those who have used them most. (92-3)

This kind of skepticism, counter-balanced to the
sentiment found elsewhere in the novel, is almost
totally, and conspicuously, absent from the film.

When it is not being used to establish and maintain
tone in the novel, Forster's wit is put to other, related
use. Sometimes the narrative voice shares "secrets" with
us, thus establishing a rapport between us and the
narrator, a rapport that is a very useful rhetorical tool
to Forster. It draws the reader more tightly into the
events of the novel, and it also gives one a closer
understanding of its characters. Often, we are led to
understand them better than they do themselves. This can
happen through little, passing narrative insights, such
as when we are told of the "ideals" adhered to by the
society of Lucy's family, which ideals she has always
accepted: "their kindly affluence, their inexplosive
religion, their dislike of paper-bags, orange-peel, and
broken bottles." (127) Or it can come about in larger,
more meaningful turns of the plot, as when, in an example
seen earlier here, we listen in on what Cecil "could not
know. . .was the most intimate conversation they had ever
had." Similar to that instance is one in which Lucy

makes, to Miss Bartlett, what she thinks is "rather a good speech." The narrator, however, cautions us about the speech: "The reader may have detected an unfortunate slip in it." The situation--not repeated in the film--is this: Lucy has been attempting to mitigate, to Charlotte, George's having behaved "like a cad" in Italy. That he kissed her must have been, she insists, an "unconscious" bit of misbehavior on his part:

> "I fell into all those violets, and he was
> silly and surprised. I don't think we
> ought to blame him very much. It makes such
> a difference when you see a person with
> beautiful things behind him unexpectedly." (172)

There are, in fact, two slips in that final sentence, but taken together they constitute a single one. First, if Lucy were to be consistent in adopting George's "unconscious" perspective, then the last pronoun ought to be "her," not "him." More importantly, when Lucy entered the "terrace" at Fiesole where George kissed her, the violets were all in front of her. ("From her feet. . . violets ran down in rivulets and streams and cataracts...." [80]) She has, in fact, recollected the scene from her own perspective.

Always, Forster derives many effects from allusion. His best ones serve as aids to characterization, and atmosphere, and theme. One of the most fruitful in A Room with a View is the song that Lucy sings, as Freddy and Mr. Beebe listen, right after Cecil has departed

Windy Corner. It is Lucy Ashton's song from The Bride
of Lammermoor. What makes it function perfectly is one's
recollection of how Scott used the song originally to
underscore the character of his Lucy (Miss Honeychurch's
namesake?). "The words she had chosen seemed
particularly adapted," Scott tells us, "to her character.
. . ." Lucy Ashton "was particularly accessible to
[impulses] of a romantic cast." But she too seldom acts
in accord with any impulses of her own, for "in her
exterior relations to things of this world Lucy
unwillingly received the ruling impulse from those around
her." And Scott uses this descriptive sketch as
foreshadowing: "It usually happens that such a compliant
and easy disposition, which resigns itself without murmur
to the guidance of others, becomes the darling of those
to whose inclinations its own seemed to be offered, in
ungrudging and ready sacrifice."[3] Lucy Ashton, of
course, comes to a tragic end; Forster's Lucy will be
spared such tragedy, because she will desert, just in
time, that army of darkness whose ranks would have been
pleased to receive her inclinations as a sacrifice. That
Lucy Honeychurch should sing Lucy Ashton's song at this
particular stage of her adventures is a kind of Freudian
slip (Note that it is "a song that Cecil gave her" [220])
much like those that Joyce has his characters commit,
especially in Dubliners. It should also be noted that

the song works in the service of theme and characterization, even if one does not recognize the allusion, although its function is greater once one does. The film, as we have already observed, finds equivalents of its own to this kind of allusion by Forster, but the less expansive function of the film's allusions points up how fruitful those of the novel are.

Forster also makes several references in this novel to the verse of A. E. Housman, of whom Mr. Emerson's views could remind one, although Housman does not seem to have been the model for Forster's character. Not surprisingly, it is Mr. Emerson who first quotes Housman, so naturally that Lucy hardly realizes at first that he is reciting lines:

> "From far, from eve and morning,
> And yon twelve-winded sky,
> The stuff of life to knit me
> Blew hither: here am I."   (30)

The naturalness of his quoting is as indicative as the lines are. He knows how much of life is "twelve-winded" accident, but he knows too that human endeavor, toward love and celebration, can overcome whatever sorrow fate causes. Furthermore, the reader who knows Housman well, or who bothers to check, realizes that the remainder of the poem Mr. Emerson quotes (it is number XXXII in A Shropshire Lad) demonstrates that Emerson's source-- Housman and/or Terence, his speaker--feels the same way:

> Now--for a breath I tarry
>   Nor yet disperse apart--
> Take my hand quick and tell me,
>   What have you in your heart.
>
> Speak now, and I will answer;
>   How shall I help you, say;
> Ere to the wind's twelve quarters
>   I take my endless way.

Later in the novel, the same poem is alluded to by George
Emerson, in his insistence to Mr. Beebe that coincidence
explains the reuniting of all the parties who had met at
the Pension Bertolini:

> "It is. I have reflected. It is Fate.
> Everything is Fate. We are flung together by
> Fate, drawn apart by Fate--flung together,
> drawn apart. The twelve winds blow us--we
> settle nothing--" (148)

That George has not yet come to a mature sharing of his
father's view of the world and its people is indicated
by the one-dimensional interpretation that he appears to
have given to Housman's poem. Once again, the film's use
of allusion, on a lesser scale, recalls to mind the
greater function of allusion in Forster's novel.

Perhaps even more than he does elsewhere, Forster
favors aphorism in _A Room with a View_. Examples so
abound that we must settle here for a representative
sampling. One that establishes a model for several
others is in a reflection by Lucy upon its being
"impossible to rehearse life." Forster elaborates upon
her thought:

A fault in the scenery, a face in the audience,

> an irruption of the audience on to the stage,
> and all our carefully planned gestures mean
> nothing, or mean too much.   (154)

This metaphoric portrayal of life as stage drama, or as
performance art of some kind, is continued in a borrowed
aphorism that Forster gives to Mr. Emerson: "'"Life,"
wrote a friend of mine, "is a public performance on the
violin, in which you must learn the instrument as you go
along".'" (236) The friend whose line this is originally
is Samuel Butler.[4]   One of the narrator's wittiest
remarks bears, not surprisingly, upon religion: "Paganism
is infectious--more infectious than diphtheria or piety.
. . ." (174)   Perhaps a close second is the use of an
aphorism by one of the Emersons (it is not clear which,
but it is an Emerson quoting Thoreau): "Mistrust all
enterprises that require new clothes." (144)   The phrase,
however, that might stand as the motto for this novel
comes to us from the narrator as part of a commentary
upon Lucy's playing of Schumann.   What that playing
captures is "the sadness of the incomplete--the sadness
that is often Life, but should never be Art. . . ." (140)

The importance of aphorism here is as another of
those rhetorical devices that cause the reader to warm
to the narrative voice, and to trust its wisdom, its
experience of the world.   So, likewise, does Forster's
use of metaphor and analogy endear itself--and him--to
the receptive reader.   This is an aspect of style,

dependent as it is upon sheerly verbal qualities, that is extremely difficult for any film to duplicate, particularly since Forster's metaphors, extended or not, are so simultaneously fanciful and accurate. Some of them are used to crystallize a truth that the narrative needs to establish just for the moment, but establish vividly. Such a one is that which Forster employs to make clear to us the kind of almost universal response that betrothals generate.

> The chief parallel--to compare one great thing
> with another--is the power over us of a temple
> of some alien creed. Standing outside, we de-
> ride or oppose it, or at the most feel sentimental.
> Inside, though the saints and gods are not ours,
> we become true believers, in case any true
> believers should be present. (109)

This is used to explain the not-quite-hypocritical expressions of happiness conveyed by Freddy Honeychurch and Mr. Beebe, upon the announcement of Lucy's engagement to Cecil.

Elsewhere in the novel, metaphors are more than a one-time thing; some have ramifications far beyond their immediate context. For instance, Cecil, when introduced to the reader, is not only described as being "mediaeval," but, more specifically, is likened to "a Gothic statue." (99) This makes him in some ways admirable, but overall ambiguous: "Well educated, well endowed, and not deficient physically," he is still not a perfect choice for betrothal, since "[a] Gothic statue implies celibacy, just as a Greek statue implies fruition." (100) Beyond giving the reader a start toward a proper perception of Cecil Vyse, this metaphor resonates throughout the novel. Indeed, the entire chapter in which it appears is titled "Mediaeval." But other aspects of "mediaevalism" are explored in other parts of the book. While Lucy is still in Italy, she has already begun to veer away from conforming to a female stereotype that Forster calls the "mediaeval lady." Significantly, Charlotte Bartlett draws a profile of the type, while explaining to Lucy what makes some things "unladylike":

> It was not that ladies were inferior to men;
> it was that they were different. Their mission
> was to inspire others to achievement rather than
> to achieve themselves. Indirectly, by means of
> tact and a spotless name, a lady could accomplish
> much. But if she rushed into the fray herself
> she would be first censured, then despised, and
> finally ignored. Poems had been written to
> illustrate this point. (46)

Forster hastens to point out that this type did not vanish with the Middle Ages, but still "lingers in our midst," although "the creature grows degenerate." (47) Perhaps it is just as well, then, that George Emerson is clearly not "mediaeval":

> . . .it was hopeless to look for chivalry in
> such a man. He would do her no harm by idle
> gossip; he was trustworthy, intelligent, and
> even kind; he might even have a high opinion
> of her. But he lacked chivalry. . . . (52)

This, of course, is at a time before Cecil has entered

the novel,and when Lucy still thinks the chivalric a desirable quality (although one sees clearly in the above passage that Forster does not). Eventually, although after the reader has discovered the same, she will realize that medievalism is a point of separation between George Emerson and Cecil Vyse, for "the only relationship which Cecil conceived was feudal: that of protector and protected. He had no glimpse of the comradeship after which the girl's soul yearned." (179) The author's final word on this useful metaphor is in the title of the novel's concluding chapter, when George and Lucy are alone together in Italy: "The End of the Middle Ages."

It must be clear from the foregoing that Forster creates any number of ironies in his novel, many of which, being singularly verbal, are difficult if not impossible for a film to duplicate. Even little ironies loom huge in this novel, such as Lucy's accidental encounter with George Emerson, which changes everything. The accident occurs the same way in the film, but, unless one knows Italian, the ironic joke is difficult to catch in the film. Lucy, on the outing to Fiesole, is virtually banished from the company of Charlotte and Eleanor Lavish. Seeking to find Mr. Beebe, she approaches their Italian driver. However, she cannot remember Italian for "clergyman," so having begun to ask "'Dove. . .("Where")?'" she finishes: "'Dove buoni uomini?'" ("Where are the good men?") The Emersons having impressed the driver as "good men," he leads her to George Emerson, who, in the violet-covered terrace, kisses her. (78-80)

The preceding example is one of linguistic irony (mostly). What textbooks call "irony of situation" is also abundant in <u>A</u> <u>Room</u> <u>with</u> <u>a</u> <u>View</u>. Perhaps it is at its most prevalent in Chapter 17, "Lying to Cecil." This is where Lucy terminates their engagement. In the previous chapter, she had summoned George Emerson to her --he had been playing tennis with Freddy and others at Windy Corner--and informed him that he must go away from the house and out of her life. He had expressed incredulity at the idea that she should still intend to marry Cecil. George's objections to that betrothal were, among others, these: that Cecil is someone who "'should know no one intimately, least of all a woman'"; (193) that no one can ever talk to Cecil without "'feeling tired'"; that Cecil is more comfortable with "'things--books, pictures'" than he is with people; that Cecil has made a habit of "'protecting and teaching you and your mother to be shocked, when it was for <u>you</u> to settle whether you were shocked or no'"; that Cecil, in short, is "'the type who's kept Europe back for a thousand years.'" (194) Lucy went from that confrontation back to the tennis court, to inform Freddy that Emerson "'has

had to go.'" Freddy then urged Cecil to complete a
foursome so that they might continue the tennis-playing.
When Cecil refused, the "scales fell fom Lucy's eyes,"
and she decided to break their engagement.

Now, she confronts Cecil, to carry out that
decision. She chooses a time that fits perfectly the
feminist ironies that underlie much of this novel: it is
"the moment before bed, when, in accordance with their
bourgeois habit, she always dispensed drinks to the men."
(198) Cecil's first line of response is, typically, a
blunder: He informs Lucy that she is not herself, she
must be "tired," thus of course hitting upon one of the
key issues in Lucy's encounter with George Emerson. (199)
She, meanwhile, presents but little solid reason, at
first, for wanting to be disengaged. She does not have
the proper education, and he refused to play tennis with
Freddy; even to herself these are apparently not
convincing. And, the whole time, Cecil is better behaved
than ever, until Lucy grows "more and more vexed at his
dignified behaviour. She had counted on his being
petty." (201) So, she commences to cite more compelling
reasons why it must be all up between them. The first
is that Cecil is "'the sort who can't know anyone
intimately.'"
When a "horrified look" comes into Cecil's eyes, Lucy
moderates that charge, but launches into a series of

indictments not unfamiliar to the reader: She "'won't be protected,'" but must be "'trusted to face the truth'"; he wraps himself up "'in art and books and music'"; (201) most of all, he has been "'all right as long as [he] kept to things, but when [he] came to people'--" At this point, Lucy stops, as the irony comes near to dawning upon her. Forster turns the irony up one more notch, before ending the chapter, as he has Cecil come near to a very accurate--and, naturally, accidental--perception, observing that Lucy seems a different person on this evening, expressing new thoughts in a new voice. When Lucy demands that he be more specific, he is: "'I mean that a new person seems speaking through you'," he says, with clear admiration. Lucy, just as unconsciously, rises to that bait: "'If you think I am in love with someone else, you are very much mistaken.'" (202)

It is typical of Forster that Lucy is no more perceptive in this scene than Cecil is. The author has treated his protagonist here almost as Swift does Gulliver in those scenes (conversations upon warfare with the Prince of Brobdingnag, e.g.) in which the character's absence of self-awareness is a shared joke between author and reader. Lest one think that Forster has treated his main character, his educable character, with little respect, it must be remembered that this is the chapter in which Lucy enters, albeit temporarily, the army of darkness. It must also be noted that any film would be hard-pressed to duplicate the manner in which, once again, it is language that produces irony in this story.

Finally, one finds segments of Forster's prose wherein the very diction precludes any conversion to photography. No non-verbal medium could hope to reproduce such a passage as the following, which is the last paragraph in Chapter Twelve (titled, whimsically, "Twelfth Chapter") of the novel:

> That evening and all that night the water ran away. On the morrow the pond had shrunk to its old size and lost its glory. It had been a call to the blood and to the relaxed will, a passing benediction whose influence did not pass, a holiness, a spell, a momentary chalice for youth.
> (152)

Even if one attempted to duplicate this in a series of pictures (which would immediately be an odd choice, for it is not meant to be at all literal), one could at best show the pond diminished at sunrise from what it had previously been. Lost in the "translation" to the visual would be the concept of the water's having run away, of the pool's having possessed a glory, of its having been not only a call to the blood, but a benediction (whether or not a passing one); lost, too, would be the idea of influence, let alone a spiritual, a religious influence. In short, the essence of the paragraph would be lost. A viewer of a pictorial version could, to be sure, provide his or her own essence. But one must need then substitute one's own genius for Forster's--not an easy or comfortable replacement.

So, while much was kept, much was lost.   And much of that which did not transform is what makes Forster's fiction the uniqueness that it is.

1. E. M. Forster, <u>A</u> <u>Room</u> <u>with</u> <u>a</u> <u>View</u> (New York, Vintage, 1961). The novel was originally published in 1908. The scene referred to here is in the last chapter; see especially pp. 202-3.
References hereafter will be to this edition, with page numbers in parentheses in the text.

2. E. M. Forster, <u>Aspects</u> <u>of</u> <u>the</u> <u>Novel</u> (New York, Harcourt, Brace & World, 1954). See p. 240ff. Future references will be to <u>Aspects</u>, followed by page number, in text.

3. All of the quoted material is from Chapter Two.

4. The film's concession to this is in <u>The</u> <u>Way</u> <u>of</u> <u>All</u> <u>Flesh</u> being one of the books Mr. Beebe discovers in the Emersons' library. It is not there in the novel's equivalent scene.

<u>ORDINARY</u> <u>PEOPLE</u>

"Ordinary People" is something of a rarity. Not only is it an improved version of the story told in the Judith Guest novel on which it is based, but it is an improvement in a singular way. The film, which marked the directing debut of Robert Redford, is more ambiguous than the novel; it establishes ambiguities and ironies that are functional, that aid the development of theme. Furthermore, it gains its ambiguities by episodes that it added to the story. As we have seen elsewhere here, a film often is a lesser version of the novel it adapts, literally (that is, quantitatively) and artistically, because of what it must cut. But Redford and screenplay-writer Alvin Sargent, both of whom won Academy Awards for this film,[1] included important scenes and lines not in the original version; these additions, along with some changes to the sequence and the emphases of the novel, help create a film that transcends its source.

As is always the case, some elements of this novel would not translate precisely into film. Consequently, some of what goes well in the novel is absent from the film. As is also typical, the first casualties are the sheerly verbal strengths of the novel: some good lines are lost, metaphors and symbols do not all work as well,

and Guest's most skillful uses of narrative point-of-
view are sacrificed. This last trait is one that the
film must find compensations for, since Guest puts point-
of-view to some fairly sophisticated use. Throughout
much of the novel, the narrative perspective is "almost"
Conrad's; it is not quite his voice that we hear, but
more nearly his thoughts. Yet, the language employed is
only sometimes Conrad's vernacular; it is qualified by
what Hugh Kenner has usefully termed "The Uncle Charles
Principle."[2] That is, other idioms intrude--those of
Con's father, his grandfather, his psychiatrist, the
general public; it is a somewhat choric effect, but it
is also a constant revelation of Conrad's personality,
intellect, and so forth. More-or-less alternately,
chapters are similarly filtered through the consciousness
of Calvin Jarrett, Con's father. At times, Guest's trick
lies in making us realize that we can hardly tell the
difference. Thus, at the beginning of Chapter 5, someone
arrives at the office of Dr. Berger, the psychiatrist.
We are at first inclined to think it might be Calvin, as
he had talked, near the end of the preceding chapter, of
making such a visit. The fifth chapter begins:

> The building is shabby, and inside, the lobby
> is hot and dark. He glances at his watch; too
> dark in here to make out the numbers. The crisp
> and sunny day he has left outside has nearly
> blinded him.[3]

For the next paragraph and more, the thoughts and

perceptions are not precisely identified. The concerns expressed ("looks like a great neighborhood for muggings"), the self-urgings ("get on it no backing out now"), the vacillating (he has toyed with the idea "all week not going just not showing up") could be Calvin's. Not until we are told, later, that he "is to meet his father at his office" do we realize it is Conrad making the visit. The realization of how much they talk/think alike reminds us of how close these two are, which will be important throughout. The film cannot do this in precisely the same way.

As always, the novel is able, in descriptive passages, to employ language that will not work easily into dialogue and therefore is practically unavailable to the film-maker. So good lines vanish, such as this metaphor depicting Conrad's typical early-morning condition:

> The small seed of despair cracks open and sends experimental tendrils upward to the fragile skin of calm holding him together. (2)

Nor will "metaphor" in other senses adapt conveniently. Time, among other considerations, prohibits the film from creating a motif, as the novel does, of Conrad's enjoyment in singing with his peers:

> Choir is the one time of day when he lets down his guard; there is peace in the strict concentration that Faughnan demands of all of them. (19)

In the film, Faughnan does not appear as choir-director,

and, while Conrad seems to enjoy singing, it is not clear that any "strict concentration" is required of him there.

Similarly, the novel is able to make more meaning of the title than is the film. "Ordinary people" is what the Jarretts want to be, what they struggle to be. Calvin needs almost desperately for them to return to ordinary lives, and the implication is that Beth needs ordinariness even more than he. When Conrad comes home from school one evening and reports to his dad that he made an "A" on a test, his first such grade in this, his first term back in school, they sit and read the newspaper together while Beth prepares supper. The point-of-view at this stage is Calvin's:

> They are ordinary people after all. For a time they had entered the world of the newspaper statistic; a world where any measure you took to feel better was temporary, at best, but that is over. This is permanent. It must be. (87)

This is the kind of insight that is best conveyed by—that perhaps can only be conveyed by—a character's thoughts.

At other times, the novel demonstrates another power that lies in the ability to depict characters' thoughts. Very often, what can be thought in but a few words, and thought in an evocative fashion, would require a thousand pictures to duplicate. Such is the depiction, here, of one of Conrad's passing thoughts, one that makes a useful contrast with his fondness for singing in the high-

school choir. He has, at this point in the novel,
invited Jeannine "to have a Coke" and is now thinking
about where they should go:

> Not Pasquesi's. It is always crowded after
> school; filled with people that he knows, and
> yet doesn't know any more. The windows are
> opaque with the steam of bodies. Just walking
> by the place reinforces his sense of separation.
> (94)

This can almost be conveyed by pictures, until that final
sentence. And it is an unwieldy, perhaps unrealistic,
observation to put into dialogue. It is not at all
certain that Conrad could verbalize this.

However, not all of the novel's quantitative
advantages provide qualitative gain, and the film
benefits from this fact. One thing, for instance, that
the film does not even attempt to keep is the novel's
portrayal of Calvin's background. Although his mother
was alive and apparently in good health while he was
growing up, he was raised in an orphanage in Detroit, an
"odd kind of orphanage: most of the kids had at least one
living parent. . . ." (7) He has some recollection of
his mother, but has "no memories of being any man's son."
(7) His surname, Jarrett, was his mother's family name.
But he has survived these unpromising origins to become
a Lake Forest tax attorney, "supporting his family, his
boys, in style...." (9; emphasis is the novel's.) The
inclusion of all this provides a window of opportunity

for Redford and Sargent. The novel tries to get too much established too quickly where Calvin is concerned, and it never quite becomes convincing. For all we can tell in the film, which omits all of these background details, Cal has always been a privileged person. But that works no less well. In fact it works better, especially when we arrive at Calvin's scene with Dr. Berger.[4] His contention there that "all life is an accident" should not be any viewpoint that he is trying out for the first time (as it clearly is) if he in fact had the background, the variety of experience that Guest wants him to have had.

Guest's novel, as source material, provided the film-makers with several advantages: an engaging plot, themes that are easily accessible but of some substance, dramatic and emotional content that comes near everyone's potential domestic experience, and characters who are interesting if none too deep. But it also brought another attractive aspect: if its strengths are almost perfectly adaptable to film, its weaknesses can either be adjusted or excised.

One of the ways in which this novel, although it is not a long one,[5] sets itself up to be trimmed by a screenplay-writer is in its tendency to do too much telling of what it could show--or has already shown. Conrad's fight with Stillman is a perfect example. Con always, just as Berger has been telling him, lets anger build too much and works too hard at restraining it; then, occasionally, as here, it overflows. When Calvin is told about it, he discovers what comes as no great surprise to the reader--that it is the first fight in which Con has ever been involved. Still, Guest cannot stop with that somewhat superfluous bit of insight, but must have Calvin tell Conrad that he owed himself this outburst, for he does such too seldom; and then she feels it necessary to have Calvin think:

> Not just to comfort, it is the truth. A disposition like an angel's, Ellen [Con's grand-mother] used to say. Sunny and sweet, he never got mad. And that wasn't good. Everybody has resentments, everybody has anger. . . . (17)

The other dimension of Guest's Ordinary People that helps make Redford's "Ordinary People" a comfortable transformation is its simplifying of almost all its issues, its shying away from the pursuit of complexities. We see this at its clearest in Calvin's visit to Berger. While there, Calvin makes an observation that is--for him, certainly, and probably for more than a few readers--fairly disturbing: "'Hell, all life is an accident, every bit of it--who you fall in love with, what grabs you, and what you do with it....'" (135) Berger, somewhat typically, ducks the question: "'That sounds more like the philosophy of a drifter than a tax attorney from Lake Forest,'" he replies, and they move on as though he had rebutted the protest that was in Cal's claim. This is perfectly acceptable in terms of character, as Berger is hardly the first psychiatrist to avoid a philosophical direction that might complicate the counselling process. And since he is not, in this instance, counselling a "drifter," the strategy is effective. But the novel never really confronts the issue any more directly than Berger has; it tends instead to evade, or to simplify, its own toughest themes. The consequence of this evasion is paradoxical: it lessens the importance of the novel, philosophically at least, while it simultaneously renders it more readily adaptable to film.

Other instances of excessive simplification are all over the novel: Conrad is rather too ethically perfect, Calvin too wishy-washy, Beth too bitchy. Berger is alternately too cute and too heroic. And any inferences we are pointed toward are easy answers--the main one being that openness plus psychotherapy equals panacea. Tacked onto this is that psychiatric cliche of popular art: once you've put the problem into words, preferably aloud, you're cured. Would that any of life--psychiatry above all--were this simple.

Normally, when film-makers choose to adapt a novel, the immediate problems are those of cutting and simplifying. In this case, those problems are greatly reduced, as cutting is easy, and simplifying is unnecessary. So Redford and Sargent were able to add to their source material whole scenes as well as dialogue and to produce a version of the story that is more ambiguous and more sophisticated than the novel.

The first addition that the film makes is a scene in which we see Beth alone. Already, this is a significant difference, for in all of the novel, Beth is never directly perceived by the reader; instead, one sees her through the eyes of Calvin or Conrad, or interacting as part of a group. Isolating her in the film, even for a moment, works in approximately the same way as does the novelist's giving narrative point-of-view to any single character: it is an innately sympathetic device. In this scene, we see Beth come home from shopping. She drops parcels in Conrad's bedroom, then starts toward her own; but, on a whim, she stops and enters what had been the bedroom of Buck, the son now deceased. She sits a while on his bed and looks pensive, perhaps mournful. When Conrad comes home from school, his appearance in the doorway of the room startles her, and Beth blurts "Don't do that!" Three times in the next few seconds Conrad apologizes. He is very nervous in her presence, she hardly less in his, and they clearly cannot talk with each other. He volunteers information about what and how he is doing at school, and the scene ends. While it has moderated her character, this glimpse of Beth has not been purely sympathetic to her. When she enters Buck's room, we cannot help but remember that earlier, when she and Calvin came home late at night, she went past Con's room without a look, while Cal spotted a light under the door and went in, having knocked first, to see if Con was all right. We notice also that she did not ask Con, in this scene, anything about his day or his school-work. Still, we become aware of some emotional capacity in her, however slight.

Just as long and no less important is another additional scene, this one taking place in the backyard of the Jarretts' home. Conrad reclines upon a patio lounge; it is autumn, late afternoon. Beth, seeing him, puts on a jacket and comes out to ask if he needs a sweater. We hear the music up and under this scene, the first time Pachelbel's tinkly "Canon" has been present since the scene in Buck's room. When Beth asks Con what he has been thinking about, he first says "Nothing." As before, they are ill-at-ease in each other's company. Then he tells her that he was recalling a pigeon which once took up residence in their garage. They both reminisce about this until Con recalls, pointedly, "That was the nearest we ever came to having a pet." Beth, just as purposefully, deflects the conversation to talking about the neighbor's dog. Eventually, they both talk at once, each ignoring the other, until Con begins to yap like a small dog. Beth then pauses, looks at him awhile, instructs him to put on his jacket if he means to stay outside, and goes in. It is not clear whether Beth has diverted the conversation because she does not want to talk about having never allowed the boys to have a pet, or because she cannot talk about their childhood (perhaps because it painfully recalls Bucky), or because she cannot talk about anything with negative connotations, anything that might be perceived as failure on her part. Perhaps, too, she just cannot --possibly for this latter reason--talk to Conrad. But we also have to remember that much of the failure to communicate in this particular scene is the result of Conrad's behavior as much as, or more than, Beth's. She did care about his possibly being cold; that was why she came out initially. When she asked what he was thinking about (and she did), he became the evasive one. He rebuffed her effort, albeit a somewhat clumsy effort, to be friendly. However, in the scene's conclusion, Conrad follows his mother into the house, looking sincerely repentant, and asks if he can help set the table. Then, in a plaintive tone, he begins, "Mom...," as though he certainly would tell her that he loves her, or, at the very least, that he wishes to make up. They both freeze for a beat, then the telephone rings. It is one of

Beth's friends calling, to whom she says, "No, no, I'm not doing anything," then settles in to hear some gossip. "Did she really?" she says, and laughs loudly. The moment is lost, and Beth has retreated into her shell. Con, meanwhile, recalls--or fantasizes--a scene in the backyard a few years previous, with his mother being regaled by Buck's aggressively upbeat personality and boisterous humor. Not only is this scene not in the novel, but nothing there is so nearly derogatory to Conrad or so nearly favorable to Beth.

A third added scene also centers upon Conrad and Beth; once again, it mitigates, if it does not soften, Beth's elsewhere steely character. The Jarrett family members are taking pictures of one another, in various combinations. It is fairly obvious that Beth does not want to have her picture taken with Conrad, not, at least, if it requires their standing next to each other, calmly, for a long time. But Con indulges in a rare outburst of impetuous anger and startles the whole family (his grandparents are also present). The scene sets up two subsequent items, both important, though in different ways. The later one is the "Christmas tree" scene; while Calvin and Conrad are trimming the tree, Beth comes home, having learned that Con has quit the swim-team without telling his parents. A harsh encounter ensues. As Calvin says later, the whole thing "could have been handled better," but Beth can easily convince herself, when Con blows up at her, that this is more of his bad temper, brought on perhaps by the indulgence he receives from his therapist. The picture-taking scene does, in fact, follow immediately Berger's encouraging Con to express feelings and not to expect all feelings to be good feelings.

The tree-trimming scene is a long-range consequent to the photo session. The scene that immediately follows the photography debacle is, in its own way, no less significant. After Con's outburst of temper, Beth (typically) tries to cover by announcing that she'll fix lunch now. Her mother hurries to the kitchen when she hears a crash, to find Beth picking up a plate she has dropped--or thrown? The two women talk, briefly, about Conrad's "case," and Beth's atitude, mainly, is the same toward him as usual: "I don't think," she tells her mother, "he's happy in school. I don't think people want to be with him. He provokes people." How she thinks she knows this, especially since she never asks him about school, is anyone's guess. However, in the same scene, she picks up the two halves of the broken plate, and opines, "I think this can be saved. It's a nice, clean break." Apart from the obvious symbolism--unconscious on Beth's part--in her remark, there is a literal importance that, again, moderates the hardness of her character. An odd literary parallel occurs. One is reminded, whether Sargent meant for us to be or not, of the alienated Silas Marner, choosing to mend his earthenware water-jug as an act of natural piety.

To one of Conrad's appointments with Berger, the film adds some dialogue. Con remembers a moment right after Bucky's death, when his father came to his room to talk. As Con remembers it, he looked at his dad's shoe and thought that it might crack off, because "he was so uptight." At the same time he knew there was something he should say, something that "John Boy on the Waltons would've said." Berger cannot get an answer to "What would John-Boy have said?" and the scene ends. Its full relevance will be clear only in, literally, the film's last minute.

Calvin finally gets himself to visit Berger, as he does in the novel. The scene between them is essentially the same. However, the film adds a scene following that visit. Calvin comes home from Berger's office; while he is still in the garage, Beth opens the door from the kitchen to see if he is coming in. Instead, he informs her that he needs to tell her something. He barely begins, "When I was getting dressed for Buck's funeral...," when Beth does one of her usual interceptions: "Calvin, what's wrong with you?" When he insists that she hear what he wants to say ("it won't hurt you to listen"), her refusal is explicit: "I won't listen to that. No one in their right mind would listen to that," although she doesn't yet know what "that" is. What he needs to tell her is that while he was nearly frantic with grief on that occasion, she was concerned with how he should dress. The contrast between them then is underscored by the contrast now, when she will not even listen; in this contrast there is considerable foreshadowing.

The film's final addition is one of its best. After their return from Houston, Beth awakens and realizes Calvin is gone from their bed. Coming downstairs, she finds him seated in the dark, by himself, quietly weeping. He explains why he has been crying, concluding with: "I don't know if I love you anymore. And I don't know what I'm going to do without that." Beth goes immediately upstairs to begin packing and there undergoes the most genuine emotional reaction we have yet seen her allow herself, although just for an instant. In the novel, the decision to separate seems to be more exclusively hers. "'When you suggested a counselor,'" she says, "'that's when I knew.'" (234) The film's version, once again, adds a bit of fruitful ambiguity to both characters.

There is one other significant alteration made by Sargent and/or the film's editor, Jeff Kanew. The

sequence of the story's last half-dozen events is
changed, and the difference not only gives an emphasis
that the novel lacks, but makes virtually a new meaning.

After Conrad's fight with Kevin Stillman, there is,
in both novel and film, a brief but important
conversation between him and Joe Lazenby. "Laze," at
one time the closest friend of both Con and Buck Jarrett,
tries to get Conrad to talk about missing Bucky, but
fails. "I don't know why," he says to Con, "you want to
be alone in this."[6] Although Con does not explicitly
respond to that line, his actions thereafter make a
consistent progression toward "letting in" other persons.
The sequence of events in the film emphasizes this
progression in a way that the novel's episodes,
alternating betwen Con in Illinois and his parents in
Texas, do not.

As soon as he leaves Lazenby and goes back to his
grandparents' home, Conrad attempts to call Karen. His
motivation is not perfectly clear, but it seems likely
that he needs more than ever to share his feelings with
someone, and a friend with whom he was hospitalized would
be a natural sharer. He learns, as we have seen, that
Karen has killed herself. Anguished, and in desperation,
he calls Berger; of course his analyst will have to do
some sharing with him--it is what he is paid to do. But
when he meets with Berger in the doctor's office--a

crucial, final turning-point--he discovers that Berger wants also to be a sharing and caring friend. From that revelation, Conrad goes immediately to Jeannine's home, where he apologizes for having shut her out when, on their one date so far, he had been on the verge of divulging things to her that he previously had told to no one except doctors. Interestingly, the film, in keeping this scene, has cut out one of the novel's scenes between Conrad and Jeannine, in which they consummate the ultimate sharing. That a film should opt for less sex than the not highly erotic novel it is based on is almost revolutionary. Furthermore, the film's replacement scene is endearingly funny, as well as warmly sentimental.

The film's next scene takes us to Houston and the vacationing Beth and Calvin. They engage in a bitter verbal exchange, constituting Beth's coldest, bitchiest moment. "I cannot respond," she explains, speaking of Conrad, "when someone says 'Here, love me, I just did this great thing.' I just can't." At about this point, what was probably already clear to the viewer becomes clear to Calvin as well--Beth is not a giving, sharing person, either as spouse or as parent. Just as this altered sequence stressed a progression of Conrad's developing ability to share himself with others, so this contrasting of Beth (with Jeannine, as well as with Con) emphasizes the same point. The culmination of this sequence that the film has created will be, appropriately, in the ending. Immediately after Beth has left, Conrad joins his father on the patio, where he professes that he loves him. "I love you too," Calvin replies; simple as it is, it is the first such exchange Con has made with anyone. It is also what he was unable to say to his dad previously. He is becoming adept at "letting in" other people.[7]

Beth Jarrett is not as fully developed a character in this film as one might wish. We do not get to know her well enough to make credible all her paradoxes. We do not get enough exposure to her to understand just what the fears and apprehensions are that keep her from giving love, that keep her turning inward. Still less do we know what caused them. But neither is she as one-dimensional in the film as the novel allowed her to be. The more complex view of her that the film presents is emblematic of the whole network of differences between Guest's novel and the Sargent/Redford film. This is one of those unusual occurrences in which film-makers took a decent-if-not-great novel and made it into something more complex, more subtle, more ambiguous, and less ordinary.

1. This film received a number of Academy Award nominations, including the oddity of two in the same category--Judd Hirsch and Timothy Hutton (who won) for Best Supporting Actor. It also won Oscars for Best Film, Best Screenplay (Adaptation), and Best Director. Sargent, whose screenplay for The Sterile Cuckoo is discussed elsewhere here, had come a long way since that early in his career. Among his credits in the interim were the screenplays for "Paper Moon" and "Julia"; he also won an Academy Award for the latter. It is odd too that Donald Sutherland, who gives a splendid performance in this film, was the only one of the featured actors not to receive a nomination.

2. See Hugh Kenner, Joyce's Voices (Berkeley: U. of California Press, 1978). He expands upon the principle ("the narrative idiom need not be the narrator's") in the second chapter.

3. Judith Guest, Ordinary People (New York: Random House, 1976), p. 34. References hereafter will be to this edition, with page numbers in parentheses in the text.

4. The film's version of this scene will be examined in more detail shortly. It is the first of two consecutive scenes in which Sutherland's acting is spellbinding. This partly explains a manner in which reviews commonly refer to this film as, for example, "An actor's piece...," an unusual description for a film based on a novel. See, e.g., Halliwell's Film Guide, Eighth Edition (New York, HarperCollins, 1991), p. 827.

5. In paperback, the novel runs 245 pages.

6. The line is also in the novel.

7. The novel's ending is different. There, in an epilogue, Conrad goes to Joe Lazenby's home, and they leave to play golf together. It, too, is satisfactorily effective, sentimental, and conclusive--it completes a cycle. While it must have been a difficult bit for the film-makers to eliminate, the film's ending, given the altered sequence described here, is right for the film.

THE PRIME OF MISS JEAN BRODIE

To examine the transformation of The Prime of Miss Jean Brodie is to indulge in a process different from the others here. Muriel Spark's novel, published in 1961, was adapted to the stage by Jay Presson Allen, in a production that opened in London in May of 1966, with Vanessa Redgrave. Later, it played the Helen Hayes Theatre in New York, where Zoe Caldwell won a Tony for her role as Miss Brodie. Then, for the 1969 film, directed by Ronald Neame, Ms. Allen wrote the screenplay, based (so film credits tell us) on the play. This time, Maggie Smith played Brodie, for which performance she received an Academy Award.

In looking at this singular transformation--from novel to play to film--one gains insight to the methods of Muriel Spark; once again, much of this learning results from the omission or distortion of those methods in the play and, particularly, in the film.

The plot is probably the simplest aspect of Spark's novel. Miss Jean Brodie, a spinster, teaches at the Marcia Blaine school for girls in Edinburgh. She plays favorites with the ten-to-twelve-year-olds whom she teaches; the half-dozen particular favorites, those she labels the "*creme* *de* *la* *creme*," form a group known throughout the school as "the Brodie set." The novel follows them through their years in the school, in Brodie's class and beyond, during which time Miss Brodie has a romantic tryst with Gordon Lowther, the singing teacher, although she appears to be in love with the art instructor, Teddy Lloyd, a married man. The headmistress, Miss McKay, is suspicious of Brodie's unorthodox teaching methods, but is never able to charge her with any dereliction that would deserve dismissal. As the girls of the Brodie set grow older, one of them, Sandy Stranger, has an affair with Teddy Lloyd herself. Shortly thereafter, Miss Brodie's political exhortations urge a girl, not part of the "set," to seek her brother, fighting in the Spanish Civil War, and she is killed in the attempt. Sandy, who will years later convert to Roman Catholicism and become a nun, "betrays" Brodie to Miss McKay, who fires her.

As a novelist, Muriel Spark proceeds by subtleties, indirections, ambiguities, and, perhaps most of all, by leaving things unsaid. These are characteristics that seldom adapt well to a stage-play and almost never are compatible with a film since these two are more exoteric art-forms than a novel. Furthermore, she makes rather sophisticated use of narrative point-of-view and of disrupted chronology. Neither of these methods will adapt easily to stage or screen. Finally, she has her own notions about the function of "suspense":

> . . .suspense isn't just holding it back
> from the reader. Suspense is created even more
> by telling people what's going to happen. Be-
> cause they want to know <u>how</u>. Wanting to know
> <u>what</u> happened is not so strong as wanting to know
> <u>how.</u>[1]

To Spark, "construction," in a novel as in poetry, is virtually everything. So it would seem that any attempt to capture the methods or the meaning of one of her novels on stage or on screen would be doomed to failure. In a sense, that's precisely what happens with "The Prime of Miss Jean Brodie." The play is not a disaster, and the film is not awful; but neither of them captures the essence of Spark's novel—or of Spark as an artist—for reasons that we shall examine here.

First of all, what is changed in following Miss Brodie from novel to play to film is chronology—or its absence. The play opens with Sister Helena, the former Sandy Stranger, receiving a visitor, one Mr. Perry, a journalist from the United States. The story then is told, in the play, in a series of flashbacks, although not all of them could be stored in Sandy's memory, as several events took place when she was not present. The time-frame for the events in the play's flashbacks is 1931 to 1938. The novel begins in 1936, jumps backward to its earliest point, 1930, then follows the main time-

line up to Brodie's dismissal, apparently in 1939. But
the narrative moves within that line almost constantly,
and there are jumps forward to brief scenes as late as
1958, years after Miss Brodie has died. The film, on the
other hand, moves constantly, evenly, progressively
forward from its starting-point in 1932, until the
ending, with Brodie's "betrayal" and dismissal, about
1937.

The novel's anti-chronological scheme is important
to Spark, presumably because it is true-to-life. Memory
generally works in an unchronological manner. As she
begins her autobiography, Curriculum Vitae, Spark
announces much the same sort of method:

> My childhood in Edinburgh, so far as my
> memory stretches back (to when I was three or four
> and on to my school-days) occurs in bright
> flashes, illuminating every detail of the scene.
> It would falsify the situtation to try to connect
> my earliest years in a single narrative.[2]

Whatever the reason, she follows this method throughout
this novel. When we first learn any details of the
novel's ending, it is in a "flash-forward" in time: "It
was twenty-eight years after Eunice [Gardiner, one of
the Brodie set] did the splits in Miss Brodie's flat that
she, who had become a nurse and married a doctor," has
a conversation with her husband in which she tells him
of wanting, when they go to Edinburgh, to visit Miss
Brodie's grave. Brodie died,

"Just after the war. She was retired by then. Her
retirement was rather a tragedy, she was forced
to retire before time. . . ..There's a long story
attached to Miss Brodie's retirement. She was
betrayed by one of her own girls. . . ."

In a 187-page novel, this quotation is on page forty-
one.[3]

At one later point, the narrative leaps ahead to
two future points, more-or-less simultaneously: An event
in 1936 causes a transition to its being remembered about
20 years later. Monica Douglas refers to it in a visit
to Sandy (now Sister Helena), who then reflects, to
herself, that she had thought of that event when, "one
day after the end of the war," she had sat in a tea-room
with Miss Brodie. So, while the narrative "holds" at
1936, we jump forward to about 1956, then immediately
backward to about 1946. This, by the way, provides the
second large disclosure of the ending. We are now on
page eighty-two.

Not long afterward, there is an oddly tucked-in
anecdote of one girl's future. Jenny Gray, at 12, feels
that she is "past" an interest in "sex research." We are
told that she will not re-experience her "sense of erotic
wonder" (118) until she is almost forty, when, in Rome,
she is standing under cover from the rain with "a man
whom she did not know very well" and suddenly feels as
though she has fallen in love with him, even though she
has been "contentedly married" for some 16 years.

"...[T]he concise happening filled her with astonishment
whenever it came to mind in later days, and with a sense
of the hidden possibilities in all things." (119)

Shortly after that, we are brought to yet another
anticipation of the "ending." (We are still, by the way,
only about three-quarters of the way through the novel.)
The whole story of Miss Brodie's nightdress being found
in Mr. Lowther's bed (an episode treated very differently
in the film) is told to Sandy by the headmistress, Miss
McKay, "at that subsequent time when Sandy looked at her
distastefully through her little eyes and. . . was moved
by various other considerations to betray Miss Brodie."
(138)

Prominent in both of these passages is a deliberate
vagueness on Spark's part. We never learn what these
"other considerations" are that motivated Sandy. We must
provide our own, as hers are part of these "hidden
possibilities" that inhere "in all things." Together,
both passages, along with the disrupted chronology,
provide a parable regarding Spark's methods of telling
a tale. That seemingly irrelevant anecdote about Jenny,
those "hidden possibilities" that "filled her with
astonishment"--these are insightful to the methods by
which the whole novel is written. This nearly
metafictive practice is not duplicatable by any play or
film.

Narrative point-of-view in Spark's novel functions
in approximately the same way as the time-leaps: it
obfuscates even as it explains; it renders everything
ambivalent. Point-of-view is constantly oblique here
("oblique" also being one of Spark's favorite words).
At numerous points the reader cannot be certain precisely
whose words, whose thoughts are being conveyed. Very
often, the narrative is, in fact, coming to us from more
than one source at a time. This sharpens our insights
as it increases them, as, for instance, in this reference
early on to the Brodie set, accompanying their teacher
on an outing: "...with the exhilarating feeling of being
in on the faint smell of row, without being endangered
by it, they followed dangerous Miss Brodie into the
secure shade of the elm." (17) Whose word-choice, here,
is "dangerous"? No one has yet described Brodie in
exactly that way, although there is already evidence that
someone in the school's administration may think her
dangerous. Quite apparently this is the little girls'
impression of what Brodie believes the headmistress to
think. This gets more sophisticated and more complicated
as the novel progresses. Eventually, we have this kind
of obliqueness: Sandy is visiting at the home of Teddy
Lloyd, the art teacher. Mrs. Lloyd, during the visit,
"disappeared to see to all her children. The Lloyds were
Catholics and so were made to have a lot of children by

force." (149) This is clearly not a judgment expressed
by the narrator; but it is not altogether Sandy's either-
-or not exclusively, anyway. In fact, precisely the same
statement has been made earlier in the novel, by Jean
Brodie. So what we have here is the narrative voice
echoing Sandy echoing Miss Brodie. Sandy unconsciously
seems to have made a judgment upon Teddy Lloyd's
religion, although we are never directly told this. With
Spark, obliqueness is all. "I don't like to spell things
out" (she has said). "I'm very much on the idea of
leaving a lot unsaid, so that a great deal can be
gathered. . . You have to live with the mystery....that's
the answer in my books."[4]

The reader of the novel finds that the "mystery"
one most has to "live with" in The Prime of Miss Jean
Brodie is the matter of what exactly motivates Sandy to
betray Miss Brodie. This is no great problem in the play
or the film, in either of which she convinces herself
that Miss Brodie is "dangerous." Indeed, in the film
Sandy seems quite the heroine for doing so. In the
novel, the mystery is not the result of any paucity of
possible motivations. Quite the opposite this time. We
have more than sufficient data for a complete
psychological portrait of Sandy, and that constitutes the
mystery.

One of the novel's most intriguing episodes is not

even partially included in the play or the film. It
seems at first not particularly relevant to the central
issues of the novel--that's often a clue that Spark is
up to something thematically. During the Easter holiday
one year (the girls are 12 or 13 at this time), a man
exposes himself to Jenny Gray. She tells Sandy all about
it, including mention of the policewoman who came to her
home to question her. This last detail becomes
"inexhaustible" to Sandy. In her mind, she identifies
the policewoman as "Sergeant Anne Grey" (Jenny has never
learned the woman's name or title). The image of the
Sergeant causes Sandy to abandon her earlier literary
fantasies--of Robert Louis Stevenson's Alan Breck and
Charlotte Bronte's Mr. Rochester--because she has fallen
"in love with the unseen policewoman," (99) whom she
finds "very thrilling." (106) She imagines herself as
"Anne Grey's right-hand woman in the Force, and they were
dedicated to eliminate sex from Edinburgh and environs."
When, in her mind, Sandy has committed herself to
assisting Sgt. Grey in gathering evidence, then "Sergeant
Anne pressed Sandy's hand in gratitude; and they looked
into each other's eyes, their mutual understanding too
deep for words." (102) Sandy urges Jenny not to tell Miss
Brodie about the flasher incident. She is uncertain of
her reasons, except that they are "connected" with
Brodie's having spent Easter at Cramond with Mr. Lowther,

the music teacher, and with her having once sent Rose Stanley on an errand to fetch some art supplies from Teddy Lloyd. Sandy sees the latter as Miss Brodie's "sending Rose to Mr. Lloyd," and her context is clearly sexual. (104)

As the apparent head of something like the sex-police (still, of course, entirely within Sandy's imagination), Sgt. Grey becomes, among other things, Sandy's alter-ego. At the same time that she envisions Sgt. Grey pressing for her to find "incriminating documents" in regard to Miss Brodie, Sandy, in her "real" life, is teaming up with Jenny on their "love correspondence" between Miss Brodie and Mr. Lowther. To Sandy, it becomes necessary in that document to "present Miss Brodie in both a favourable and an unfavourable light." (106) As the girls' last term with Brodie is drawing near its end, "nothing less than this was demanded." (107)

The one recurrent physical detail by which Sandy is described is her "tiny little eyes." They are mentioned at least a dozen times. (In the film, ironically, Pamela Franklin, as Sandy, wears round glasses that magnify the size of her eyes.) Once Spark describes them as "pig-like"; (21) once Sandy blinks them "hypocritical[ly]"; (73) one of the last times, they are "tiny eyes which it was astonishing that anyone could trust." (147) Who has most trusted Sandy, of course, is Jean Brodie. And although Spark never uses this metaphor, we realize, as Sandy Stranger gets nearer and nearer to the moment of betrayal, that those tiny, squinting eyes are also hawk-like. Sandy, indeed, has the instincts of a predator. When Jean Brodie is mistaken or misled, she then looks "beautiful and fragile" to Sandy, who preys upon this fragility: "...Miss Brodie's masterful features became clear and sweet to Sandy when viewed in the curious light of the woman's folly, and she never felt more affection for her in her later years than when she thought upon Miss Brodie silly." (163) At the last assembly of the term during which Mr. Lowther's engagement (to Miss Lockhart, the science teacher) is announced, the Marcia Blaine School faculty and staff honors them both. Miss Brodie, on this occasion, looks, to Sandy, "quite beautiful and frail." (166)

Among the aspects of Miss Brodie that impress Sandy Stranger, one stands out: Brodie is a revisionist, even (or especially) of her own past. Two years or more after she has told her girls the story of Hugh, her war-time lover who died at Flanders, she has taken up with Gordon Lowther, though the girls are sure that she is secretly in love with Teddy Lloyd. Now she revives--and revises--the war-time legend: "'Sometimes Hugh would sing, he had a rich tenor voice. At other times he fell silent and would set up his easel and paint. He was very talented at both arts, but I think the painter was the real Hugh.'" (105-6) The girls understand what is going on here, but in particular "Sandy was fascinated by this method of making patterns with facts...." (106) Much later, Sandy discovers, as do all the Brodie girls, that whether Teddy Lloyd paints one of them or another, all the portraits come out looking like Miss Brodie. Sandy, typically, has her own way of perceiving this: She "was fascinated by the economy of Teddy Lloyd's method." (Notice the diction here: "fascinated" and "method.") And that the method is, in her own term, "economical" most lastingly impresses her:

> ...it always seemed afterwards to Sandy that where there was a choice of various courses, the most economical was the best, and that the course to be taken was the most expedient and the most suitable at the time for all the objects in hand. She acted on this principle when the time came for her to betray Miss Brodie. (149)

Unlike many in Edinburgh, Sandy has not been raised by Calvinists, but at times she feels "deprived" at never having been exposed to Calvinism, as it would have been "something definite to reject." (159) But because she has her own Calvinistic predispositions and perceptions, she is able to sense, she thinks, what motivates Miss Brodie: "In this oblique way, she began to sense what went to the makings of Miss Brodie who had elected herself to grace in so particular a way and with more exotic suicidal enchantment than if she had simply taken to drink like other spinsters who couldn't stand it anymore." (160) Sandy's penchant for inferring motives is not diminished when, in her last year at Marcia Blaine, she begins to study psychology. Now, when in conversation with adults, she is almost always "calculating their souls by signs and symbols, as was the habit in those days of young persons who had read books of psychology when listening to older persons who had not." (175) Combining her psychology studies with her personal religious predispositions, Sandy finds it easy to categorize people, particularly Miss Brodie: "She thinks she is Providence, thought Sandy, she thinks she is the God of Calvin, she sees the beginning and the end. And Sandy thought, too, the woman is an unconscious Lesbian." (176)

Sandy enters into--for want of a better word--an "affair" with Teddy Lloyd, but after a year "it happened that she had quite lost interest in the man himself, but was deeply absorbed in his mind, from which she extracted, among other things, his religion as a pith from a husk....She left the man and took his religion and became a nun in the course of time." (180) She "betrays" Miss Brodie to Miss McKay because in Sandy's perception Miss Brodie is "a born Fascist...." (182) Shortly thereafter, she says goodbye to the Lloyds, and

"congratulated Teddy Lloyd on the economy of his method."
(183) At this stage, she is "more fuming...with Christian
morals, than John Knox." (183) And shortly after this,
she enters "the Catholic Church, in whose ranks she had
found quite a number of Fascists much less agreeable than
Miss Brodie." (183) As a nun,[5] she is "Sister Helena of
the Transfiguration." The "strange book of psychology"
that she has published is titled "The Transfiguration of
the Commonplace." (186) Its publication brings her "so
many visitors that Sandy clutched the bars of her grille
more desperately than ever." (186) It is there that we
leave her, as the novel ends.

There is almost no way for the play or the film to
capture the most intimate insights that the novel
provides to Spark's feelings, perspectives, or habits of
mind; but some perception of those traits is essential
to appreciating the novel. Even if these other
"versions" of Brodie had made use of the novel's
references to Dr. Marie Stopes, for instance, there would
be no way to convey the fact that Spark introduces this
historical personage in order to pay an old score. An
Edinburgh native, Marie Stopes became one of the world's
best-known crusaders for birth control, after she and her
second husband founded the Mothers' Clinic for Birth
Control in London in 1926. In the last years of her
life, curiously, she fancied herself a better poet than

scientist. Of added interest, in Spark's hostility toward Stopes, is the fact that it is not the result of an ideological objection--as one might have supposed, given Spark's religious conversion--to Stopes' professional ventures. To that--her work, that is, on birth control--Spark's response is: "on that account, [Stopes is] much to be admired."[6]

Stopes once wrote Spark to ask if it were true, as Stopes had heard, that Spark's husband had divorced her. Spark wrote back informing the good doctor that such was none of her business. Stopes replied that she felt herself "fully entitled to be informed and to make enquiries" about Spark, as she was a Vice President and long-time member of the Poetry Society, by which Spark was then gainfully employed. Spark's letter of 29 May 1948 was, she reports, her final response to Stopes:

> I have received your outrageously impudent letter of 27th May. My private affairs are no concern of yours and your malicious interest in them seems to me to be most unwholesome. You have no rights whatsoever to make enquiries about me--all enquiries necessary were made by those who appointed me and confirmed my appointment. I must say that your attitude fills me with contempt, as it would all right-thinking people.[7]

This put an end to the direct feuding, at least, although Stopes did some long-distance sniping at Spark thereafter. But to those who know Spark (through her fictional and scholarly works and her autobiography), it comes as no great surprise when we are told that the "legions" of Miss Brodie's "kind" of "war-bereaved spinster[s]" go about "preach[ing] the inventions of Marie Stopes." (62-3)

Given this tendency of Spark's to pursue a private and personal agenda in her fiction, it strikes a reader as particularly odd that religion in general, conservative religion in particular, religious conversions, and Roman Catholicism all take such a beating in this novel, for Spark herself, in 1954, became a convert to the Roman Catholic Church, and her religious views seem always to have had a conservative and authoritarian nature. The most influential person in her school years, one Christina Kay--the model, in fact, for Jean Brodie--imparted religious opinions to her girls that struck favor in Spark, then and later.[8] Among others, there was this: that "Land of Hope and Glory" was "basically anti-Christian." This is the lyric that Arthur Christopher Benson wrote in 1902 to go with Edward Elgar's "Pomp and Circumstance" (the melody played at every American graduation ceremony). The particularly objectionable lines, to Miss Kay, were these: "Wider still and wider Shall thy bounds be set; God who made thee mighty, Make thee mightier yet." Now it might have seemed to most of us that the idea of God's allowing an upwardly mobile spiral of humankind's progress had long since been accepted by all Christians. Even Tennyson found it a pleasant prospect--see, e.g., section 118 of In Memoriam. But Miss Kay did not find it acceptable. And Spark's response? "Of course, she was quite right."[9]

Yet, in this important novel by this religiously conservative, (in many ways) old-fashioned convert to Catholicism, there is an almost constant disparagement of, if not religion itself, then the people who are its most ardent practitioners. Sandy, as we have seen, found many "Fascists" among Catholics. Eunice Gardiner, for a while, takes a "religious turn"; the phase does not last long, but "while it did she was nasty and not to be trusted." (88) Over and again, we are impelled toward the conclusion that those in the novel who most prominently "have" religion are those least to be trusted. In addition to Brodie and Sandy (and, temporarily, Eunice), they include Teddy Lloyd, the snooping, ubiquitous Miss Gaunt, and the sewing teachers, Alison and Ellen Kerr, of whom Brodie says, "they are too much in with Miss Gaunt and the Church of Scotland." (119)

When Jean Brodie's religious ardor is characterized, it too is portrayed negatively. She goes to church every Sunday, but to a different one as often as possible. She has a fondness for almost every Christian denomination except the Roman Catholic, which she abhors. It seems to her a church of "superstition," and, more than most, it discourages thought among its followers. "In some ways, her attitude was a strange one, because she was by temperament suited only to the Roman Catholic Church; possibly it could have embraced, even while it disciplined, her soaring and diving spirit, it might even have normalised her." (125) This is not flattering to Miss Brodie; nor would we expect it to be, as the rest of the novel does not make her heroic. But neither is it kindly considerate of Catholicism or of the reasons for which one might turn to it.

Immediately following this delineation of Miss Brodie's religious proclivities, the novel moves again to its most suspect case of discovered religious zeal- -Sandy Stranger. "It was twenty-five years before Sandy had so far recovered from a creeping vision of disorder that she could look back and recognise that Miss Brodie's defective sense of self-criticism had not been without its beneficent and enlarging effects; by which time Sandy had already betrayed Miss Brodie and Miss Brodie was laid in her grave." (126) Not coincidentally, Sandy has also by then become a nun, presumably by way of seeking an antidote to that "disorder" she perceived; that antidote is what everyone in this novel seems to seek in religion. Perhaps as a consequent of that quest, virtually all religion in the novel seems as Sandy once, obliquely, describes it--fascistic. This oddity is not lessened or at all explained by anything Spark has to say about her own conversion. When friends ask her why she did it, she "can only say that the answer is both too easy and too difficult."[10]

We have been seeing here, among other things, that the novel's characters, especially Miss Brodie and Sandy, are both better and worse than those of the play or the film.[11] Similarly, the novel, on the one hand, is more sombre than either of the other "versions." Neither of them refers to Miss Brodie's admiration of Hitler, "a prophet-figure like Thomas Carlyle, and more reliable than Mussolini...." (143) On the other hand, it is also more humorous than either. While the play and the film are not without their funny moments, neither of them includes some of the novel's best humor. For instance, in the novel, Sandy reports to Miss Brodie that Teddy Lloyd "looked very romantic in his own studio." When Brodie wonders why that should have been so, Jenny suggests, "I think it was his having only one arm," to which Brodie rejoins, with logic and accuracy, "But he always has only one arm." (140) The dark side to this humor is also typical of the novel, more than of the other two. Occasionally, too, the humor is linked to point-of-view, as in the following instance, which reflects the thinking of Gordon Lowther. He has been worried about his relationship with Jean, and

> In the midst of this dissatisfaction had occurred
> Ellen Kerr's finding of a nightdress of quality
> folded under the pillow next to Mr. Lowther's
> in that double bed on which, to make matters
> worse, he had been born. (153)

However, not all of this novel's wit and humor is
dependent upon the characters. At times, it comes in
the narrative voice, even in description:

> There was a wonderful sunset across the
> distant sky, reflected in the sea, streaked
> with blood and puffed with avenging purple
> and gold as if the end of the world had come
> without intruding on every-day life. (140-41)

Again, there is a macabre aspect to this humor, as well
as an implicit religious subject-matter. Not
surprisingly, some of the harshest wit and darkest humor
is reserved for direct religious references. The
churches of Edinburgh feature "emblems of a dark and
terrible salvation which made the fires of the damned
seem very merry to the imagination by contrast, and much
preferable." (158) And a central tenet of Scottish
Calvinism, we are told, is "that God had planned for
practically everybody before they were born a nasty
surprise when they died." (159)

The play and the film make other departures that
one might pursue: neither includes the character of Joyce
Emily Hammond, making it necessary for Mary Macgregor to
be the character who goes in search of her brother during
the Spanish Civil War. Both disregard the basic nastiness

of Teddy Lloyd. (Imagine a film passing up a chance to exploit the villainy of a character; in fact, the film at times wants to make him admirable.)   There are also odd additions and relocations, especially to the film: In it, Miss Brodie and Teddy Lloyd have been lovers previously, whereas, in the novel, they never are. Jean Brodie's speech about her ancestor, Willie Brodie, comes at the end of both play and film, where it takes on more importance than it deserves.   And Miss Mackay, particularly in the film, becomes a soap-opera shrew, an almost farcical character, rather than a suitably thoughtful, careful antagonist to Miss Brodie.   These changes all seem to render the play and the film less "Sparkian" than they might have been.

It doesn't matter, in our context here, whether the play is good or bad, whether the film is better or worse. Neither is able to capture--neither had a chance of capturing--the essence of Muriel Spark's methods. Obliqueness, disrupted chronology, the constantly evocative quality of the prose, a deliberate vagueness that makes one read between the lines, occasional metafictive tendencies, and the mysterious arrangement of strands of motivation--none of these are techniques that translate easily. As a summary of these techniques, let Ms. Spark have the final word:

In fiction, plausibility is the big thing.

Veracity. Veracity is in details, not necessarily
leading anywhere--just chance details, throw-away
things that have got nothing to do with anything.
I like to sometimes open a paragraph just by
saying something and then forgetting it. Just a
reflection, and then forget that, get on with the
story, because that's very often the way people
think. I'm very interested in fictional methods fo
persuading people that what you're saying is
true. It's an illusion, but there are many, many
methods of creating this illusion.[12]

That will work, <u>does</u> work, on the printed page; but it

won't play, and it won't film.

251

1. Stephen Schiff, "Muriel Spark Between the Lines," The New Yorker, May 24, 1993, p. 42.

2. Muriel Spark, Curriculum Vitae (New York/Boston: Houghton Mifflin, 1993), p. 17.

3. Muriel Spark, The Prime of Miss Jean Brodie (New York: Plume/Penguin, 1961). References hereafter will be to this paperback edition, with page numbers in parentheses in text.

4. Schiff, p. 43.

5. Sandy's eventually becoming a nun is never referred to in the film.

6. Curriculum Vitae, p. 174.

7. Curriculum Vitae, p. 175.

8. It is odd that, while Brodie is based upon Christina Kay (see Curriculum Vitae, p. 56), it is the headmistress whose name, McKay, is so nearly that of Spark's best-remembered teacher.

9. Curriculum Vitae, p. 62.

10. Curriculum Vitae, p. 202.

11. This is also somewhat typical of novel-into-film transformations. See the discussion of the same phenomenon in the chapter on One Flew Over the Cuckoo's Nest.

12. Schiff, pp. 40-41.

THE FRENCH LIEUTENANT'S WOMAN

One of the best essays on Fowles's work (Malcolm
Bradbury's in <u>No</u>, <u>Not</u> <u>Bloomsbury</u>) is entitled "The
Novelist as Impresario"[1] and takes as its central image
one of the "many disguises of the novelist," the one in
which he enters the final scene of <u>The</u> <u>French</u>
<u>Lieutenant's</u> <u>Woman</u>.[2] In that appearance, his second,
Fowles describes—and disguises—himself as possessing
"a distinct touch of the flashy." He has, in fact "more
than a touch of the successful impresario about him."
(362) Bradbury goes on to show that this is but one view
of Fowles provided by the novel. It is accurate enough
of almost any good novelist, "for in any strong fiction
there is indeed a touch of the flashy, and filling
theatres is one of the businesses of the confident
novelist." (280) But there is another Fowles present in
this novel, just as there are—as we shall see—two of
almost everything in it. That other Fowles is a serious,
reflective observer, a teacher of sorts, not only of
subjects psychological, but also moral and philosophical.
To Bradbury, the central fact of Fowles's
impresario/teacher career is its demonstration that "the
capacity to learn through fictions is essential."

(Bradbury, p. 285)

Now this is certainly true, and the explorations of Fowles's fiction that it leads Bradbury to make are exceptionally insightful and useful. It is curious, however, that Bradbury omits one of the other ways in which Fowles sees himself in The French Lieutenant's Woman. It is a way highly germane to Bradbury's central point, and it is a way that includes but transcends that of teacher (and, perhaps, also of impresario): Fowles portrays himself in the novel as a preacher, a minister, indeed prophet, of the "church" of existentialism.

In the first appearance of the character who is obviously Fowles himself, we are told that

> there was something rather aggressively secure
> about him; he was perhaps not quite a gentle-
> man. . .an ambitious butler (but butlers did
> not travel first class) or a successful lay
> preacher--one of the bullying tabernacle kind,
> a would-be Spurgeon, converting souls by scorch-
> ing them with the cheap rhetoric of eternal
> damnation. (315-16)

Later in that same appearance he is referred to as "the prophet-bearded man." (316) He stares at Charles, who is nodding off, as though wondering what to do with him. Then, in the concluding paragraphs of this chapter, Fowles informs us that it will be necessary for him--as the modern novelist trying to write a Victorian novel- -to write two endings. Fiction, he tells us, is always a fixed fight; the side the novelist favors will win.

The skill of the novelist is in disguising the fact that the fight has been fixed. Additionally, we judge writers of fiction by "the kind of fighter they fix in favor of." (317) Aware that we will read with our usual habits intact, and will think the last ending the "real" one, he decides further to flip a coin to determine the order in which the alternate endings will appear.

All of this business in the fifty-fifth chapter relates to Fowles's role as impresario; but it relates no less to his role as preacher and prophet. He has not abandoned the "godgame,"[3] nor his part in it, even as he announces his metafictive choices. But the god that he presents, that he portrays, that he leads Charles to recognize, is the god Fowles had characterized earlier, in the thirteenth chapter, as the "only...good definition of God: the freedom that allows other freedoms to exist." And he noted at that time that he too "must conform to that definition." When, therefore, the modern novelist plays God--as Victorian novelists did regularly--he must do so "in the new theological image, with freedom [the] first principle, not authority." (82)

Much of the foregoing is recalled by one who studies the transformation of Fowles's novel into film, for in Karel Reisz's film, with screenplay by Harold Pinter, religion is conspicuous by its absence. Except for a couple of passing references (e.g., Mrs. Poulteney's speaking of the state of her soul) and one brief scene in a churchyard--which, but for the peal of an organ, could have been anywhere--religion is not relevant in the film.It is almost everywhere in the novel, albeit sometimes in an unconventional manner. Implications of conventional religion run through the entire novel, from the rejections of Darwinism by Mr. Freeman and Mrs. Poulteney, et al, to Charles's being foresworn to the premises of duty, honor, and whatever else can cause a person to see the soul as essential and body as necessary but inconvenient baggage.

More to Fowles's point, however, is the way that "religion" functions in the very form and telling of his story. The modern novelist does play god--albeit a different being from the God played by Dickens and Thackeray--as seen in the acknowledgement by Fowles-the-modernist that "we wish to create worlds as real as, but other than the world that is." (81; italics in text.) That acknowledgment leads, in turn, to the discussion of "gods" in the "new theological image" cited above. Clearly, the "prophet-bearded man" who eyes Charles in the railway carriage, wondering what he might do with him, plays a god-like role in this image. And the action

of that same intrusive figure, when he appears the second
time, is the deed of an omnipotent being: he turns time
back by a quarter-hour.

This playing of the godgame by the author and his
impresario alter-ego (or, in this case, altar-ego?)
underscores the manner in which religion conditions the
life of Charles Smithson. Through three-fourths of the
novel, Charles is inclined to think in religious figures-
-to think, that is, in terms of religious influences.
Thus, when Sarah first seeks him out, he feels
"flattered, as a clergyman does whose advice is sought
on a spiritual prombem." (115) And when he does not, at
first, respond to a later summons from her, he feels like
"Pontius Pilate." (189) Religion is more than mere
decoration, here; it is a subtle, restrictive influence
upon Charles. When Fowles is accounting for what caused
(or might have caused, had they happened) the events of
the first, and clearly bogus, "ending," he cites "the
personification of a certain massive indifference in
things--too hostile for Charles to think of as 'God'--
that had set its malevolent inertia on the Ernestina side
of the scales . . ." (267)

Shortly thereafter comes the turning-point in
Charles Smithson's religious history. Following his
sexual encounter with Sarah (a ninety-second interlude
can hardly be called love-making), Charles wanders the

streets of Exeter, until he comes to "a small redstone church" and suddenly feels a "need for sanctuary." (280) There he tries to pray but is unable to. "No communication was possible." (282) However, he converses--with himself, apparently, in the role of Christ--and he recognizes his choices: to remain in the "prison" his age calls "duty, honor, self-respect," and be "comfortably safe," or to be "free and crucified." (284) Then, in "a sudden flash of illumination, Charles sees the right purpose of Christianity"; it is "To uncrucify." That is, "to bring about a world in which the hanging man could be descended," and smile in peace, not grimace in agony. (285) Henceforth, Charles is liberated, almost completely, from the dictates of his age; he moves toward a "cruel but necessary. . .freedom." (287) When he leaves the redstone church, he has been "shriven of established religion for the rest of his life." (288)

This image of Fowles as prophet of existentialism, made sharper for us by the contrast of the filmed version of the story, is more relevant to this novel than it is to his others, since the reader, too, is possessed of a "cruel but necessary freedom" in this case. Compared to any more orthodox novel, The French Lieutenant's Woman allows--and necessitates--choices. At the same time, the existential aspects of this novel sneak up on a reader, for its setting far pre-dates Sartre or Camus, or even

most of the world's awareness of Kierkegaard. Fowles was
conscious of this from the outset. In an essay he wrote
for Harper's prior to the novel's publication--perhaps
even to its completion--Fowles made this clear:

> My two previous novels were both based on
> more or less disguised existential premises.
> I want this one to be no exception; and so I
> am trying to show an existentialist awareness
> before it was chronologically possible.[4]

In fact, in this anachronism lies one of Fowles's most
clever reversals (about which, more later): "One can
almost invert the reality and say that Camus and Sartre
have been trying to lead us, in their fashion, to a
Victorian seriousness of purpose and moral sensitivity."[5]

Virtually all of Fowles's existential/religious
theme was lost to the film from the first moments of its
conception. One of the earliest decisions made by Pinter
or Reisz or both was to parallel Fowles's metafictive
devices by a cinematic equivalent: they would do a film-
within-a-film.[6] While this was in many ways an ingenious
choice, it carried certain disadvantages. There would
be neither time nor facility for capturing the equivalent
of Fowles's exploration of Charles's motives, second
thoughts, impulses, and so forth. We almost never see
a ruminative, reflective Charles in the film. Since the
film has to tell the Anna-Mike story as well, it cannot
afford nearly the concentration upon Charles that we find
in the novel.

Again, the conspicuousness of an omission recalls
to the reader/viewer how prominent something was in the
original version. The film's story--being doubled, and
with more time constraints to begin with--does not nearly
attempt to duplicate the novel's process of motivation.
In Fowles's story, motivation for Charles to escape his
attachment to Ernestina and act upon the attraction he
feels toward Sarah accumulates over a convincingly long
period. From the beginning, he finds her father, Mr.
Ernest Freeman (even names are Victorian paradoxes,
here), somewhat repellent, especially that gentleman's
view of Darwin ("'You will never get me to agree that we
are all descended from monkeys'. . ." [227]). That
aversion is compounded by Charles's awareness of how
perfectly Mr. Freeman fits the age in which they live,
while Charles knows that much of what his respectable age
believes, indeed insists on (including, for example,
nulla species nova), is "rubbish." (45)

This repulsion is matched by an attraction. When
Charles first sees Sarah, and especially when he first
hears her story, not only is he struck by her beauty,
but by what a mystery she represents. This is an appeal
to Charles the scientist as well as the man. When he
first tries to speak to her, he gets her "noli me
tangere" look. (74-5) Previously she has looked "through
him" and he has had the feeling of being perceived as "an

enemy." (14-15) When he tries to talk about her to
Ernestina, it seems to him that he would be committing
"a sort of treachery, both to the girl's real sorrow and
to himself." (76) All of this is to suggest, at least to
Charles, that, even though Sarah may be an unapproachable
enigma to others, he has some chance of understanding
her.   And he is more perceptive of her than is anyone
else in Lyme Regis: he alone notices her "sense of
injustice." (87) Much later, when she has disappeared
from Lyme, Charles guesses where she is, even before she
sends him a message, and he is aware that he's the only
person in Lyme who knows.   In the early stages of the
relationship, he is "flattered," as we have seen, to be
sought out by Sarah for counsel and advice. (115) Their
acquaintance makes him more self-perceptive as well;
Sarah   exposes   his   own   disguises--his   "cryptic
coloration"--to himself. (118-19) Late in the novel,
reference is made, in connection with Sarah, to the
riddle of the Sphinx. (344) Throughout the novel, Charles
has felt as though he were the man who could solve that
riddle.

At the same time that Charles is becoming aware of
the   depth   of   intellect   and   interest   that   Sarah
represents, he is getting to know Ernestina better, and
the more closely he knows her, the more he is aware of
her shallowness, her "mere cuteness." (122) A "sugar

Aphrodite," Ernestina is, at best, perfectly conventional. (207) At her worst, she is somewhat mean-spirited, as when she takes the side of Mrs. Poulteney against Charles--and against Sam and Mary and young love, at least among the lower classes. Following this exchange, Charles concludes that he will have to teach Ernestina a "lesson in common humanity." (89) The manner in which Charles's doubts about Ernestina and his curiosity about Sarah work in tandem is one example of Fowles's astute use of "rhythm" in this novel.[7] Immediately after Charles has heard Sarah's "confession" and recognized how "remarkable" and "baffling" (153) a woman she is, he has a conversation with Tina that reminds him that his affianced has "been given no talent except that of conventional good taste." (154) Charles fancies himself "not like the great majority of his peers and contemporaries," and his early contacts with Sarah make him "aware of a deprivation": he is headed toward a perfectly conventional future with a perfectly conventional young woman. That future has become, to Charles's consternation, "a fixed voyage to a known place." He seems to intuit that Sarah could save him from this. (107) Amateur Darwinist that he is, Charles wants to be a naturally fit creature of free will; his reluctance to encourage further contact with Sarah suggests to him that he is not. Simultaneously, his

Darwinistic view of the world makes him almost the only person in Lyme capable of not blaming Sarah for her circumstances. (99) After Charles and Dr. Grogan have discussed Sarah for the second time, and Charles has confessed to the little Irish doctor his involvement with her, he fears that he has "condemned her to avoid condemning himself. . . ." Switching rapidly between religious and Darwinian images, he chastises himself as a "Pontius Pilate" and concludes that he has "no more free will than an ammonite." (189) It is at that point that he violates his agreement with Grogan and sets out to answer Sarah's summons. The evolutionary metaphor recurs: As Charles heads back toward Lyme in the bogus "ending,"[8] he sees his fate clearly. "He was one of life's victims, one more ammonite caught in the vast movements of history, stranded now for eternity, a potential turned to a fossil." (262) Having imagined this as his fate, he must make exertions of his free will in an effort to avoid it.

That Charles may be "disinherited" by his uncle changes everything in his relationship with Ernestina and, indirectly, provides yet more motivation for Charles to dissolve his engagement and pursue Sarah. Were he to marry Tina, he could no longer bring to the marriage a title, an estate, etc. Materially, they would now make an uneven start. "As the future master of Winsyatt he could regard himself as his bride's financial equal; as a mere _rentier_ he must become her financial dependent." (174) Thus, Charles becomes more approachable game for Mr. Freeman, who must think that Charles will now be more susceptible to his entreaties that his son-in-law take an active part in the family business. And, sure enough, Mr. Freeman offers Charles a partnership. (227) This causes Charles to feel "obscurely debased; a lion caged." (228) More even than his marriage itself, the consequences of that marriage seem ready to imprison him. Additionally, the discovery that Sir Robert Smithson intends to marry brings a response from Ernestina that hardly constitutes her finest moment; she seems to Charles "only too reminiscent of the draper's daughter. . .worsted in a business deal." (162) Again, typical of this novel's "rhythm," Charles learns, in the instant following this impression, that Sarah has been dismissed by Mrs. Poulteney and has disappeared.

As much as her beauty, her mystery, her intelligence, and her wish to be independent attract Charles to Sarah, so does his becoming convinced that he can "save" her--from fate, from society, from the small-mindedness of the age, and not least of all from madness. Inadvertently, Dr. Grogan confirms this belief of Charles's, after Sarah has suggested it. If Sarah were able to reveal her feelings to a sympathetic listener,

Grogan tells Charles, she would be "cured." (127) Sarah
has already told him: "'I am not yet mad. But unless I
am helped I shall be.'" (117) Furthermore, Grogan feeds
into the sexism of Charles by emphasizing his/their
superiority to Sarah: "'You must not think she is like
us men, able to reason clearly, examine her motives,
understand why she behaves as she does.'" (127) Later,
when sketching a scenario of Sarah's behavior and
inferring her motives, the doctor casts Charles as both
the "Good Samaritan" and Sarah's "savior." (178) Thus,
Charles feels obligated to assist Sarah; "he [has]
detected a clear element of duty." (134) Despite his
sexism, and the not-very-ardent state of his democratic
sympathies, Charles is a man who can be appealed to
through his sense of justice and fair play.
Consequently, Sarah's situation--her being oppressed, as
an intelligent, visionary female, by virtually every
custom of the age--appeals to him powerfully. In the
scene in which she "confesses" everything to him, he
becomes at least partially aware of this appeal: "What
had on occasion struck him before as a presumption of
intellectual equality (therefore a suspect resentment
against man) was less an equality than a proximity like
a nakedness, an intimacy of thought and feeling hitherto
unimaginable to him in the context of a relationship with
a woman." He recognizes that here is a "remarkable

woman," and the feeling which that invokes in him is "not of male envy: but very much of human loss." (147) Since he was already feeling an obligation to take care of Sarah, Charles is overwhelmed by a sense of duty after he has taken her to bed.[9] When Sarah says that she knows he cannot marry her, he answers "I must." (276) Later, he will realize that, duty apart, he wants to marry her, but for now he is sure that to do otherwise will cause him to feel "eternally guilty in his heart." (277) It is immediately after this that he recognizes the necessity to "uncrucify."

As we have seen, Pinter and Reisz early on decided, in effect, to exclude the religious dimensions of Fowles's story and most of the insights to Charles Smithson's thought processes. What they elected to keep, mainly, was the romantic element. Pinter has declared that he and Reisz "refined it to be what we finally found to be a love story. . .although of a rather bizarre kind."[10] Not only is this a defensible choice because the observation is perfectly true, but their seizing on it maintains one other essential characteristic of the novel: Part of what gives it its metafictive quality is that Fowles is as fascinated by Sarah as Charles is—to say the least. In speaking of the origin of the book, Fowles acknowledges as much. The image rose in his mind of a woman standing on a quay, and he knew instantly that

he "wished to protect her." That is to say, he goes on:
"I began to fall in love with her. Or with her stance.
I didn't know which."[11] This is part of what complicates
the novel. To allow Charles to win her, the novelist
would have to let her go from himself. In Mantissa[12]
Erato chides Miles Green--and Fowles simultaneously
chides himself,but also excuses himself--for his sexist
offenses. She insists that Miles abandons all his women
when he has finished with them; he argues that he gives
them all possible freedom.[13] Indeed, he contends that one
of his books would have had an unprecedented twelve
endings, except that the female dominated it, and him,
and he was left with only three endings.[14] In its use,
then, of parallel love-stories, the film is true to the
spirit of the novel. In other ways, it preserves more
than the spirit, and these preservations, too, give one
insight to the novel, and probably provide the reason for
Fowles's seeing the film as "a brilliant metaphor for"
his novel.[15]

Probably the most important part of the novel that
the film retains is its feminist theme.[16] It does more,
in fact, than retain; it expands and adds to that theme,
for it carries it over from Sarah's life into Anna's.
When first we see Anna after the opening credits, the
first time, that is, that we see her in her own person,
she and Mike are in bed together, in her room. Awakened

by the telephone, he answers it. To Anna's expressed fear that now "they'll know. . ." Mike replies cavalierly: "Good. I want them to." Later, Anna, reading up on the Victorian period, realizes that Sarah is right when she says, in their script, "If I go to London, I know what I should become." Again, Mike shows no great concern; indeed, he responds with a crude and casual joke. Anna perhaps begins to perceive her all-too-conventional part in an all-too-common relationship. In any case, she starts to identify with her character, Sarah. We see and hear her, as Sarah, deliver her line: "I am nothing; I am the French Lieutenant's--whore!" Immediately thereafter, we see her, as Anna, on a sea-side picnic with Mike. He asks her why she is sad, and she denies that she is; it is clear to us, however, that she is sad, and as she looks into the distance, she seems to "see" herself as Sarah (as our film makes the transition) heading past Mrs. Fairly and toward her doom in Lyme. The final underscoring of Anna's merging of her two identities is in the scene when, as she leaves the film location for London and her visit with David, Mike says he must "have" her. Her response is "You just had me--in Exeter."

Not only does the film wage a feminist theme with Anna's story, but with Sarah's as well. Even such subtle devices as sequence work to generate sympathy for the "plight of woman" in the Victorian era. At one point, the cry of a woman being assisted by Dr. Grogan with a breeched birth (in "the asylum") is followed by a shot of Sarah, in the Undercliff, crawling toward shelter from the raging weather, having been banished from the household of Mrs. Poulteney and, de facto, from Lyme. The nearest that the film comes to explaining Sarah's motives (which Fowles allegedly told Reisz and Pinter not to do)[17] is in her offering Charles this justification for her not having summoned him to London sooner: "It has taken me this time to make my own life. . .to find my freedom."[18]

In pursuing this theme, Reisz and Pinter are being true to their source, for the novel displays Fowles's feminist instincts. The condition-of-woman question in the Victorian age is one that intrigues him, and one to which he apparently devoted much of his historical research for this novel. So few opportunities does the age provide for women such as herself--or women in general--that Sarah does "know what [she] should become" if she were to leave Lyme for London. Her choices, throughout, are few. Fowles reenforces this opinion with historical fact: Exeter, in 1867, had something like a red-light district because of all the runaway "undone girls and women." Nor was Exeter unique; "all the larger provincial towns of the time had to find room for this unfortunate army of female wounded in the battle for universal masculine purity." (217) Still later, we see much the same to be the case in London, where consequences of the battle are exemplified by the story of the "other" Sarah. (246-9) Using footnotes occasionally, and drawing upon E. Royston Pike's book Human Documents of the Victorian Golden Age for "countless minor details,"[19] Fowles presents such telling historical evidence as the fact that, in London of the time, "one in sixty houses was a brothel." (211; this chapter is prefaced by a lengthy quotation, on the state of girls, from the Children's Employment Commission Report of 1867.) Lest we think that discrimination against women in the Victorian age worked only in extreme cases involving prostitution, Fowles elsewhere, and in a somewhat different context, cites Dr. George Drysdale's 1854 forerunner to a sex manual: "Any preventive means [i.e., contraception], to be satisfactory, must be used by the woman, as it spoils the passion and impulsiveness of the venereal act, if the man has to think of them." (213n; italics in text.) And by way of indicating the divided nature of the age (what he elsewhere calls its "schizophrenia" [288]), he notes that one might mark one of the very days of the novel's setting as "the beginning of feminine emancipation in England." It was on March 30, 1867, that John Stuart Mill introduced a female suffrage clause to the Reform Bill; this hardly gave emancipation a hopeful beginning--the clause was struck down by a 196-to-73 vote.

As we have seen previously, Charles is considerably more sexist than he knows he is--or, probably, wants to be. When he does not share information with Ernestina, it is (one time, at least) because she has "neither the sex nor the experience to understand the altruism of his motives." (134) Granted, "altruism" here is sheer rationalization by Charles, but as surely as he knows that Ernestina lacks experience, so does he believe that her gender is a block to understanding. In this capacity, the young Smithson is more than usually useful to Fowles. Two particular qualities that Sarah possesses to which Charles is, at first, blind are "passion and imagination." His inability to see these is a conditioned non-response: "He could not, for those two qualities of Sarah's were banned by the epoch, equated in the first case with sensuality and in the second with the merely fanciful. This dismissive double equation was Charles's greatest defect--and here he stands truly for his age." (153) Sarah, to the contrary, seems to represent a much later time. When she gives Charles that "come clean" look that she frequently does, she is at her most unfathomable to him, for "We can sometimes recognize the looks of a century ago on a modern face; but never those of a century to come." (146) She is aware that "in another world, another age, another life," she might have married him. (278-9) At last, Charles, too, recognizes that Sarah "would have been at home" in the more up-to-date, more liberated United States. (339)

By the time that he comes to this realization, Charles has been greatly altered by his relationship with Sarah. And one of the several tentative, partly-true explanations of Sarah's actions that Fowles allows us to make is that she has deliberately used Charles as part of her progress toward self-liberation. It is in the second ending, the (ostensibly, for Charles) unhappy ending that we see that possibility, as he does also. There he more-or-less accurately perceives himself as having been "no more than a footsoldier, a pawn in a far vaster battle. . .[which] like all battles. . .[has been] not about love, but about possession and territory." Sarah is dressed for this confrontation "in the full uniform of the New Woman." (347) However, his being used in this manner--if he has been used--is not altogether bad for Charles. Through this battle, he has learned more about the nature and the necessity of freedom. After he has committed the venereal act with Sarah, recognized the need to "uncrucify," and broken his engagement to Ernestina, Charles begins "to understand one aspect of Sarah better: her feeling of resentment,

of an unfair because remediable bias in society." (320)
So near is he to generic enlightenment, that he is able
to speak to Grogan of the "obfuscating cant our sex talks
about women. They are to sit, are they not, like so many
articles in a shop and let us men walk in and turn them
over and point at this one or that one--she takes my
fancy. If they allow this, we call them decent,
respectable, modest." (310) While Sarah goes on to
achieve independence, Charles is impelled toward
authenticity.

The second important aspect of Fowles's theme that
the film retains is the contrast that the novel
frequently reenforces between the Victorian age and our
own. This contrast has been implicit throughout this
essay. It is seen in the feminist and the religious
themes, in Charles's being "disinherited" and finding
trade unacceptable because he was a gentleman born, in
the status of Ernestina, and in the several ways in which
Charles "stands. . .for his age." Sometimes this contrast
serves to remind us that the Victorian period was rather
more complex than we might lead ourselves to think.
There are, after all, cases in which their highly
developed sense of duty caused Victorians to behave with
admirable ethics. So does "duty" operate here. For
instance, following his epiphany in the church at Exeter,
Charles does not go back to Endicott's Family Hotel and

Sarah, though a "modern man would no doubt have gone straight back there." Instead, he makes his "first task" to "cleanse himself of past obligations." (288) It would be irresponsible of us not to respect him for this.

However, complex though it may have been, it <u>was</u> a repressive age as well. Its self-contradictions regarding sex are significant. It was "an age where woman was sacred; and where you could buy a thirteen-year-old girl for a few pounds"; where Bowdler was a public hero, "and where the output of pornography has never been exceeded." (211-12) An individual who would be free in that age, which is to say from that age, found some of its dictates no easier to escape for their being expressed in subtle and profound ways and sources. In Charles's main moment of "ilumination," in the church at Exeter, he seems "as he stood there to see all his age." (285) He begins to hasten away from ideas that Fowles locates for us in Tennyson, specifically in the fiftieth stanza, or "poem," of <u>In</u> <u>Memoriam</u>:

> There must be wisdom with great Death;
> The dead shall look me thro' and thro'.

Charles revolts "against these two foul propositions," and starts to see that "his previous belief in the ghostly presence of the past had condemned him, without his ever realizing it, to a life in the grave." (286) He has begun to move--for better or worse--toward a singularly modern freedom.

Still, in the long run, Fowles makes contrasts
between the two ages, in order, mainly, to reverse,
complicate, or obliterate them at key moments. Thus
Charles, entertaining the infant daughter of Sarah the
prostitute, experiences a "profound and genuine intuition
of the great human illusion about time, which is that its
reality is like that of a road," when the truth is "that
time is a room, a now so close to us that we regularly
fail to see it." (252) He is, at this point, coming to
see time in a much more random manner than that which
had beset him in the novel's early stages. And when the
two ages are most directly contrasted in the novel--in
regard, that is, to their widely differing modes of
playing the mating game--the contrast is not entirely in
our favor. It is possible, Fowles suggests, that the
Victorians

> chose a convention of suppression, repression and
> silence to maintain the keenness of the pleasure.
> In a way, by transferring to the public imagina-
> tion what they left to the private, we are the
> more Victorian--in the derogatory sense of the
> word--century, since we have, in destroying so
> much of the mystery, the difficulty, the aura of
> the forbidden, destroyed also a great deal of the
> pleasure. Of course we cannot measure comparative
> degrees of pleasure; but it may be luckier for us
> than for the Victorians that we cannot. (213-14)

It is just here that the film emphasizes the novel's
contrast between the two ages. As viewers, we are struck
by the differences between the way Anna and Mike conduct

"courtship"--which is, of course, precisely what they do
not conduct--in their own persons, and the way they
eventually unite as Charles and Sarah in the "inner
film." As Anna and Mike, sharing what never seems to be
a particularly happy arrangement, they represent
precisely what Fowles speaks of in the above quotation:
two modern "lovers" who have destroyed the pleasure by
destroying the "mystery." This accounts, in part, for
the perception by most viewers that Irons and Streep are
much more likeable as Charles and Sarah than they are as
Mike and Anna, a difference which further serves the
film's contrast between the two centuries.

Some of the novel's symbolism is noticeably absent
from the film. Not surprisingly, most of what is missing
is symbolism that complicates matters in the novel. A
single pattern will serve as an example here. This is
a cluster of symbolic references that create the
possibility, in the reader's mind, that Sarah's motives
in pursuing Charles may not be totally admirable, may in
fact be vengeful.[20] The pattern begins in the
"confessional" scene on the Undercliff. Sarah has bought
time with Charles by bringing him, on their previous
encounter, two tests which he then "felt. . .in his
pockets," recognizing "some kind of hold she had on him."
(115) Now she tells him the story of her having met
Varguennes, and while she speaks, she plucks "a little

spray of milkwort from the bank beside her, blue flowers like microscopic cherubs' genitals. . . ." (138) The simile is sufficiently bizarre to arrest our attention; but no sooner has it done so than Sarah begins "to defoliate the milkwort." (139) Much later, a single verb reactivates our perception of this symbolic business. In their immediately post-coital scene, Sarah realizes that Charles has "discovered the truth" about her Varguennes story. But even before he can accuse her of having lied, she has "forestalled, castrated the accusation in his mind." (278) "Castrated" in this context could be an innocent enough term, even though made somewhat redundant by "forestalled"; but it becomes rather more ambivalent to the extent that it evokes the earlier castration symbol. Particularly does this become so when, near the novel's first ending--first of the last two, anyway-- Charles accuses Sarah of not only having put a dagger in him, but of having "delighted in twisting it." That this suggested image of a cutting, stabbing Sarah is meant to be classically Freudian is enforced by Charles's perceiving himself a casualty in a "battle" having to do with a "terrible perversion of human sexual destiny." (355)

However, while the film omits some patterns of symbols that Fowles makes use of, it adds some of its own, and in those additions, ironically, the film emphasizes important methods and habits of the novel. Like Fowles's novel, the Pinter/Reisz film creates numerous parallels, mirrorings, analogs. Some of these are drawn between characters, others between scenes, or images, or motifs. However they are drawn, they remind one of the various analogs at work thematically in the novel: comparisons and contrasts between two eras; comparisons of the states of men and women (in both ages); and differences (but ultimately similarities, too) between modes of art in two centuries. It is no overstatement to say that the entire novel is built upon analogs. It is constantly binary; rather like Catch-22, almost everything that happens in it happens twice. Not only is it "diachronic,"[21] but its author makes two entrances as a character in the work; there are two Sarahs, each with an infant daughter; and, of course, there are two endings.[22] Lines are repeated, often by a different character in a similar situation. Thus, Charles's exclamation when Sarah comes upon him in Ware Commons, having followed him there--"Miss Woodruff!. . .How come you here?" (113)--is echoed much later by her query when he finds her in London--How came you here, Mr. Smithson?" (347) And the paired members of the Ernestina-Charles-Sarah triangle repeat several of one another's lines in highly ironic contexts. Just a few pages after Sarah has professed being "not worthy" (278) of Charles, when he has discovered her lie about Varguennes, he goes back to Lyme to confess himself "not worthy" of Ernestina. (294) The latter insists that what he is telling her is that he has never loved her. (295) In one of the endings, Charles similarly insists to Sarah: "Then what you are saying is that you never loved me." (352) Ernestina's frustration, when she sees that Charles is not to be dissuaded from breaking their engagement is expressed in the line, "And that is all what I say means to you?" to which he responds, "It means a great, a very great deal to me." (297) Again, it is in the penultimate ending that Charles has an identical exchange with Sarah:

> "What I say means nothing to you?"
> "It means very much to me. So much I. . . ."
> (350; ellipsis in text)

Fowles also ascribes similar behavior to some of his characters, in ways that cause a reader to associate those characters, even though they may be dissimilar in many ways. Thus we see Ernestina likened to Mrs. Poulteney, for they react to Mary, Mrs. Tranter's servant, in much the same prudish, censorious way. Indeed, this comparison is made explicit at one point, when we are told that Ernestina has given Mary "a look that would not have disgraced Mrs. Poulteney." (67) Later, they will be the two female characters to perform typically Victorian faints, Mrs. Poulteney's described as "a not altogether simulated swoon," (195) and

Ernestina's as "the catatonia of convention." (300) And, in a scene already looked at here, they join forces in an argument against Charles, on the very subject of Sam and Mary's romance. (Chapt. 14) The film, by the way, retains all of this comparison.

Sometimes, the novel means for these match-ups to work on us contrastively, to convey to us opposite qualities or circumstances of the characters, and thus clarify them in our minds. Charles, as we have seen, fancies himself "not like the great majority of his peers and contemporaries." (107) Yet he is quite bound by convention. Sarah, to the contrary, feels herself enslaved by society and its conventions, although it is clear to us that she has kicked herself free of most of society's dictates. In a similarly contrastive way, the very different situations of Sarah and Ernestina are clarified. Sarah's working-class father caused her to be instilled with--in her own words--"a natural respect, a love of intelligence, beauty, learning"; (138) Ernestina, "[l]ike so many daughters of rich parents . . .had been given no talent except that of conventional good taste." (154) At the same time that their relative situations are rendered clear to us by this contrast, the matter of which of them has been less well outfitted for her life is made more ambiguous.

These examples of analogous process which the film

replicates are a miniature, a precis, of the method that dominates the novel. Not only are many items paired by Fowles, but the pairing almost invariably provides a tension that is meaningful. One of the metaphors that Fowles uses to represent a novel, as we have seen, is that of a "fixed fight." A prizefight, or any contest, is, of course, an example of tension, wherein sympathies, expectations, and/or hopes are tugged one way, then another. But a fixed contest is a doubling of such, for it adds the opposition between an audience's expectation (of a "fair" match) and the reality. Fowles's metaphor is particularly apt for his own novel, which uses this kind of opposition almost constantly. Consider, for example, what it does with the insertion of the "La Ronciere incident." The case of a French Lieutenant (yet another doubling), Emile La Ronciere, is recounted in a pamphlet given to Charles by Dr. Grogan, at the time that Sarah has disappeared from Lyme, and Charles has, in effect, confessed to Grogan that he is in love with Sarah, but has vowed that he will never see her again. Grogan plans to keep a meeting with Sarah in Charles's stead, and, in the meanwhile, he wants the younger man to read up on the effects of sexual deprivation upon hysterical women, as this seems to be relevant to Grogan's "diagnosis" of Sarah.

The pamphlet relates the circumstances that brought

La Ronciere to trial: a sixteen-year-old girl, Marie de Morell, daughter of La Ronciere's commanding officer, charged that he appeared in her bedroom on the night of September 24th., 1834, and, among other things, "forced her to raise her night-chemise and wounded her in the upper thigh." (184) Fowles's narrator, as does the pamphlet from which Charles reads, takes an unwavering pro-defense position: "The number of circumstances in the accused's favor was so large that we can hardly believe today that he should have been brought to trial, let alone convicted." (184) And in describing the trial, that narrative voice is no less partial. The president of the court, we are told, "under the cannon-muzzle eyes of the Baron [Marie's father] and an imposing phalanx of distinguished relations," refused to allow cross-examination of Mlle. de Morell. At last, it is reported that La Ronciere was convicted--"by social prestige, by the myth of the pure-minded virgin, by psychological ignorance, by a society in full reaction from the pernicious notions of freedom disseminated by the French Revolution." (185) And then the novel gives two full pages to "repeating" the portion of the pamphlet that Grogan had marked for Charles, the testimony, on La Ronciere's behalf of one Dr. Karl Matthaei, "a well-known German physician of his time," on the subject of hysteria (especially, or perhaps exclusively, in young

285

females) and its sexual causes. All of this is designed to cause a shock to Charles Smithson and to force him to reconsider his relationship with Sarah. But only in a footnote does there come the final word on La Ronciere. There Fowles acknowledges that a 1968 account of the case by Rene Floriot, in Les Erreurs Judiciaires, indicates that La Ronciere, although he was finally exonerated and rehabilitated by an 1848 re-trial, did in fact enter Marie de Morell's room on the night in question, in order to produce, for his fellow-officers, a lock of her hair--"but not from the girl's head." The wound to her thigh "was caused by a pair of scissors." (188n) That the original court, despite what Fowles's narrator has led us to believe, did not wrongfully convict an innocent man (but at worst wrongfully convicted a guilty man) is not the main consideration here. That Grogan's analysis of Sarah's "case" is not precisely well-founded is also not central. What is the main point is the by-play between Fowles the author and the novel's narrator or central consciousness. Grogan, with the support of that narrative voice, presents the case to Charles in one way, and Fowles presents it to us in another; but he has had to go outside the novel, as it were, to make his case. The footnote stands in opposition to the text proper.

In the novel, Victorians are said not to have been fond of paradox, of ambivalence; (197) yet Fowles describes what he calls, with some justice, a "Victorian schizophrenia." (288-9) In that context, the "best guidebook to the age," in Fowles's opinion, is probably Dr. Jekyll and Mr. Hyde. It is appropriate, then, that a novel which juxtaposes that age against ours employ its own "schizophrenic" methods.

This kind of juxtaposing--making character analogs reflect other kinds of parallels--is one of the novel's qualities that is most consistently retained by Pinter and Reisz. The parallels between the modern couple and the Victorian one(s) are particularly fruitful. One such is observed by Joanne Klein, in writing about Pinter's screenplay:

> Although Anna's freedom correlates with Sarah's in several respects, it differs in more significant and consequential ways. A Sartrean nausea afflicts Anna; her freedom is so great that it paralyzes her, and she cannot choose. Unlike Sarah, she cannot defy convention, because convention barely exists.[23]

This is not merely true of these two characters, but is an insight to their respective eras. What was difficult for many Victorians to cope with was the paucity of freedom; what is sometimes difficult to cope with in our century is the excess of freedom.

Similar analogies between fortunes of the main couples (Anna-Mike and Sarah-Charles) in the two films continuously function. Immediately after Charles has sent Sarah to Exeter, Anna informs Mike that she is leaving for London; the two male characters are left alone. Later, when Charles returns to Exeter to find Sarah gone, the film cuts from his look of exasperation to an exasperated Mike dialing Anna's London hotel room--and reaching David.[24] Then, while Charles is searching London streets for Sarah, Mike is trying to locate Anna in London. While they are still on location, he asks whether he'll get to see her there; on the train, when he is seeing her off, he pesters her about it again; he attempts to reach her there by telephone;[25] finally, at the garden-party, he demands to see her, though she puts him off until "at Windermere," which he observes will be "the last scene."

Symbolically, the film adds to this pattern of repetitions and duplications through considerable use of mirrors, windows (and other glass), and water--another reflective surface. The inspiration for these devices might even have come from the novel. There, Charles sees his reflection at a key moment--while he is breaking his engagement to Ernestina:

> He caught sight of himself in a mirror;
> and the man in the mirror, Charles in
> another world, seemed the true self. The
> one in the room was what [Ernestina] said,
> an impostor; had always been, in his re-
> lations with Ernestina, an impostor, an
> observed other. (299)

Once again, this motif--of a Charles who watches Charles, as well as of doubling of many other characters and

events--is ubiquitous in the novel, and the film retains
it through a host of images. The very first shot we see
in the film is of Meryl Streep's face in a hand-mirror;
as Anna, she is being made-up and costumed to play
Sarah.[26] Mirrors will thereafter recur frequently. The
main instances involving Sarah are when she first
interviews with Mrs. Poulteney (an echo is prominent here
also); when she is setting a trap for Charles at
Endicott's Hotel; and when she does her self-portrait,
from her reflection in a dressing-table mirror. The
portrait, seen against a background of windows, could be
titled "Despair." Charles is no less prominently
mirrored. When Grogan quizzes him as to whether he is
in love with Sarah, Charles leans on a mirror-topped
mantel. After his game of "real tennis" with his lawyer,
Montague, and after he has instructed the latter to send
Sarah money, he appears to give a wistful look into a
mirror as he knots his necktie. The room in which
Charles unbethroths himself from Ernestina is framed by
a mirror at one end and windows at the other, which serve
as alternating backgrounds. Windows consistently
function as motifs in the same manner as mirrors.
Charles looks out the window of his inn, "The Cups," and
sees in his mind a vision of Sarah repeated from much
earlier. Mike stands pensively in a window--from over
his shoulder, we see his reflection in it--while, behind

him, Anna half-wakes and calls out, "David." Sarah, as she awaits the arrival of Charles at Endicott's Hotel, hears a train as she looks out a window. Other forms of "looking-glass" are prominent. When we first see Charles, he is hunched over a microscope. Twice we see him peer through a telescope, both times looking for Sarah. Grogan, too, has a telescope which, he jokingly suggests, he uses to watch mermaids. All this is reminiscent of the opening of the novel; in its first chapter, we are told what the "local spy" might see were he "focusing his telescope" on Charles and Ernestina. In the film as in the novel, water is often the background, but especially when Charles is notified of Sarah's having been found, when the two are re-united at the significantly-named Windermere (in a scene played against a wall of windows overlooking the lake), and when "their" film ends and they row out upon that lake.

In addition to these uses of symbolic images, the film does figurative mirrorings that, once again, put viewers' minds on two tracks, much as the novel does. Repetitions make likenesses that are sometimes unexpected. Charles hums softly while he works, Sarah hums as she walks. They make almost identical gestures when first they meet,[27] she putting a hand to her blouse-front, he to his necktie--gestures that reaffirm gender, perhaps. This scene is interrupted by a shot of Sam picking flowers, thus mirroring Charles, as both, albeit at different levels of overtness, are practising courting behavior. Twice Charles tears up explanatory notes he has just begun to write, one to Sarah and one to Mr. Freeman. There are two cast-parties, at each of which Mike is rebuffed when attempting to get together with Anna. On location, when Mike insists that he "must" see Anna in London, she has just said "Okay," when a metallic, PA-system voice says, "Mike, we need you in make-up." He responds with a mechanical "Yes"; Anna mimicks his "Yes," and then repeats, "Yes." Later, she will make a similar mechanical response to a similar insistence of his, at the garden-party. Sometimes, transitions provide parallels. One of the more effective of such sequences occurs when Charles has sought Grogan at "the Asylum." That scene fades on the scream of a woman whom Grogan is assisting with a breech delivery. The cut is to Sarah struggling up the Undercliff in the rain. The sequence provides one of the film's best moments on "the state of woman."

In one more way, the film preserves some of Fowles's method and structure. As the novel uses analogs-- repetitions, duplications, parallels--both to make likenesses and to make contrasts, so does the film create analogs of both kinds. Reversals in fortune or contrasts between the states of characters are often underscored

by bits of symbolism. When, for instance, Charles visits
Mr. Freeman at the latter's office, in order to ask his
permission to marry Ernestina, his potential father-in-
law opens French doors to show Charles how the family
business thrives; this is in the context of his inviting
Charles into that business, a prospect which is clearly
distasteful to the young man. A few short scenes later,[28]
Mike, in a conversation with Anna, rises from the bed to
close the window against the sound of a helicopter. This
seems to be a reminder of Charles's inability to prevent
incursions into his life of industry and technology
(i.e., modernity). In the short run, his prospects seem
low, relative to those of Mike, whose romantic life
flourishes at this point. Elsewhere, Charles's position
in his growing relationship to Sarah is subject to
reversals, and these too are conveyed in part by symbolic
means. Eye-contact (yet another kind of visual motif)
or its absence is significant. In the earliest
encounters between Charles and Sarah, she avoids looking
at him; gradually, that's reversed, and he often cannot
meet her gaze. Similarly, episodes of hiding present a
reversal: On the occasion of their second meeting on the
Undercliff, Charles hides at Sarah's bidding; their
conversation has been interrupted by the approach of
hunters, perhaps poachers. He insists "It's really not
necessary to hide," but it is clear that she is being

protective of him. Later, their roles change in this regard; when they meet in the churchyard, he instigates hiding, although presumably not to protect her. Reversed images and scenes remind us of the differing fates of Mike and Charles, right to the end of the film. Mike loses Anna in (or should that be from?) the same room in which Charles has won Sarah. That scene--the final re-uniting of Charles and Sarah--took place, as analog to Charles's "unbetrothal" scene with Ernestina, against a wall of windows and a lake in the background. Now, when Mike returns to the same room, Anna is outside, in an automobile, and the viewer recalls her having been in one earlier, going to and from a fitting, while Charles desperately searched London for some trace of Sarah.

At least once, a series of repetitions represents a pattern of complete reversal in fortunes of the characters. Charles makes four visits to the home of Mrs. Tranter, Ernestina's aunt. The first is to propose to Ernestina; on the second, he is alienated from her somewhat, by her siding with Mrs. Poulteney against him, and he receives a clandestine note from Sarah; when he next returns, it is to lie to Ernestina about his trip to London, which in fact he makes in order to have Montague provide for Sarah; the last time he comes to the house, it is to break his engagement. On the next-to-last visit, at Ernestina's command, he kisses her, in order to "seal [his] promise" to her; he returns to tell her he is breaking that promise.

The film's most complicated use of reversals involves the cross-overs made by Anna and Mike from their "real" into their fictional personalities. As though they had little or no authentic identities of their own, they assume the masks of their characters. At first, they both do this. In the screenplay, Pinter has written a scene in which Anna and Mike meet in a London bar, and he informs her that Exeter is where he'll "have" her. In the film's final version, this scene is omitted, but another with nearly the same conversation is retained: When Anna is leaving the film's location to go to London, Mike insists that he must "have" her; Anna answers, "You just had me. In Exeter." Then Mike begins to confuse Anna with Sarah. "You weren't in your hotel room," he tells Anna. "In Exeter." He is speaking to Anna at her hotel room, with David, in London. Meanwhile, Anna has started some cross-over associations of her own. Immediately following the scene in which Charles tells Sarah that they "must never meet alone again," we see Anna and Mike alone on a beach. He asks what's wrong because it is clear that she is sad. After the scene in which Charles sends Sarah away from Lyme, Anna says goodbye to Mike because she is leaving for London. As they talk, a set-man urges her to "think of us" when

she's away. "Oh, I will. . ." says Anna, and her hand
goes to her hair in a gesture that we see Sarah use when
she is being both coy and untruthful as Anna is here.
We first saw it in the "confessional" scene when Sarah
told Charles about Varguennes. We see it again when she
is setting a trap for Charles at the hotel in Exeter.
By the middle of both the inner and outer films, it is
clear that Anna is more together, more poised, when being
Sarah than when not. Especially is this so in the
rehearsal scene.[29] To Mike's annoyance, Anna is confused
and klutzy, until she gets into character; then she truly
gets "into" that character: self-reliant, -assured, -
contained. But during her week with David, Anna starts
to separate from Sarah. At her costume-fitting, she says
enthusiastically, "I'm going to like her in this." And
while she has switched over and back, Mike remains stuck
in the nineteenth century with his vision of a non-
existent character. Thus, at the film's end, he calls
out, "Sarah!"

Virtually all of these analogs--be they parallels
or reversals or whatever--are brought together in the
film's ending(s). Returning to the glassed-in room at
"Windermere," Anna looks closely at herself in a mirror;
almost simultaneously, she peers at the wig she wore when
portraying Sarah, now hanging in symbolic detachment.
After her retreat, Mike comes in pursuit of her and calls

out the wrong name; then he sits before the bank of
windows and again smokes a cigarette. As the credit-
lines run, the film repeats the ending of the "inner
film," with Charles and Sarah rowing out on the lake.

"Though much is taken, much abides," says Tennyson's
Ulysses. So it is here. If the film had to sacrifice
some of the fullness of the novel, yet its frame and a
good deal of the spirit was preserved. Above all, the
film keeps, and makes us more mindful of, the novel's use
of repetitions and analogs, its creation of "rhythm."
And, in the process, it keeps much of the metafictive
spirit of the original. Often, in Fowles's work, a
prevailing tension is the result of metafiction. In The
Magus, Mantissa, here in The French Lieutenant's Woman,
and especially in A Maggot, almost constant self-
contradiction goes on; details work against one another,
characters disagree about the meaning of events, and the
narrative voice takes various sides. We, as readers, are
often uncertain of precisely what we know. We are all
a bit like Nicholas Urfe in the hands of Maurice Conchis.
Reisz has claimed that he and Pinter all along intended
to confront an audience's passivity:

> "We're challenging them by saying 'Look, we're
> making a fiction here--are you coming with us
> or not? And what do you think about it?'

We're colluding with them."[30]

This kind of audience involvement goes a long way toward matching one of Fowles's achievements. As does the reader, the viewer shares Charles Smithson's journey toward a "cruel but necessary freedom." Once again, Fowles, the self-styled prophet of liberation, has reminded us that liberation was ever painful.

1. Malcolm Bradbury, _No, Not Bloomsbury_ (New York: Columbia U. Press, 1988).

2. John Fowles, _The French Lieutenant's Woman_ (New York: Signet, 1969). References hereafter will be to this paperback edition, with page numbers in parentheses in text.

3. This Fowlesian term is especially prominent in _The Magus_. It refers to attempts at divine ordination, particularly those made by mortals.

4. Fowles, "Notes on Writing a Novel," _Harper's Magazine_, July, 1968, p. 90.

5. Fowles, _Harper's_, p. 90.

6. Leslie Garis, "Translating Fowles into Film," _New York Times Magazine_, 30 August 1981, pp. 24-5, 48, 50, 52, 54, 69.

7. As it is used here, the term comes from E. M. Forster, in _Aspects of the Novel_. It is used more extensively, and explained, in the chapter here on _A Room with a View_.

8. One must remember that the events of that non-ending are later revealed to have taken place only in Charles's imagination.

9. The order of predication in that last clause is debatable, but certainly Charles thinks he has done the taking. Note, too, that his wish to be protective of Sarah puts him into conflict with Fowles. See below.

10. Garis, p. 54.

11. Fowles, _Harper's_, p. 88.

12. Fowles, _Mantissa_ (Boston: Little Brown, 1982).

13. Fowles, _Mantissa_, pp. 94-5.

14. Fowles, _Mantissa_, pp. 127-8.

15. Fowles, "Foreword," to Harold Pinter, "_The French Lieutenant's Woman_": _A Screenplay_ (Boston/Toronto: Little Brown, 1981), p. xii.

16. Some of this has already been examined here.

17. See Garis, especially p. 25.

18. In the novel it is not she who summons him.
    Montague is informed by Sam Farrow of her
    whereabouts, and he notifies Charles.

19. Fowles, "Acknowledgements," prefatory to the novel,
    p. 8. In the USA, Pike's book is published as
    "Golden Times": Human Documents of the Victorian
    Age (New York: Schocken Books, 1972).

20. Here is more of the "tension," the playing-off
    between opposed possibilities, that this essay will
    examine shortly.

21. Fowles's term. See "Foreword" to Pinter's
    screenplay.

22. Technically, there are three endings, but surely no
    reader is taken in by the pretenses of the first,
    as it occurs more than a hundred pages prior to the
    last. When this essay speaks of two endings, it
    means to discount that one in Chapter 44.

23. Joanne Klein, Making Pictures: The Pinter
    Screenplays (Columbus: Ohio State U. Press, 1985).

24. The credit lines give this character's name as
    "Davide" (as it is pronounced); in the screenplay,
    it is "David."

25. As will be shown shortly, a scene in the screenplay
    in which they do meet is omitted from the film's
    final version. See Pinter, p. 67.

26. Our last look at her will also be in a mirror; see
    below.

27. This is when they meet on the Undercliff;
    previously, they have seen each other, from a
    distance, on the quay.

28. See the summary of scenes in Appendix A.

29. In Appendix A, this is scene #16.

30. Harlan Kennedy, "The Czech Director's Woman," <u>Film Comment</u>, 17 (Sept.-Oct. 1981), p. 28.

CONCLUSION

A number of inferences about film, but even more about novels, may be drawn from the preceding essays. One such might be that, in the case of novel-to-film transformations, the film is almost always a miniature version of the novel. But what goes into that quantity is nearly always worth examining, if one wants to learn what constitutes the/a novel. Clearly, the quantitative difference need not make a negative qualitative difference; the quantity factor occasionally works "backwards." One of the disappointing aspects of The Caine Mutiny is that the film had so much opportunity to be better, partly because of the novel's trimmable excesses. Instead, the makers of the film found other ways to be different from the novel, with such consequences as we have seen.

One can make other kinds of comparisons and juxtapositions, starting from the basic model employed here. One is the examining of more than one novel by the same author and the respective transformations of those novels into films. Twenty years after John Nichols had written The Sterile Cuckoo, he co-wrote the screenplay for Robert Redford's adaptation of his later novel The Milagro Beanfield War. In this case, the film was a much more successful transformation, partly because the later novel has considerably more excess to it than did the earlier. The Sterile Cuckoo is a tighter, more spare novel than the sprawling, comic-epic Milagro.

A novel, one discovers, is less bound by the demands of realistic portrayal than is a film. That was seen in the chapter on Shoeless Joe and "Field of Dreams," and especially in the summary there of Charles Lamb's argument about Shakespeare's plays. A camera (or any number of cameras) will never prove as flexible, as all-encompassing, as an active imagination. In a preface to one of her novels, Ursula LeGuin contends that a reader in the grip of a good novel is in a state of temporary insanity--a point worthy of reflection. The same could not be as accurately said of one's viewing of a film. Film typically goes further--almost necessarily goes further--than a novel to meet the reader's need to effect a "suspension of disbelief." This does not contradict the "Apollonian-Dionysian" dichotomy made in the essay on One Flew Over the Cuckoo's Nest; paradoxically, the novel is also capable of being more rationally intervening or analytical.

When having examined enough transformations, one also reaches some explanations of the cliche that "great novels make bad films," etc. Its converse should read: "Good [but not great] novels might make good or even great films." This is best exemplified here by "Ordinary

People." Probably the ideal transformation would start with a novel composed of a good plot, a few compelling characters, and one central theme. The novel would preferably be short--fewer than 300 pages, say--or would have some quantity of material that could be excised, as not being germane to the central plot or the one theme. Its quality should not be too reliant upon fine prose, on the development of characters by interior monologue or to great depth, or on any complex use of narrative point-of-view. An even more likely beginning for a fiction-to-film transformation would be a good short-story, but with the exception of a few film-makers, those who made "The Dead," for instance, or "Babette's Feast," or "The Rocking-Horse Winner," that is a preference whose day has not yet come.

Even when the transformation is as nearly perfect as one could hope, there are likely to be elements of a well-conceived and well-executed novel that just will not be transformed. This is perhaps best demonstrated in the essay on A Room with a View. And when, as in the clever and intelligent transformation of The French Lieutenant's Woman, the director, the screenwriter, the film-editor, et al, find a near-perfect equivalent of something not quite duplicatable photographically, we will likely see why it was essential that the novel proceeded in the inimitable fashion that it did.

<u>APPENDIX A</u>

A scene-by-scene summary of "The French Lieutenant's Woman."

The following is a list, in sequence, of the scenes
that make up the film "The French Lieutenant's Woman."
Immediately following it, in Appendix B, is a chapter-
by-chapter synopsis of the novel. The purpose of the
inclusion of these is that the reader should have at
least one example of a way in which a film may "follow"
its fictional source. "Scene" is used here in its common
theatrical sense of actions happening in one place at one
time. When the locale changes in the film, or the time
changes by more than a moment, then the numbering changes
here; in other words, when a new "equilibrium" is
established, that constitutes a new scene. However,
there is not a change in the numbering here merely to
denote the entrance or exit of actors.

Readers who wish to pursue this transformation
through one more step should examine also the published
version of the screenplay by Harold Pinter, and the
essays on that screenplay by Joanne Klein and Shoshana
Knapp (see Bibliography).

PRELIMINARY: In the first shot, we see the face of Anna, in a hand-mirror. She is being made up to play (we will learn) Sarah Woodruff. When a voice-over asks if she is "ready," she nods; then a board is held up to designate "32/2," the voice announces "Action," and we go into Sarah's walking toward the quay, while the credit-lines run.

SCENE #1: A street along "The Cobb." We see Sam flirting with women vendors. The camera moves inside the inn, and we see Charles unable to concentrate on his work at a microscope. He summons Sam to "Get the carriage ready."

SCENE #2: Charles and Sam in the carriage, enroute to Mrs. Tranter's.

#2A: Inside, Charles asks to see Ernestina, alone. Mary fetches Ernestina and helps her dress. Charles waits in the parlor, wringing his hands. He and Ernestina go together to the conservatory, where he proposes marriage and is accepted. Meanwhile, Sam and Mary watch from the kitchen window and provide commentary. ("'E's 'ome an' dry," is Sam's observation.)

SCENE #3: A telephone rings in the room where Mike and Anna lie in bed. He answers and takes the message for her: she is wanted in make-up. She is concerned that now people working on the film know that she and Mike sleep together, but he treats it casually.

SCENE #4: A car picks up Anna. As it drives away, Sarah's music is the transition to the next scene.

SCENE #5: Sarah draws, seated on a stairway of her former employer's home. Mr. Forsythe, the vicar, informs her that "Miss Duff" left no provision for Sarah in her will; he agrees to find her a situation. It is clear that she has no money.

SCENE #6: Charles rides in a carriage, through a factory-and-warehouse district, to Mr. Freeman's office. They talk, and again Charles is "accepted."

SCENE #7: On the quay, Charles and Ernestina go for a walk. He suggests returning, for the wind is strong. Spotting Sarah at the end of the breakwater, he goes out to advise her that she is in danger. Sarah's theme-music is up full, as she turns to Charles with a look by which he is entranced.

SCENE #8: Back at Mrs. Tranter's, Charles and Ernestina discuss "Poor Tragedy" (i.e., Sarah). Charles's response to the report on gossip concerning her is "How banal."

SCENE #9: Sarah arrives for her interview with Mrs. Poulteney. A servant tries to talk to her, then runs when she hears someone approaching. As Mrs. Poulteney issues moral demands upon Sarah, her voice echoes, and Sarah sees her own image in a mirror fading, as she apparently "shuts out" her new employer.

SCENE #10: Anna and Mike sit on a bed. She is researching for her role; he is working a crossword-puzzle. They discuss statistics she has discovered in regard to Victorian prostitution. Mike again seems rather callous in regard to such matters, although Sarah is seriously concerned about the historical condition of women.

SCENE #11:   At   the   flintbeds,   Charles   is   at   work
searching out specimens.   Through a telescope, he sees
Sarah out walking.   He runs through the woods in order
to meet her "accidentally."   They are about equally
flustered at this meeting.   Charles's behavior is
(somewhat ironically) mirrored by an interspersed scene:

     #11A: Sam picks flowers for Mary, while on his way
to Mrs. Tranter's.

SCENE #12: At Aunt Tranter's, Sam delivers the flowers
to Mary at the door, first Charles's bouquet for
Ernestina, then his own gift to Mary.

SCENE #13:   Charles stops for a glass of milk at The
Dairy.   The dairyfarmer identifies the passing Sarah as
"The French Leftnant's hooer."

SCENE #14:   A resumption of #12.   Mary takes the flowers
upstairs to Ernestina, who chides her for paying
attention to Sam.   Ernestina, for the first time, looks
like a censorious prude, even something of a hypocrite.

SCENE #15:   On the Undercliff, Charles pursues Sarah,
ostensibly just to apologize for having disturbed her

earlier. She not only indicates that she would "prefer
to walk alone," but also urges him to "Please tell no one
that you have seen me in this place." Does she know that
this will work backwards--that is, that she will be the
one who will give away her presence here? It is not
certain; but, for the first time, she makes eye-contact
with Charles on that plea, and, as she walks away, she
swings her purse jauntily.

SCENE #16: Anna and Mike at "home" rehearse a scene. He
directs their work, somewhat impatiently. Anna stumbles
through the first doing of the scene, but when she snaps
into character, suddenly _she_ seems in charge. Mike looks
a bit surprised. There is an abrupt cut to:

SCENE #17: They are doing "for real" the scene they have
just rehearsed privately. In the woods, Sarah almost
falls, Charles catches her, he looks into her face, and
they nearly kiss. Hearing someone drawing near, Sarah
leads them into cover. Charles makes an offer to help
her establish a life elsewhere than Lyme. He also urges
her to speak of her troubles. It is at the end of this
scene that Sarah divulges that her Frenchman "will never
return.--He is married."

SCENE #18: [Voice-over is again the transition.] Mrs.

Poulteney is haranguing Sarah for her having been seen walking in the Undercliff. She orders her servant to confine her walks to approved places.

SCENE #19: The Poulteney contingent calls on Mrs. Tranter. Ernestina and Charles are on review. Mrs. Poulteney speaks of the current "gross disorders in the streets."

SCENE #19A: Mary and Sam are seen in the kitchen, where Mary identifies Mrs. P. as the former employer who "kicked [Mary] out in the street." Sam advises: "Poison her tea."

SCENE #19[Cont'd]: Sarah gives Charles sidelong looks, then a surreptitious note. Mrs. Poulteney informs on Mary and Sam's flirtation; Charles comes to Sam's defense, and in the ensuing disagreement, Ernestina sides with Mrs. Poulteney.

SCENE #20: Pursuant, presumably, to her note, Charles and Sarah have a clandestine meeting in a churchyard. He berates her for arranging the meeting. Her defense is in her desire to confess to him: "I have. . .sinned. You cannot imagine my suffering." When someone comes out of the church, they hide, this time at Charles's instigation. He reluctantly agrees to meet her and hear her story.

SCENE #21: Mike smokes a cigarette at the window of their room, while Anna sleeps. She wakes, calls "Davide?" He says, "No, it's Mike." Drowsily, she reaches for him and says, "Come back." Mike rejoins her in bed.

SCENE #22: Charles visits at Dr. Grogan's home. He is looking at pictures of apparently hysterical women as the scene opens. The two men admire Grogan's telescope, and they share brandy. Charles finds a way to introduce the topic of "Poor Tragedy." Then Grogan shares with him the theories of a Dr. Hartmann concerning "obscure melancholia," Grogan's diagnosis of Sarah. At Charles's inquiring, Grogan assures him that if she could confide the true state of her mind to someone, "she would be cured."

SCENE #23: The longest scene in the film has Charles and Sarah meeting in the Undercliff for her confession. She tells her "story" of Varguennes, the French Lieutenant. Her face is almost always centered in this scene; his is mostly not. But when she gets to "I saw that I'd been an amusement to him--nothing more," this is no longer the case. Now they share the screen, for now Charles's reaction is equally important. Throughout, she has been somewhat coquettish in mannerisms. Now she swings around a tree, then starts to let down her hair--literally, that is. "I did it so that. . .I should be. . .the outcast that I am," she confides. Charles, visibly attracted, visibly disturbed, suggests again that she leave Lyme. Again, they are interrupted, this time by the sound of a boy and girl dallying in the woods. As they watch the young couple, Sarah smiles delightedly; now Charles is clearly smitten. "We must never meet alone again," he declares.

SCENE #23A: Anna and Mike on a beach. "What's the matter?" he asks. "You look sad." "I'm not," she replies; but she clearly is. She looks into the distance and sees Sarah departing the scene that "surrounds" this interlude.

SCENE #23 [cont'd]: The meeting in the woods concludes. Sarah goes down from the cliffs and is seen by Mrs. Fairley. Clearly, she could have avoided being seen. The music is tremulous and ominous.

SCENE #24: In her upstairs room at Mrs. Poulteney's, Sarah draws her own portrait. It has a look of despair.

SCENE #25: Charles, clad in a robe, in his room. A note comes under his door. Sarah is at the Undercliff.

SCENE #26:   Charles   seeks   Grogan   at   his   home.
Unsuccessful there, he goes to him at the "asylum," where
Grogan is delivering a baby. The only patients we see
or hear are women.   Grogan informs Charles that "Miss
Woodruff has disappeared. . . .Go to my house. Wait for
me."

SCENE #27: Sarah struggles up the cliffs in the rain.
She reaches the shelter she has sought.

SCENE #28: At his home, Grogan brings out a copy of The
Origin of Species and "swears" on it that "Nothing...will
go beyond these walls." He then gives to Charles, who
has asked his advice, a summary of Sarah's actions and
speculations on her possible motives. (Grogan has spoken
to Mrs. Fairley.) Charles defends Sarah so staunchly,
that Grogan observes, "My dear man, you are half in love
with her." In protesting that "nothing indecent has
passed between us," Charles tacitly admits to the charge.
He promises to honor his vows to Miss Freeman, and Grogan
volunteers to see that Sarah is taken care of.

SCENE #29: Back in his room, Charles looks out at the
quay. He "sees" the unforgettable face of Sarah, as he
saw her that first time. The music plays Sarah's theme.

SCENE #30:   Contrary to his agreement with Grogan, Charles walks to the Undercliff. He finds Sarah asleep in the shelter. They kiss. Mary and Sam intrude upon them, and Charles bullies Sam into leaving, while urging him strongly to tell no-one. Then Charles returns to Sarah and persuades her to leave Lyme. "I shall never see you again?" she asks. "No" is his answer.

SCENE #31: Anna emerges from a trailer on location. To Mike she announces that she is off for London, where David will meet her. Mike responds in monosyllables. "Think of us," a set-man suggests. "Oh, I will. . ." Anna answers, and her hand goes to her hair flirtatiously, just as Sarah has done earlier.

SCENE #32: Charles orders Sam to go to London, to "Open up the house." Sam worries about his "future."

SCENE #33: Charles goes to Mrs. Tranter's. He gives Mary a coin, a reward for her silence; when he is out of sight, she bites the coin. He finds Ernestina practicing archery. She is upset that he must go to London, ostensibly to speak with her father. She demands a kiss to seal his promise that he will return shortly.

SCENE #34: Sarah struggles up a hill (again), this time with luggage, in Exeter. She goes to Endicott's Family Hotel.

SCENE #35: Charles and his attorney, Harry Montague, play "Real [Royal] tennis." Charles plays with fury. In the locker-room later, he orders Montague to send money to "a Miss Woodruff." The lawyer double-takes slightly at the amount: fifty pounds. "And I want," Charles adds, "to hear nothing more about it."

SCENE #36: Charles takes a carriage to his London home. To Sam, when he finally answers the door, he snarls, "Where have you been? Are you deaf?" To Sam's request to speak with him, Charles answers a curt "No."

SCENE #37: Charles gets drunk with his old college chums, Nathaniel and Sir Tom. They decide to end the evening at "Kate Hamilton's," but as Charles makes for the exit, he staggers into tables, then collapses.

SCENE #38: A messenger delivers, to Charles's London home, a message from Montague. Sam rifles it. When he brings it to Charles, who is "sleeping it off," we learn that the note is in Sarah's hand; it says, "Endicott's Family Hotel."

SCENE #39:   Sarah, at Endicott's Hotel, lays out a "trap." She tries her shawl and gown over a chair; she glances at a mirror and her hand goes to her hair again.

SCENE #40: Charles writes a letter to Sarah urging "No further communication. . .," then tears it up. Sam tries out his "business" idea on his master. He would need capital of about "two hundred eighty pounds" to open a shop; he has about thirty.
Charles refuses, then consents to "think about it." Sam, ordered to prepare for travel, is surprised at the destination: "To Lyme, sir?"

SCENE #41: Their train stops at Exeter, and Charles and Sam alight. They will stay the night before hiring a carriage, because "It's going to rain."   Charles instructs Sam to get a room, while he is "going to stretch [his] legs."

SCENE #42: Charles goes to Endicott's Family Hotel. At the front desk he pretends to be a "gentleman of the law." He is conducted upstairs to Sarah's room; he is told that she has "turned her ankle." (It is not clear that she has not.) As they try to talk, he is extremely nervous, and she cries softly. Embers from the fireplace get on her shawl. Charles stamps them out, then adjusts her shawl around her, and they kiss passionately. He carries her to bed, where they consummate, hurriedly and fumblingly, their relationship.

SCENE #42A: Sam finds the hotel. Through the window, we see him talk to the landlady.

SCENE 42 [cont'd]: In post-coital conversation, Charles causes Sarah to admit that he was her "first." She then tells him the real story of Varguennes. He must away to Lyme. "You must give me a day's grace," he tells Sarah. "You will wait for me, won't you?" She does not answer.

SCENE #42A [cont'd]: Sam stands in the street, watching the window of Sarah's room.

SCENE #42 [concl'd]: With his coat on, Charles takes his farewell from Sarah. She still has not promised to wait. She assures him: "You have given me the strength to live." After he has left, she appears to cry.

SCENE #43: In another train station, Mike runs to Anna's car, with a sandwich for her. He indicates that he must "have" her, and she replies, "You just had me--in Exeter."

SCENE #44: Ernestina reacts to hearing Charles's voice

at the door of Aunt Tranter's home. He has come to sever their engagement. "I am not worthy of you," he tells her. Ernestina is alternately upset, pleading, then angry: "My father will drag your name. . .through the mire," she screams. Over her voice, the scene shifts to:

SCENE #45: Charles tries to write to Mr. Freeman, but tears up this letter also. Sam comes in and stays just long enough to inform Charles that he is leaving his employ: "I have to consider my own situation."

SCENE #46: Charles returns to Endicott's. "The young lady's left, sir," he is informed. "On the three o'clock to London." He rushes upstairs to check for himself, but Sarah is gone. He screams at the landlady to leave him alone. He stands, looking exasperated, in a doorway. Cut to:

SCENE #47: Mike, at his home, dialing the telephone. In Anna's hotel room, David answers, and Mike hangs up. David looks, rather knowingly it seems, at Anna. To his wife, Mike suggests a "lunch" for some of the cast. His wife agrees, asking at the same time, "Are you all right?" Back in the hotel, David answers the telephone again, says "I give you Anna." She and Mike arrange the luncheon party, while David manipulates a calculator. In the conversation, Mike accuses Anna of having been gone from her hotel room--in Exeter.

SCENE #48: Charles hires an investigator, Mr. Grimes, to find Sarah. To Grimes's question of whether Sarah wants to be found, Charles admits, "I cannot say."

SCENE #49: By car, Anna is taken to the film's wardrobe shop.

(This scene will be completed in three short takes.)

SCENE #50: Montague reads a legal summons to Charles. Mr. Freeman is bringing an action against him. Montague anticipates an "ugly document."

SCENE #49 [cont'd]: Anna is picking out clothing for Sarah. Her response to one outfit is "I'm going to like her in this."

SCENE #50 [cont'd]: At the offices of Aubrey and Baggot, Mr. Freeman's Solicitors, Charles hears read the document he is asked to sign. In it, among other things, he "forever forfeits the right to be thought a gentleman." After brief contemplation, he signs. Once more, the scene is juxtaposed with Anna's costuming.

SCENE #49 [concl'd]: Anna goes back to the car, smiling. In the distance, the sound of children, as though the costume-shop were near a school.

SCENE #51: Charles, in a carriage, searches London for Sarah. Several times he thinks he has found her. The scene is something of a "descent into the underworld," as it takes Charles through factory areas and red-light districts. Finally, he starts to head off somewhere with a prostitute.

SCENE #52: Mike's daughter, Lizzie, welcomes Anna and David to the Sunday luncheon party. The camera wanders through the gathering. David asks Mike if "they [have] decided how they are going to end the movie," since, as he notes, "the book has two endings." Mike seems to evade the question. Anna admires the garden of Mike's wife, Sonia. "I really envy you," Anna says. "I wouldn't...if I were you," is the reply. The actor playing Sam sits at the piano performing Mozart for "Ernestina." After much pursuit, Mike gets Anna alone--too late. "We've got to decide what we want," he insists, but she must leave hurriedly.

SCENE #53:   Over the "inside" film is juxtaposed the legend "THREE YEARS LATER." Charles, sitting at seaside somewhere, is given a cable. It is from Montague: "She is found."

SCENE #54: At the lake at Windermere, the last scene of the "inner film" is acted out. Sarah lives with and works for a family named Eliot. She has her own art studio, and has been doing her own artwork, rather well. She goes by the name "Mrs. Roughwood" for convenience. It was she who contacted Montague. The best explanation of her past behavior she is able to give Charles is, "There was madness in me at that time. . . .It was unworthy." He insists that she must say that she has been evil and that she never loved him; in the argument, he pushes at her, and she falls. As he kneels over her, she admits, "I called you here to ask your forgiveness." He grants it: "I must--forgive you." They kiss, and the scene fades into their rowing out, through a gateway, onto the open lake.

SCENE #55:   At the final cast-party, on the set at Windermere, Mike tries to get Anna alone, again.   She starts to leave, he follows; she goes up to her dressing-room and looks at herself in a mirror. As Mike is following, he stops briefly to say goodbye to the actress

who played Ernestina and gives her a short peck on the
cheek. She looks after him, longingly it seems. By the
time he gets up to the room in which the last scene of
the "other" film was staged, Anna is gone. As does Mike,
we hear a car start up outside. He goes to the window
and calls out, "Sarah!"

POST-FINAL: Over the final credits, the "other" ending
is repeated, with Charles and Sarah rowing out at
Windermere.

APPENDIX B

The <u>French</u> <u>Lieutenant's</u> <u>Woman</u>

PLOT SUMMARIZED BY CHAPTERS

Chapter 1.

The date and the place are precisely established:
late March of 1867, in Lyme Regis, on Lyme Bay, near the
quay that is east of cliffs known as Ware Cleeves. We
see Charles and Ernestina, neither yet identified,
walking.

Chapter 2.

The young couple now identified, Charles summarizes
his meeting with Ernestina's father. Charles and
Ernestina see Sarah Woodruff, known locally as "Tragedy"
or "The French Lieutenant's . . .Woman." (The fishermen,
Tina tells us, use a "gross name" instead.) She is
walking on the breakwater; Charles, realizing she is thus
endangering herself, goes out to warn her. She does not
respond, except to look at him briefly; he sees "an
unforgettable face. . ." in which there is "no artifice.
. .no hypocrisy, no hysteria, no mask. . . ." He feels
afterwards, however, that the look fixed him as an enemy.

Chapter 3.

Following a quote from The Origin of Species, noting
that the "structures" of many living creatures "have now
no very close and direct relations to present habits of
life. . .," we are given a description of Charles
Smithson. He is thirty-two years old, descended from
baronets, has been something of a dilettante, but is not,

at present, "essentially a frivolous young man." He would like, perhaps, to do something serious in paleontology, although he is somewhat lazy. Since his years at Cambridge, and the obligatory spiritual/sexual crisis, he has become a "healthy agnostic," though as Fowles observes in a footnote, Huxley would not coin that term until 1870.

Chapter 4.

We are introduced to Mrs. Poulteney, the severely moralistic widow who employs Sarah. In flashback to one year previous, we see how they came together. Mrs. Poulteney wished to do something charitable, out of worry, in her later years, over the current standing of her spiritual stock. The young vicar of Lyme, Mr. Forsythe, suggests that she take in Sarah as a companion, who would also conduct the Scripture-readings for the household, since the chief servant, Mrs. Fairley, no longer reads well.

Chapter 5.

As Charles was two chapters previous, Ernestina is now described: "Ernestina had exactly the right face for her age . . ." It turns out she has practically all of the proper attributes for the Victorian age. Even though she is in small ways willful, she is above all dutiful. She even looks upon her coming marriage, and particularly the sexual aspects thereof, primarily in terms of that Victorian watchword, "duty." (The prefatory quotation to this chapter, from In Memoriam, is on sex, love, death and moral duty.)

Chapter 6.

As will be a pattern in this novel, the sixth chapter picks up where the fourth ended. We are still in that period a year prior to the story's "present tense," when Mrs. Poulteney is considering taking in Sarah. Mr. Forsythe lingers on his visit, to describe Sarah's recent past and her present situation. Mrs. Poulteney is persuaded to bring Sarah in for an interview; following it, we learn that Sarah accepted the position because Mrs. Poulteney's home commands a good view of the sea--and because Sarah at the time was penniless.

Chapter 7.

There remains one character to be introduced in this early going. Here we meet Sam Farrow, Charles's man-servant, who is falling in love with Mary, a maid at the home of Mrs. Tranter, Ernestina's aunt with whom she resides in Lyme. The relationship between Charles and Sam is friendly, even jocular, although Charles keeps it distant also. It is clear that he takes seriously a responsibility that he feels as paternalistic employer. Sam is likened to (undoubtedly his literary namesake) Dickens's Sam Weller. The difference between the two

Sams is that "the first was happy with his role, the second suffered it." Fowles also sees this as a difference between 1836 and 1867.

Chapter 8.

As Ernestina is indisposed, Charles sets out on a day's fossil-hunting. He is in search of "tests," or echinoderm, the petrified sea urchin ("sand dollars" in the United States). The outing gives Fowles the opportunity for more century-contrasting, particularly since, to our thinking, Charles is ludicrously outfitted, in heavy flannel and a long coat, plus "stout nailed boots" (for hiking on rock-covered beaches). But, to Fowles, Charles's being dressed so as to be ready for anything represents his--and his era's--being constantly prepared for discovery, and that readiness in turn implies the Victorian age's acknowledgment that discovery would determine the all-important future. Contrasted to this, in Fowles's view, is the present-only orientation of our age. These Darwinian instincts of Charles Smithson's will be constantly useful to Fowles.

Chapter 9.

Again, we go back two chapters, and learn more of Sarah's taking a position in the household of Mrs. Poulteney. Too, we get some information about Sarah's background. Her father, obsessed with an awareness of nobility a long way back in his ancestry, educated her

out of her class, "but could not raise her to the next."
Thus, too polished and sophisticated for any man who came
near her--and too impoverished to come near any other
kind--she seemed doomed to be a spinster.

Sarah ingratiates herself to Mrs. Poulteney in two
ways: she is able to recognize and remedy problems among
the staff and her scriptural readings are genuinely
moving, for, while "Mrs. Poulteney believed in a God that
had never existed. . . .Sarah knew a God that did." Mrs.
Fairley, a servant "whose only pleasures were knowing the
worst or fearing the worst," shocks her employer by
reporting to her that Sarah has been seen walking "on
Ware Commons."

Chapter 10.

We rejoin Charles on his test-hunting expedition,
and he enters Ware Commons, an "English Garden of Eden"
on this 29th day of March, 1867. The beauty of the place
makes him a bit sad, for he is unable, as a 20th-century
man might do, to be happy with what he possesses at the
present moment. In the midst of this reverie, he
blunders upon a woman sleeping in the woods and
recognizes the French Lieutenant's Woman; she has not
seen or heard him. He pauses to gaze at her a while.
She awakens, they stare at each other for several
seconds, then Charles apologizes and retreats to a fork
in the path, at which he takes the steeper route. The

chapter ends: "Charles did not know it, but in those brief poised seconds above the waiting sea. . .the whole Victorian Age was lost. And I do not mean he had taken the wrong path."

Chapter 11.

When Ernestina at last gets up, it is just in time to receive flowers from Charles, delivered by Sam, who paused at the door to flirt with Mary. Ernestina, rather prudishly, not to mention hypocritically, cautions her against having anything to do with a man who comes from London.

The second half of the chapter recalls the courtship of Charles and Ernestina, and indicates what a good Victorian match could be made between his gentlemanly rank and her father's wealth. It also makes clear how attracted each was by the other's ironic humor, and how much "natural sexual instinct" they "imprison" within themselves.

Chapter 12.

Thinking he has put "Tragedy" completely behind him, Charles tramps out of Ware Commons and onto a farm called, locally, just "The Dairy." He stops to purchase a glass of milk; while he drinks it, Sarah passes. Charles catches up with her, and her look again has "an extraordinary effect on him," seeming as it does to "both envelop and reject him." He tries to speak with her (he is still apologetic for having disturbed her nap), but her look rebuffs him. "Do not come near me," her eyes seem to say.

In the second part of the chapter, Charles takes a gift of ammonite to Ernestina. So lyrical is he in describing the Undercliff, where he walked, that Ernestina calls him "entranced," and jokingly suggests he's been dallying with wood nymphs rather than hunting fossils.

The chapter's final segment explains Mrs. Poulteney's shock at the end of Chapter Nine; Ware Commons is, among other things, a local lover's-lane. What Mrs. Poulteney imagines going on there is worse by far than the actuality. She and Sarah have a tense encounter, and the old woman orders her servant not to walk there again. At chapter's end, Fowles has Sarah poised at her bedroom's open window, at one o'clock in the morning, apparently contemplating jumping from it. This prompts the author to the questions which close the chapter:

> Who is Sarah?
> Out of what shadows does she come?

Chapter 13.

This chapter provides a turning-point, of sorts, beginning with the answer to the questions posed in the last chapter: "I don't know." Speaking to us, intrusively, in his own voice, Fowles confesses that he has been trying, in style and in diction, to write a Victorian novel, but has realized the difficulty of that task for a modern writer, for it requires him to play God. The contemporary novelist knows, Fowles suggests, but one definition of God--"the freedom that allows other freedoms to exist." Therefore, Fowles must at times, however unVictorianly, allow his characters autonomy. So developed is this habit, he reports, that it sometimes defeats planning. If we insist on believing that Fowles is putting us on, that all of this has nothing to do with his novel's themes (or the themes we demand that it have), he cannot, he tells us, argue further; but we shall have then earned his suspicion.

To conclude the chapter, Fowles gives us the "facts": Sarah knew she'd be seen going past the Dairy, but did so mainly because she had overslept and knew she was late. Also, "Charles's down-staring face had shocked her; she felt the speed of her fall accelerate. . . ." This will be the nearest we ever come to getting anything like Sarah's point-of-view.

Chapter 14.

Charles accompanies Ernestina and Mrs. Tranter in paying an obligatory social call upon Mrs. Poulteney. As the latter holds forth opinionatedly on her always-limited range of subjects, Charles observes that Sarah

labors "under a sense of injustice"--and does "singularly
little to conceal it." In making this observation,
Charles perceives something that "had escaped almost
everyone else in Lyme."

Chapter 15.

Charles, back at his inn, pretends to be sending
Sam back to London; thus he learns that Sam's overtures
to Mary are an expression of genuine affection. Charles
promises to speak with Mrs. Tranter to find whether she
will permit Sam's attentions to Mary.

Chapter 16.

Six days later, Charles returns to where he had
previously found Sarah on "that wild cliff meadow." He
had seen there that day piles of fallen flint, and Fowles
suggests that it "was certainly this which made him walk
[now] to the place." (This is one of several places in
which the "certainty" of Charles's motives will be
suggested ironically.) Sure enough, he comes upon Sarah
again. Her coat is caught in some brambles on the steep
path, and as she pulls it free, she slips in the mud and
falls. Charles helps her up, then to the ridge above.
He offers to enlist the aid of Mrs. Tranter in securing
her a position elsewhere, perhaps in London. She insists
that she has "ties" in this region. But when she is
walking away, in refusal, Charles tells her that if the
"French gentleman" truly wishes to find her, he will do

so anywhere. To his amazement, Sarah informs him that the "gentleman" will never return, as he is married. As she disappears, Charles realizes that she is much more enigmatic than his smug superiority as a man-of-the-world had led him to think.

Chapter 17.

Charles realizes that Sarah has made him "aware of a deprivation" in his life. While he had always thought his future filled with diversity, it now has become "a fixed voyage to a known place." In contrast to Charles's thoughts of his affianced, we see the Tranter kitchen, where Sam, against a specific prohibition from Charles, courts Mary. Shortly thereafter, Charles secures Mrs. Tranter's permission for Sam's courtship.

Chapter 18.

Three days later, Charles again goes exploring, this time forbidding himself to go anywhere near the spot where he twice previously encountered Sarah. Accordingly, he goes northward and upward from that meadow, only to be surprised by her silently coming upon him. Clearly, she has followed him; furthermore, she has brought a gift: two tests, excellent specimens. There is a price: she wants to tell him her story. Obviously, the tests are to compensate him for his time and attention. Why has she chosen him? He is well-traveled, educated, and a gentleman; she fancies that he will be at least understanding, possibly kind. At last he agrees; and this time he does not even try to convince himself that he will tell Ernestina, though in so choosing he feels some sense of shame.

Chapter 19.

We get to know something of Doctor Grogan as he and Charles, after a dinner party, go to the doctor's "cabin" for a nightcap. They will discover that they share a passionate interest in Darwin. Before that, however, they discuss Sarah's "case"--Charles has introduced it--which Grogan has already diagnosed as "obscure melancholia." To Charles's main question--what the result would be if she could confide her feelings to a sympathetic other--Grogan's response is instant: "'She would be cured.'"

Over the course of the evening, Charles again realizes that Ernestina is more cute than acute, but again convinces himself that this must not be held against her. Later, he and Grogan reveal themselves to be, contrary to their own self-perceptions, not very democratic, even less progressive, and woefully sexist. Meanwhile, in an interpolated scene, we see Sarah in bed at Mrs. Poulteney's with a young, slightly ill and even more lonesome servant, named Millie. Ignorant of lesbianism, partly aware of the carnal, but "as inocent as makes no matter," Sarah is sheerly befriending the

young maid. They make an interesting and clear contrast
to the "two lords of creation" in Grogan's apartment.
Chapter 20.

Charles goes to the meeting with Sarah, able to
believe now that he goes out of a sense of humanitarian
duty. They find a secluded dell, and Sarah tells the
story of herself and Varguennes, how she fell for the
injured, shipwrecked sailor while he was recuperating in
her employers' house, how she followed him--when he had
healed--to Weymouth, met him at an inn, and (in her
words) "'gave myself to him.'" But she could not marry
him thereafter, so she "married shame"--she deliberately
became the "French Lieutenant's Whore" (she knows people
use the term). It was "a kind of suicide." By it, she
set herself beyond the pale, beyond and outside of human
society. Charles recognizes that he--listening,
sympathizing, visualizing--is "at one and the same time
Varguennes enjoying her and the man who sprang forward
and struck him down."
Chapter 21.

Sarah finishes her story. Charles recognizes the
great "human loss" in there being no one, except perhaps
himself, to recognize what a "remarkable woman" she is.
As they are about to leave together, they are nearly
intruded upon by Sam and Mary, walking (and dallying) in
the woods. He tells her that they must never meet alone

again. When all is clear, they part, separately.

Chapter 22.

Returning to his hotel, Charles chides himself for toying with danger, then forgives himself because he "has cured [Sarah] of her madness." Back at the White Lion, he learns that he has been summoned to the family estate at Winsyatt by his Uncle Robert. He informs Ernestina, who again begins planning which family home she will decorate after Charles inherits his estate. Chapter 23.

Charles has little idea why he has been summoned. He is not eager to be an heir in any case. But "Duty" is always "his real wife, his Ernestina and his Sarah," so he goes. Meanwhile, we are told how Sarah returned from her clandestine meeting with Charles. Rather than maintaining cover, "she walked boldly" into the open, past the cottage at the Dairy, "in full view of the two women" who chatted there. One of them was Mrs. Fairley. Chapter 24.

We learn, as Charles discusses it with Ernestina, why he was called to Winsyatt. His uncle plans to marry. This, especially considering that there could be progeny, means that Charles is in danger of being "disinherited." Meanwhile, there is news buzzing in Lyme: Mrs. Poulteney has dismissed Sarah Woodruff. Charles worries on two levels: for her safety and that he might have been seen with her.

Chapter 25.

At the White Lion, Charles receives two notes from Sarah, one asking him to meet her, the other, in French, telling him where she'll be. After cautioning Sam that, "'though it is not important at all,'" he is to "'speak of this to no one,'" Charles finds he cannot avoid thinking of Sarah. While Sam quite apparently forms suspicions, Charles leaves the hotel.

Chapter 26.

It is revealed that Sam has ambitions; he would like to go into business, but lacks capital. It is broadly hinted that he is not above blackmail. In a flashback to Winsyatt, we find out that Sam learned the truth of Charles's plight from the servants there. While we are there, we see a bit of Charles's interview with his uncle.

Chapter 27.

Charles goes to see Grogan. He informs the doctor that he has heard from Sarah (for whom a search-party is looking), then confides to Grogan, almost completely, his interest in her. Grogan, not altogether inaccurately, summarizes his view of the attraction, drawing three conclusions: that Charles is "'half in love with her,'" for which he should not harshly blame himself, as she has "'eyes a man could drown in'"; that Sarah '"deliberately invited'" Mrs. Fairley to report her walking in Ware

Commons; that her motive was, and is, revenge.
Befuddled, Charles insists that he will honor his vows
to Ernestina. Grogan volunteers to call off the search-
party, to make the rendezvous with Sarah in Charles's
stead, and to see that she goes to a "private asylum" run
by an efficient and kindly friend of his in Exeter.
Charles agrees to defray the cost.

Chapter 28.

As Charles departed from Grogan, the doctor gave
him a book containing an account of the La Ronciere case.
Although he at first finds it persuasive, Charles, after
reading it a second time, begins to see discrepancies
between Sarah's behavior and the cases described. Now
he is convinced that he transferred judgment of her to
Grogan, because he was concerned only with appearances,
because he has "no more free will than an ammonite." He
changes his mind and sets out, despite his pact with
Grogan, to find Sarah.

Chapter 29.

Once Charles is back in the Undercliff, all is
different from the evening before. One's notion of
"reality" is altered here: the "heart of all life" beats
in a "wren's triumphant throat." Charles can stand in
this Eden, "but not enjoy it." He fancies himself similar
to Sarah in this. That Hardy-esque bird (cf. "The
Darkling Thrush") dominates the scene; Charles can "only

envy the wren its ecstasy."

Chapter 30.

Once again, a new chapter brings a switch in perspective and a backing-up in time. We see Sarah being dismissed by Mrs. Poulteney. It is a nicely ambiguous scene: her behavior recalls Grogan's analysis of her deliberate self-destructiveness, but at the end of the chapter she weeps in despair.

Chapter 31.

Again, we return to the time at the end of the chapter-before-last. Sarah is in the barn, sleeping. Charles is moved by "a desire to protect," among other desires he is less conscious of. After she wakes, Sarah's "wildness" seems to him like that in the singing of the wren. An encounter of "intense repressed emotion" follows, then Sarah confesses that indeed she did make sure Mrs. Fairley saw her emerging from the Commons. As Charles looks at her closely, trying to determine why, the Victorian age is again lost, and they kiss. Charles pushes her away, runs from the barn and right into "yet another horror," which is "not Doctor Grogan."

Chapter 32.

We see Ernestina on the previous evening, troubled because she offended Charles by her attitude over the Winsyatt business. She repents in her diary, then goes back to bed relieved; the narrator misleadingly

speculates that she "must, in the end, win Charles back.
. . . ." Meanwhile, she sleeps through a drama downstairs.
Sam has been ordered by Charles (the night before) to
prepare to leave. Mary collapses in tears at the news,
and Aunt Tranter gives her the morning off, in order for
her to say goodbye to Sam.

Chapter 33.

We learn that the "horror" for Charles at the end
of Chapter 31 was his face-to-face encounter with Sam
and Mary, "out walking." Charles informs Sam that he is
assisting Sarah, with Dr. Grogan's awareness. It is
clear that Sam will be discreet, and both master and
servant seem to know that "a shrewd sacrifice" has been
made. Although Charles had been considerably aroused a
minute before, as soon as Mary and Sam have left, "Duty"
once more comes "to his aid." He advises Sarah to go to
Exeter; he and Mrs. Tranter will assist her there. She
agrees, even though Charles assures her they will never
meet again. Telling her that she is a "remarkable
person," to which she assents, he also vows that he will
never forget her.

Chapter 34.

Charles goes to Ernestina to tell her he must go to
London to explain his changed circumstances to her
father. He takes a by-now familiar stance: "I know my
duty." She pouts but consents. In leaving, he sees Mary

and gives her a coin, which she tests by biting.

Chapter 35.

We get another digressive chapter, in which Fowles
adds to the contrasts between the centuries. While ours
is more indulgently open (and openly indulgent) about
sex, yet the preceding century had contradictions aplenty
in that regard. Fowles's prime example of the tension
"between lust and renunciation" that "structures the
whole age" is that which possessed, but also motivated,
Thomas Hardy, whom Fowles designates "the perfect emblem
of his age's greatest mystery."

Chapter 36.

Exeter is described, particularly that section of
the city containing the Endicott Family Hotel, a part of
town often come to by "fallen" and/or deserted women from
other cities. Sarah has taken a room there. She returns
to it from a shopping trip on which she has bought a
teapot and mug, some tea and a meatpie, a nightgown and
shawl (each of which compliments her hair), and a roll
of bandage. With the aid of ten sovereigns from Charles,
she is "simply enjoying the first holiday of her adult
life."

Chapter 37.

Charles goes to his meeting with Mr. Freeman. The
latter is surprised at the news, and momentarily
suspicious. The gentleman in him overwhelms the

business-man, particularly after he has read the letter
Charles brings from Ernestina, and he agrees that the
prospects of the "alliance" have not been seriously
marred. Then he presents Charles with a dilemma: he
wants Charles to succeed him in the business, to enter
it even now as a partner. After all, he points out, we
must all adapt to changes in the environment in order to
survive. Charles cannot refuse outright, but within
himself he feels that he is "a gentleman; and gentlemen
cannot go into trade." Thus he feels, now, like "a lion
caged."

Chapter 38.

From Mr. Freeman's office, Charles attempts to walk
to his club in St. James. As he wanders, getting lost,
he contemplates his status: he feels analagous to a
"superseded monster," a "poor living fossil." Even more
clearly, Fowles sees Charles trapped in history. He is
part of a uniquely human evolution, part of a "self-
questioning, ethical elite," who live by certain rules,
which rules cause their own destruction, but ultimately
"brace or act as structure for the better effects of
their function in history." Abandoning, for the moment,
his attempt to escape, Charles take a hansom cab to his
club, for milk punch and champagne.

Chapter <u>39</u>.

Arriving at his club, Charles falls in with two former fellow-students, with whom he gets stupidly, nostalgically drunk. He is taken rather than goes to a "noted Bagnio," Ma Terpsichore's. He is both aroused and disgusted by the exhibition there. He leaves by himself, intending to go home, but has his cab stop to pick up a streetwalker. He is first attracted by her "auburn hair," her eyes, and her "vaguely wistful stance." Later he realizes she is "not really like Sarah." He goes to her home.

Chapter <u>40</u>.

Charles extracts from her the story of the prostitute's life. She was abandoned while pregnant, took up the profession out of desperation, and has no regrets. Though fighting off nausea, Charles stalls for time by drinking yet more wine. At last she makes overtures, and they head toward the bed. Once again, Charles is "two people" (one drunk, one horny). As he leans into her bed, he asks her name. It is "Sarah". Charles vomits upon the bed.

Chapter <u>41</u>.

The story moves forward, to the next morning, with Charles severely hung-over. But it soon flashes back to the ending of his evening before. After she'd cleaned up, his streetwalker friend hailed a cab while Charles

dressed. The baby in the next room began to cry, and
Charles comforted her. The child and the scene and his
ability to help braced him, and Charles imagined himself
"suddenly able to face his future. . . ." He told this
other Sarah that she was a brave, kind girl, paid her
five sovereigns extra, and left.

Chapter 42.

In Charles's Kensington residence, the story resumes
on the morning after his night out. We see a letter he
sent to Grogan before departing Lyme, as Charles now
reads the answer. Grogan does not suspect why he was
unable to find Sarah; Charles is "not discovered."
Another message is in but three words, an address. He
burns it. Sam wants a conversation with his master,
which turns out to be about his ambition to be a
shopkeeper. Charles confides (what Sam already knew) the
news about Uncle Robert, and Sam reminds him, ". . .'You
knows I knows 'ow to keep a secret'." The meaning is not
lost, and Sam now knows that he owns "a lever." As the
chapter ends, with plans to return to Lyme, Charles muses
upon Sam's behavior and attitude; there are too many
"orders beginning to melt and dissolve." He does not
know all--Sam steamed open the three-word letter before
delivering it.

Chapter 43.

We begin to veer once more into the metafictive,

perhaps even more than we did in Chapter Thirteen. The "events" related in the latter half of this chapter will be altered later in the novel, for it is in this chapter that we start into the first--and completely bogus-- ending to the novel. Fowles begins the chapter by debating, aloud as it were, whether one finds "more color for the myth of a rational human behavior in an iron age like the Victorian" than in others. He then has the would-be-rational Charles, convinced that Sarah's case has been disposed of in the best way possible, stop in Exeter, where he and Sam must change from railway to carriage, then continue on toward Lyme. Charles has accepted his fate, though he still sees himself as a "victim" and as "a potential turned to a fossil."

Chapter 44.

Although he returns to Lyme late at night, Charles goes right to Mrs. Tranter's, where he enjoys a contented reunion with Ernestina. He commences a confession to her about "that miserable female at Marlborough House. . .poor Tragedy," and it tapers off in an ellipsis. "And so [Fowles informs us] ends the story. What happened to Sarah, I do not know. . .," and he heads into a thoroughly conventional Victorian ending, accounting for all the main participants, including Mrs. Poulteney, whom we last see descending into Hell. Charles and Ernestina lived in love until she died, a decade before he would;

their union produced seven children, etc. . . . .

Chapter 45.

The metafictive process continues. Clearly, no one is deceived by the first "ending"; the reader still has a hundred pages of book in her/his right hand. We might also have noticed, Fowles points out, the "small matter" of Charles's being given a life-span of "nearly a century and a quarter." Sure enough, we learn now that the events we have just read of took place only in Charles's imagination as he approached Exeter. Now the action reverts to that of Chapter 43, but this time Charles informs Sam that they'll spend the night. He goes for a walk, perhaps to "'attend Evensong at the Cathedral.'" Sam is not fooled, and follows Charles to Endicott's Family Hotel.

Chapter 46.

Allowing the landlady to think him "a gentleman of the law," Charles is directed to Sarah's room. She appears to have "turned her ankle" in a fall and is a temporary invalid. Charles realizes again her beauty and knows why he has come: "to see her again. . .to possess her, to melt into her, to burn, to burn to ashes on that body and in those eyes." Amid almost constant imagery suggesting his release, his being a "prisoner" now "set free," he carries Sarah to the bedroom, where, in a brief but passionate embrace, they consummate their affair.

Chapter 47.

Charles is awash not in "postcoital sadness" but in "horror." All morality seems to him fled from life. Still, he insists that he will marry Sarah: "'I must. I wish to. I could never look myself in the face again if I did not.'" He pleads with her to give him "'a day or two's grace,'" as he cannot now think clearly what he should do. Retiring to the other room, he discovers blood on his shirt and his person; Sarah had been a virgin. As he thinks that she must after all be "mad, evil," she emerges and explains that, when she followed Varguennes, she found him with another woman and departed Weymouth at once. Charles, she says, has given her "'the consolation'" that in other circumstances she might have been his wife, and he has thus given her "'the strength to go on living.'" Beyond that, she cannot explain having deceived him. When she asserts that he "cannot" marry her, Charles does not deny it, and when she beseeches him to leave, he does so, abruptly.

Chapter 48.

Back in the streets of Exeter, Charles comes upon a church. He receives the curate's permission to visit, though the church was about to be locked up. Alone, he prays for forgiveness, but when he stares at the crucifix he sees Sarah's face. He attempts a dialogue with

Christ, or "between his better and his worse self," which keeps coming back around to a consideration of duty vs. freedom. It becomes clear to Charles that the "prison" of duty will allow him to be comfortable, while if he chooses "freedom" he will be "crucified"--a banished, hated sinner. "In a sudden flash of illumnination," Charles sees the "right purpose" of Christianity, perhaps of all religion: "To uncrucify!" If living human beings create a world "in which the hanging man could be descended," then the goal would be achieved. Charles has not leaped into atheism but has come to a humanistic view of Jesus, who now in Charles's life stands for--as does Sarah--"the pure essence of cruel but necessary. . .freedom."

Chapter 49.

Returning the key, Charles declines the curate's invitation to Confession. He is "shriven of established religion for the rest of his life." Faithful still to the demands of "Duty and Propriety," he sets out to "cleanse himself" of his previous commitment. He writes a letter to Sarah that conveys exactly what he might-- perhaps should--have conveyed to her earlier. Now, at last, he expresses feelings of love: "What strange fate brought you to me I do not know, but, God willing, nothing shall take you from me unless it be yourself that wishes it so. . . . Your heart knows that I am yours and that I would call you mine." He dispatches Sam to the Endicott Hotel, with the note and a brooch that Sarah should send back if she does not accept his proposal. Sam examines the seal on the envelope and curses "the man who invented wax." He returns to tell Charles that there was no reply. Only much later will we learn that Sam has not delivered the message; for now, we see him back in Lyme, conferring with Mary in Mrs. Tranter's kitchen. It is clear that he will get no money from Charles, but he has another idea that might succeed, if he and Mary "play [their] cards right. . . ."

Chapter 50.

Charles goes to Ernestina to break their engagement. When Ernestina raises the inevitable question of whether there is someone else, Charles seizes the possibility of easing into a half-truth. He tells her he has renewed an "attachment" of "many years" previous. Ernestina finally turns angry ("My father will drag your name...through the mire"), then falls into a faint. Charles instructs Mary to stay by Ernestina's side, then leaves, promising to fetch Dr. Grogan.

Chapter 51.

Charles finds Grogan and sends him to Mrs. Tranter's. Then he returns to his rooms, to be accosted by Sam, who resigns, hurling insults as he does so. Consoling himself with the reminder that he will soon see

Sarah again, Charles begins to write his letter to Ernestina's father. He is interrupted by the arrival of Grogan.

Chapter 52.

Back at Mrs. Tranter's, Grogan gives Ernestina a sedative, then calms Mrs. Tranter, who in turn calms Mary, by now as hysterical as her mistress was. Informed that Sam has had "bad words" with Mr. Charles, Mrs. Tranter tells Mary that she wishes to speak with Sam, and promises that she will find him a post.

Chapter 53.

Charles must confess to Grogan all that has happened since they last conversed. This is the first person to whom Charles tells all. In explaining what he has done, whether or not he justifies it, Charles makes a ringingly feminist defense of Sarah, and a summary of the plight of Victorian women in general: "'They are to sit, are they not, like so many articles in a shop and to let us men walk in and turn them over and point at this one or that one. . . .If they allow this, we call them decent, respectable, modest.'" His argument goes to the center of Grogan's own Victorian schizophrenia: "the Grogan who had lived now for a quarter of a century in Lyme and the Grogan who had seen the world." Charles is partially, conditionally absolved. If he becomes a "better and a more generous human being" as a result of all this, he "may be forgiven."

Chapter 54.

Charles returns, alone, to Exeter, anticipating a joyous reunion with Sarah. When he gets to Endicott's Hotel, he finds that she has left; furthermore, the message he had sent that morning was never received. Charles, before retiring that evening, kneels in prayer and pledges to himself that he will search the rest of his life, if need be, to find her.

Chapter 55.

We might have guessed from the prologue to this chapter that we would be headed back into metafiction, as the quotation is from Through the Looking-Glass, wherein Tweedledee and Tweedledum attempt to convince Alice that she is only given existence (as are they) by the dream that goes on in the mind of the sleeping Red King. Sure enough, into Charles's railway compartment comes a "prophet-bearded man" of "forty or so," who is "not quite a gentleman," and may be "a successful lay preacher." As Charles dozes, this man--clearly, by now, Fowles himself--watches him with a stare that becomes "positively cannibalistic in its intensity." What the visitor is wondering, we are told, is what he might "do with" Charles. Then Fowles reminds us of a fundamental principle of fiction: it always presents a "fixed fight," but disguises the fixing so as to make it look not fixed.

How will this book escape that inevitability? It will present "two versions" of that fight; and, so tyrannous is the position of the final chapter, Fowles will flip a coin to decide the order of the two endings. He does so, Charles wakes, and the "bearded man" disappears among the crowd at Paddington station. (There may be one more "in-joke" here; as the original version of The Magus ends, Nicholas Urfe is on his way to the waiting-room of the Paddington Station.)

Chapter 56.

Charles hires detectives to look for Sarah, and he searches diligently himself. While the search does not discover its object, it does bring Charles some understanding of her--why she resented a societal bias the more "unfair because remediable." Meanwhile, through his solicitor, Harry Montague, Charles is summoned to the offices of Mr. Freeman's solicitors and there is forced to sign a statement of guilt, clearly meant only to be punitive. At Montague's advice, Charles finally decides "to go abroad."

Chapter 57.

The story jumps ahead twenty months to February of 1869. Charles is still out of the country, and we see Mary and Sam, wed and living in London, where Sam is working, quite successfully, for Mr. Freeman. He boosted his stock considerably with that gentleman by conceiving a new advertising slogan for the clothier: "FREEMAN'S FOR CHOICE." (Fowles seizes the opportunity to contrast the two centuries again.) Now, Mary has spotted a person she is certain is Sarah Woodruff, and Sam appears to be choosing to act upon the sighting. In the chapter's last image, we see, around Mary's neck, the brooch that Charles once attempted to send to Sarah.

Chapter 58.

Charles wanders about Europe, never visiting for long in one place, almost never striking up close acquaintance with fellow-travellers. He has abandoned paleontology and seems to have retained little interest in any science. Ironically, poetry now attracts him. He reads Tennyson's Maud passionately, and finds --as does Fowles--Matthew Arnold's "To Marguerite" to be "perhaps the noblest short poem of the whole Victorian era." It is that poem in which "islands" that (like those of John Donne) once were parts "of a single continent" now are severed, apparently permanently, by a God who

> bade betwixt their shores to be
> the unplumb'd, salt, estranging sea.

Charles meets two engaging gentlemen from Philadelphia, and, urged by them and by Montague, he decides to go "home"--to America.

Chapter 59.

There is much in America that attracts Charles, and much that repels him. He writes somewhat better poetry here, in the place that has revived his "faith in freedom." He finds the "New Woman" everywhere, and realizes that Sarah would have been comfortable here.

Back in England, Sam arrives at the decision we saw forming two chapters ago. Shortly thereafter, Montague cables Charles: "She is found." Charles books passage at once.

Chapter 60.

This is the longest chapter in the novel, half again longer than any other. Charles arrives by cab at 16 Cheyne Walk, where Sarah, under the name of "Mrs. Roughwood," now resides, with members of the Pre-Raphaelite Brotherhood. No damsel in distress, Sarah lives in much better circumstances than Charles had pre-supposed. She comes to greet him "in the full uniform of the New Woman." Now both model and artist, she is quite liberated. As they talk, Charles is made aware that Sarah has known for some time that he was seeking her and that he had terminated his engagement to Ernestina. He feels betrayed and says as much to Sarah, who insists that he misjudges her. She informs him that there is a lady in the house who can explain everything. Charles imagines that he is going to meet Christina Rossetti; instead, the young woman who had shown him upstairs brings to him a child, a girl little more, apparently, than a year old. The realization strikes Charles: she is his daughter. Sarah returns, tells him that their child's name is "Lalage." Charles knows now that Sarah's seeming rejection of him moments before had been a test of his devotion. He also realizes now that "the rock of ages can never be anything else but love." Aware that he will probably never understand Sarah's "parables," he nevertheless embraces her, and the novel reaches another ending.

Chapter 61.

The bearded man seen in Chapter 55 returns, somewhat altered. Standing across the street, he turns his watch back a quarter-hour, then rides away in a landau. Back in the house, the story again backs up. The paragraph that has Charles saying "'No. It is as I say. You have not only planted the dagger in my breast, you have delighted in twisting it'. . . ." is repeated entirely. But this time Charles and Sarah are not reunited. Although she holds out a hand to restrain him, he stomps from the house after his "dagger" speech, imagining that he now sees "his own true superiority to her." It is not a snobbish or sexist perception this time; rather, he sees his superiority in "an ability to give that [is] also an inability to compromise." As he leaves, he passes the young woman who had shown him upstairs, and

she is holding a young child. This time it is not
explicitly established whose child this is. Charles
emerges outside, to see a "trotting landau" disappearing
in the distance.

Charles will presumably return to America. Sarah's
future is no less uncertain than his; in this ending, her
motives, too, are somewhat murky. Nevertheless, we are
cautioned by Fowles not to think "that this is a less
plausible ending to their story." Charles will probably
be all right eventually, as his life has been--to use a
popular existential term--"authenticated." He has, in
fact, "found an atom of faith in himself, a true
uniqueness on which to build," as he has also learned
that life is to be "endured." So, in the story's last
line, he walks away: "And out again, upon the unplumb'd,
salt, estranging sea."

BIBLIOGRAPHY OF WORKS CITED

Aristotle.   [See Corbett.]

Berry, Betsy.   "Forever, In My Dreams: Generic
    Conventions and the Subversive Imagination in Blue
    Velvet." Literature/Film Quarterly, v. 16, no. 2
    (1988): 82-90.

Borden, Lizzie.   "The World According to Lynch." The
    Village Voice, Sept. 23, 1986: 62-3.

Bowden, Liz-Anne, ed.   The Oxford Companion to Film.
    New York/London: Oxford University Press, 1976.

Bradbury, Malcolm.   No, Not Bloomsbury. New York:
    Columbia University Press, 1988.

Brown, William H., Jr.   "The Caine Mutiny." Magill's
    Survey of Cinema, English Language Films, First
    Series, vol. 1. Englewood Cliffs, NJ: Salem Press,
    1980.

Casty, Alan.   "The Films of Robert Rossen." Film
    Quarterly, Winter 1966-67: 91.

Corbett, Edward P. J.   Classical Rhetoric for the Modern
    Student. New York: Oxford University Press, 1965.

Corliss, Richard.   Time, Sept. 22, 1986, 86.

Epstein, Seymour.   The Denver Post, Sunday, 5 February
    1989,10D.

Forster, E. M.   A Room with a View. New York: Vintage,
    1961.

Forster, E. M.   Aspects of the Novel. New York:
    Harcourt, Brace & World, 1954.

Fowles, John.   "Foreword" to Pinter, Screenplay. [See
    Pinter.]

Fowles, John.   The French Lieutenant's Woman. New York,
    Signet, 1969.

Fowles, John.   "Notes on Writing a Novel," Harper's'
    Magazine, July 1968, 90.

Fowles, John.   Mantissa. Boston: Little,Brown, 1982.

Garis, Leslie. "Translating Fowles into Film." New York Times Magazine, 30 August 1981, 24-5, 48, 50, 52, 54, 69.

Guest, Judith. Ordinary People. New York: Random House, 1976.

Hampden, John. [See Lamb.]

Harris, Mark. Bang the Drum Slowly. Lincoln: University of Nebraska Press, 1984.

Heller, Joseph. Catch-22. New York: Dell, 1961.

Heller, Joseph. "On Translating Catch-22 into a Movie." Frederick Kiley and Walter McDonald, eds. A "Catch-22" Casebook. New York: Crowell, 1973.

Hoberman, J. The Village Voice, Sept. 23, 1986, 56.

Hollander, Anne. Moving Pictures. New York: Alfred A. Knopf, 1989.

Huck, Janet. [See McGuigan.]

Isherwood, Christopher. Prater Violet. New York: Farrar, Straus and Giroux, 1945.

Kael, Pauline. The New Yorker, Sept. 22, 1986, 99-103.

Katz, Ephraim. The Film Encyclopedia. New York: Crowell, 1979.

Kaufmann, Walter. [See Nietzsche.]

Kennedy, Harlan. "The Czech Director's Woman." Film Comment, 17 (Sept-Oct 1981), 28.

Kenner, Hugh. Joyce's Voices. Berkeley: University of California Press, 1978.

Kiley, Frederick. [See Heller.]

Kinsella, W. P. Shoeless Joe. New York: Ballantine Books, 1982.

Klein, Joanne. Making Pictures: The Pinter Screenplays. Columbus: Ohio State University Press, 1985.

Knapp, Shoshana. "The Transformation of a Pinter Screenplay: Freedom and Calculators in The French

Lieutenant's Woman." Modern Drama, 28:1 (1985): 55-70.

Krist, Gary. "The Junior Wife's Story." The New York Times Book Review, July 25, 1993: 12.

Lamb, Charles. "On the Tragedies of Shakespeare." Charles Lamb: Essays. Rosalind Vallance and John Hampden, eds. London: The Folio Society, 1963.

Layman, Richard. Shadow Man: The Life of Dashiell Hammett. New York/London: Harcourt Brace, 1981.

Life. January 16, 1956: 43.

Marcus, Fred H. and Paul Zall. "Catch-22: Is Film Fidelity an Asset?" Marcus, ed. Film and Literature: Contrasts in Media. Scranton, PA: Chandler, 1971.

McDonald, Walter. [See Heller.]

McGuigan, Cathleen, with Janet Huck. Newsweek, Oct. 27, 1986: 103-104.

Michaels, Leonard. The New York Times Book Review, August 15, 1993: 20.

Newsweek. June 28, 1954: 72.

New York Times. January 17, 1954: Sec. II, 1-3.

Nichols, John. The Sterile Cuckoo. New York: Avon Books, 1965.

Nietzsche, Friedrich. The Birth of Tragedy. In Basic Writings of Nietzsche. Walter Kaufmann, ed. New York: Modern Library, 1968.

Pike, E. Royston. "Golden Times": Human Documents of the Victorian Age. New York: Schocken Books, 1972.

Pinter, Harold. "The French Lieutenant's Woman": A Screenplay. Boston/Toronto: Little, Brown, 1981.

Plummer, William. "Pride of the Sox." Books in Canada, April 1983: 8-9.

Pratt, John C. [See Kesey.]

Rafferty, Terrence. The Nation, Oct. 18, 1986: 383-385.

Rogow, Lee. Saturday Review, 34: 17.

Schiff, Stephen. "Muriel Spark Between the Lines." The New Yorker, May 24, 1993: 38-51.

Simon, John. Movies into Film: Film Criticism 1967-1970. New York: Dell, 1971.

Simon, John. National Review, November 7, 1986: 54-56.

Spark, Muriel. Curriculum Vitae. New York/Boston: Houghton Mifflin, 1993.

Spark, Muriel. The Prime of Miss Jean Brodie. New York: Plume/Penguin, 1961.

Swados, Harvey. "Popular Taste and The Caine Mutiny." Partisan Review, 20: 248-256.

Time. June 28, 1954: 90.

Time. September 5, 1955: 48.

Time. June 15, 1970: 38-45. Reprinted in Kiley & McDonald.

Vallance, Rosalind. [See Lamb.]

Walker, John, ed. Halliwell's Film Guide (Eighth Edition). New York: HarperCollins, 1991.

Whyte, William H., Jr. The Organization Man. New York: Simon & Schuster, 1956.

Wouk, Herman. The Caine Mutiny. New York: Doubleday, 1951.

Wouk, Herman. The Caine Mutiny Court-Martial. New York: Doubleday, 1954.

Zall, Paul. [See Marcus.]

Zunser, Jessie. Cue, June 26, 1954: 16.

INDEX